WORLDVIEW

GREG LAURIE

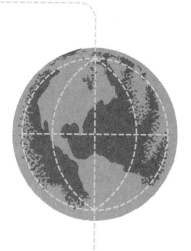

WORLDVIEW

LEARNING TO THINK AND LIVE BIBLICALLY

KERYGMA
PUBLISHING

International Standard Book Number: 978-1-61291-242-4

Published by Kerygma Publishing

Cover design by Ty Mattson

Coordination: FM Management, Ltd.

Contact: mark@fmmgt.net

Printed in the United States of America

1 2 3 4 5 6 7 8 / 17 16 15 14 13 12

CONTENTS

ABSOLUTE TRUTH

One of the most depressing situations I encounter in my ministry is when I'm talking to someone who has been a Christian for years and then find out they know virtually nothing about the Bible.

Sad as that might be, it's a reality I encounter more and more these days. It's become one of the biggest problems we see in the church today—an astonishing ignorance of what Scripture actually teaches.

People just don't know what the Bible says.

George Barna, a longtime student of America's religious beliefs and behavior, described the situation in a recent article, calling it "a crisis of biblical illiteracy."

A crisis?

Barna wrote,

How else can you describe matters when most church-going adults today reject the accuracy of the Bible, reject the existence of Satan, claim that Jesus sinned, see no need to evangelize, believe that good works are one of the keys to persuading God to forgive their sins, and describe their commitment to Christianity as moderate or even less firm?"[1]

Barna went on to point out that the most widely known verse among adults and teen believers today (and just recently quoted on national television by the president's press secretary) is "God helps those who help themselves."

The only trouble is, the verse isn't in the Bible.

Barna's study revealed that fewer than one in ten believers possesses a biblical worldview as the basis for his or her decision making and behavior.

Do you have a biblical worldview? Why is that so important?

WHAT IS A BIBLICAL WORLDVIEW?

Christian philosopher Francis Schaeffer once wrote: "As Christians we are not only to know the right world-view, the world-view that tells us the truth of what *is*, but consciously to *act* upon that world-view so as to influence society in all its parts and facets across the whole spectrum of life, as much as we can to the extent of our individual and collective ability."[2]

Worldview really matters, and everyone has one. It's not a question of whether or not you have a worldview. The question is, do you have a biblical one?

A number of different factors go into forming our worldview, or the way we see life. It's formed by the culture in which we are raised, our upbringing, the books we've read, our education, and the media to which we've exposed ourselves.

What kind of worldview do you have? It's important,

because your worldview—whatever it may be—is *comprehensive*. In other words, it will have a bearing on virtually everything you say and do, from your personal standards of morality, to the way you spend your money, to how you vote, to the way you relate to your family, to your attitude toward God and the church.

What, then, is a *biblical* worldview? In his book *Think Biblically!*, Dr. John MacArthur wrote that a Christian worldview is based on two major presuppositions:

> The first will be the eternal existence of the personal, transcendent, triune, Creator God. Second, the God of Scripture has revealed His character, purposes, and will in the infallible and inerrant pages of His special revelation, the Bible, which is superior to any other source of revelation or human reason alone.[3]

In other words, there is a living God, and He has revealed Himself in Scripture. As Christians, therefore, we believe that we can find absolute truth from the Word of God.

Yes, absolute truth is a reality in our world, regardless of what contemporary culture says, regardless of what may or may not be politically correct, and regardless of what we might *feel* to be right or not right.

We don't base our beliefs on our emotions or on what our culture tells us; we base our beliefs on what the Bible teaches. That is what it means to have a Christian, or biblical, worldview. And this will affect the way we see everything else in our lives, from now until the day we die.

C. S. Lewis said, "I believe in Christianity as I believe that the Sun has risen, not only because I see it, but because by it I see everything else."[4]

Why is this so important? Because we are living in the last days and the soon return of Jesus Christ to this earth. If ever there was a time when we needed to know our Bibles and have a close walk with Christ, the time is now.

Listen to this description of earth's final days, given to us in 2 Timothy 3:

> In the last days there will be very difficult times. For people will love only themselves and their money. They will be boastful and proud, scoffing at God, disobedient to their parents, and ungrateful. They will consider nothing sacred. They will be unloving and unforgiving; they will slander others and have no self-control. They will be cruel and hate what is good. They will betray their friends, be reckless, be puffed up with pride, and love pleasure rather than God. They will act religious, but they will reject the power that could make them godly. Stay away from people like that! (verses 1-5, NLT)

How contemporary is that? What an accurate assessment of the times in which we are living. America has never been more "spiritual" yet more immoral. You hear people throw around terms like "spiritual" and "spirituality" a lot these days. But what do those terms even mean?

A poll taken by the Barna Group a few years ago said that Americans are more interested in faith and spirituality than they are in Christianity. George Barna pointed out that Americans increasingly want to shape their own faith experience: "Americans typically draw from a broad treasury of moral, spiritual and ethical sources of thought to concoct a uniquely personal brand of faith."[5]

In other words, we customize our own religion.

THE ERA OF THE iGOD

We live in the age of the iPod, the iPhone, and the iPad. Why not the iGod? And why not iFaith? When you purchase an iPad, one of the first things you do is customize the home screen to fit your needs, right? You select the backgrounds and colors, add apps, throw others out, and basically rearrange things to meet your needs and suit your fancy.

So why not do that with your faith and your beliefs? Keep stuff that you like and makes sense to you, and delete the teachings that you don't like, can't understand, or find inconvenient. So if you believe in a God of love, forgiveness, and mercy, you can keep that. But if you are offended by the biblical teaching of a God of holiness, righteousness, and judgment, you just delete those more uncomfortable teachings. It works out perfectly.

Yes, it's all very neat and convenient. But the question is, will that god, the iGod you have created for yourself and made in your own image, be able to save you in the final day?

It has been said that God made man in His image, and man returned the favor. That is what is happening today.

MAKING OUR OWN "TRUTH"

The result of all our tinkering with the truth and remaking God in our own image is the currently popular philosophy in our culture known as *moral relativism.*

Moral relativism is the belief that there are no absolutes in life. We are all random products of an evolutionary process, and we weren't created by a personal God. There is no right or wrong, no good or evil. There is no plan or purpose, no rhyme or reason for our lives here on earth, because we're only here by chance. In the course of our brief stay on the planet, we make our own luck, create our own truth, forge our own fate, and weave our own destiny. All people are basically good, but if they happen to go bad (and what is bad?), it is simply because we are all products of our environment.

But there is something very interesting—and somewhat amusing—about people who subscribe to moral relativism. These people tend to be tolerant of just about everyone—*except* people who hold to absolute beliefs. When they encounter someone who actually believes in and holds to absolute truth, these broad-minded, progressive, accepting, oh-so-tolerant men and women suddenly become very intolerant—even angry.

Imagine, for instance, that you dared to stand up and say, "I believe that the Bible is the Word of God."

Instead of the moral relativist giving a shrug of the shoulders and saying, "Well, that is your truth, and I have my truth," they might very well say, "Why you puritanical, narrow-minded, Bible-thumping bigot! How dare you say that?" The fact is, there is very little tolerance for people who believe in absolute truth in our culture.

Now, moral relativism may sound fine in theory. But what if we were to actually put it into practice? Could anyone actually live that way? Of course not. What if someone went out tonight in your town, removed all of the traffic lights and stop signs, and painted over all of the lines in the streets? What would it be like trying to get to work the next morning? It would be chaos out there.

That is precisely what moral relativism is doing in our culture today.

A KEY QUESTION

In the pages of this book, we'll talk about the hot-button issues and the basic life questions that so many people have today. In the process, you will be able to compare your own worldview alongside a truly Christian worldview, and see where you stand.

For instance, your response to the following no-brainer Christian worldview statement will reveal a great deal about how your outlook measures up to the standard of Scripture. Here it is: *Jesus Christ is the only way to God.*

If you are a true Christian and hold to a biblical worldview, you must believe that it is Jesus, and Jesus alone, who can save you from your sin.

Why do I bring this up? Because people who call themselves Christians have said to me, "Yes, Jesus is *my* way and He has changed *my* life. But who am I to say that He is *the* way for everyone? Someone else might find God by following their own path."

No, they won't. Jesus said they wouldn't. He said very clearly, "I am the way, the truth, and the life. No one comes to the Father except through Me" (John 14:6).

The all-roads-lead-to-God philosophy is neither Christian nor biblical. It is moral relativism.

It's interesting, but sometimes you will find that non-believers have a better understanding of what the Bible teaches than so-called believers who have surrendered any pretense of a biblical worldview.

I recently read an interview of well-known atheist

Christopher Hitchens by a minister who described herself as "a liberal Christian."

In her interview, she noted that when Hitchens cited Christianity in his writings, he spoke of those who held a "fundamentalist faith." She went on to say that as a liberal, she didn't take the stories from Scripture literally and didn't believe in the traditional doctrines. For instance, she didn't hold to the doctrine of atonement, that Jesus died for our sins. So she asked him why he didn't make a distinction between the fundamentalist faith and her liberal views.

Christopher Hitchens replied, "I would say that if you don't believe that Jesus of Nazareth was the Christ and Messiah, and that he rose again from the dead and by his sacrifice our sins are forgiven, you're really not in any meaningful sense a Christian."[6]

Is it any wonder that people in our nation develop all sorts of crazy ideas about God? When the sloppy thinking of moral relativism is promoted from the nation's pulpits, men and women who seek truth have no idea what to believe. So they come up with a "religion" and a god of their own making to fill the gaping emptiness in their souls.

Our country was founded on what we call Judeo-Christian principles. More specifically, however, many of our founding fathers were professed believers in Jesus Christ. Though revisionists attempt to discount or deny this fact, a careful study of American history will affirm the truth again and again.

Founding father Patrick Henry was most famous for his statement, "Give me liberty or give me death." On another occasion, however, he said this: "It cannot be emphasized too strongly and too often that this great Nation was founded not by religionists, but by Christians, not on religions but on the gospel of Jesus Christ. For that reason alone, people of other faiths have been afforded freedom of worship here."[7]

It is our departure from this truth that has brought our nation to where we are today . . . with abortion on demand on an epidemic scale . . . with marriages dissolving at record rates . . . with the very definition of marriage and family under attack . . . with rampant, random violence stalking the hallways of our high schools . . . with the increase in suicides and the utter disdain for sexual morality.

Should we be surprised?

Not really.

The Bible says in Hosea 8:7, "They have planted the wind and will harvest the whirlwind" (NLT).

WRITTEN IN STONE

In the Ten Commandments we find absolute truth actually written by the finger of God on tablets of stone. This is truth we can believe in and depend on in a fickle, wishy-washy, morally illiterate, relativistic world.

In Scripture we read about a man who asked Jesus, "Which is the greatest commandment in the law?"

> Jesus said to him, "You shall love the LORD your God with all your heart, with all your soul, and with all your mind.' This is the first and great commandment. And the second is like it: 'You shall love your neighbor as yourself.' On these two commandments hang all the Law and the Prophets." (Matthew 22:37-40)

Jesus wasn't doing away with the Ten Commandments when He made that statement; He was simply summing them up, showing us how those commandments play out in life. If I love God with all of my heart, soul, and mind, I *won't* have any other gods before Him, I *won't* make and worship a graven image of Him, and I *won't* take His name in vain. And if I love my neighbor as I love myself, I won't steal from him, covet his possessions, or tell him a lie. So Jesus is effectively saying, "Get these two things down, and the commandments will come together for you."

The Ten Commandments are found in Exodus 20. The first four commandments pertain to our relationship with God, and the last six speak to our relationship with others. Here's another way to look at it: Commandments one to four are vertical, while commandments five to ten are horizontal.

Let's take a moment to review them.

1. *You shall have no other gods before Him.*

> And God spoke all these words, saying: "I am the LORD your God, who brought you out of the land of Egypt, out of the house of bondage. You shall have no other gods before Me." (verses 1-3)

2. *No graven images.* Sometimes people merge this commandment with the first, but they are distinct in Scripture—connected, but separate.

> "You shall not make for yourself a carved image —any likeness of anything that is in heaven above, or that is in the earth beneath, or that is in the water

under the earth; you shall not bow down to them nor serve them. For I, the LORD your God, am a jealous God, visiting the iniquity of the fathers upon the children to the third and fourth generations of those who hate Me, but showing mercy to thousands, to those who love Me and keep My commandments." (verses 4-6)

3. Do not take the Lord's name in vain.

"You shall not take the name of the LORD your God in vain, for the LORD will not hold him guiltless who takes His name in vain." (verse 7)

4. Keep the Sabbath day holy (verse 8).

And in the second section . . .

5. Honor your father and mother (verse 12).
6. Do not murder (verse 13).
7. Do not commit adultery (verse 14).
8. Do not steal (verse 15).
9. Do not lie (verse 16).
10. Do not covet.

"You shall not covet your neighbor's house; you shall not covet your neighbor's wife, nor his male servant, nor his female servant, nor his ox, nor his donkey, nor anything that is your neighbor's." (verse 17)

Commandment One: Worship the Right God
"You shall have no other gods before Me." (Exodus 20:3)

The first commandment is first for a reason. It's as though God was saying, "Get this one down. Because if you mess up on this one, everything else will fall apart. You shall have no other gods before Me."

A recent survey revealed that 76 percent of Americans consider themselves completely in line with the first commandment. They might say, "Well, maybe I've had a little trouble with a few of the other commandments, but never this one. I'm not into bowing down to idols, and I never will set another god before the Lord."

Could it be that we don't understand what that first commandment actually means? It all starts with the place of God in your life. Why is this important? You will serve what or whom you worship. Jesus said, "'You shall worship the LORD your God, and Him only you shall serve'" (Matthew 4:10). If the Lord is number one in your life, then everything else will find its proper balance. If He isn't, then everything else will fall into chaos.

Take a careful look at the wording in Exodus 20:2: "I am the LORD your God, who brought you out of the land of Egypt, out of the house of bondage." The Lord was saying, "I would like to remind you of what I have done for you already." He was reminding Israel about the fact that they were slaves to Pharaoh. Then God sent Moses to appear before Pharaoh and to demand their release. When the Egyptian king refused, the Lord unleashed a series of ten plagues against the land of Egypt.

As God wrote this first commandment down with His

own finger on a tablet of stone, He reminded Israel of what they had just been delivered from. He was essentially telling them, "Remember where you were and how I redeemed you from that situation. And don't ever put another god in My place."

We need to keep these same things in mind. God also says to us, "Remember what I have done for you. I have forgiven you of your sin, redeemed you, and brought you out of great darkness. This is what I have done for you. Now here is what you can do for Me: You can keep My commandments."

In 1 John 4:19 we read, "We love Him because He first loved us."

It all begins with the first commandment: "Have no other gods before Me." Another way to translate this is, "Have no other gods before My face."

We've all heard the expression "Hey, man, get out of my face!" Have you noticed how some people always seem to stand too close to you when they talk? I call these people space invaders. You take a little step back to give yourself some breathing room, and they'll take a step forward. You feel like pushing them away, don't you? I can't even concentrate on what they're trying to tell me when they're so close to my face.

God was basically saying here, "Get out of My face with these false gods. They're an offense to Me."

And don't imagine you can play with these substitute gods in secret. Our God is both omniscient (all-knowing) and omnipresent (everywhere present). Wherever you go, He is already there. So you can shut the door, draw the curtains, and turn out the lights, but He still sees you — what you are doing and what is in your heart and thoughts. David wrote: "If I try to hide in the darkness, the night becomes light around me.

For even darkness cannot hide from God; to you the night shines as bright as day. Darkness and light are both alike to you" (Psalm 139:11-12, TLB).

Worship of any other god is a deep offense to the Lord —and it's doing it in His face.

When we think of an idol worshipper, we might visualize someone lying prone before some creepy carved image—and people still do that in our world today. But the biblical concept of an "idol" is much broader than that. Maybe we don't give these false gods the names people once gave them, like Dagon, Asherah, Baal, Zeus, or Thor. But they are gods nonetheless.

In 1 John 5:21, the apostle says to Christians, "Little children, keep yourself from idols." The New Living Translation says, "Keep away from anything that might take God's place in your hearts." The J. B. Phillips translation of that same verse says, "Be on your guard, my dear children, against every false god!"

What does this mean? What is an idol? *An idol or a false god is anyone or anything that takes the place of God in your life.* The fact is, everyone—including atheists—has a god. It may not be the true and living God, but it is a god nonetheless that they worship and serve.

Believe it or not, idolatry comes naturally to all of us. Why? As human beings, we must worship, and we *will* worship. We were wired that way by our Creator. The human soul abhors a vacuum every bit as much as nature does and will always find an object of worship—whether on the shelf, on the altar, in the mirror, or in heaven.

But why would we worship some cobbled-together, imitation god instead of the true God? Because in our minds, it gives us control. In his book *Words from the Fire,* R. Albert

Mohler Jr. wrote, "We can pick an idol up and we can put an idol down. We can move an idol to this place, and then we can remove it to another place. The idol is at our disposal. We can hide it from our sight, or we can put it in the center of the room. We will devise our own worship because we have devised our own god."[8]

Worshipping a god of our own making gives us a sense of control. For instance, listen to this statement: "I don't believe in a god who would judge someone. *My* god is just, merciful, loving, and accepting, and would never judge anyone."

Really? Who or what is that god of yours? Where did you come up with him or her? In fact, you just made up a god of your own. And that's an idol.

A biblical worldview is believing in God as He is revealed in Scripture. It is looking to the Bible, and the Bible alone, as the source and authority for your belief. It is not what you feel, not what you've heard, not what is popular, not what is acceptable, not what is perceived as hip or cool, and not what fits in with contemporary culture.

No, it is what the Bible actually says.

As Paul wrote: "Let God be true, and every human being a liar" (Romans 3:4, NIV).

Another definition of a false god is whatever you get worked up and excited about. People get passionate about a lot of things. They may not call these things "gods," but that is really what they are. What is the focus of your life? For all practical purposes, that is your god.

Some people just worship themselves. It was Oscar Wilde who said, "To love one's self is the beginning of a lifelong romance." How true. Left to ourselves, we will love ourselves more than anything or anyone else.

I've heard it said, "The Bible teaches that we need to learn to love ourselves. Jesus said, 'Love your neighbor as yourself.' Therefore, if we learn to love ourselves, then we can effectively love others. The reason we don't love as we ought to is because we don't love ourselves."

Sorry, but I don't buy that at all.

I think you already love yourself, and I already love myself. I admit it! The Bible says, "For no one ever hated his own flesh, but nourishes and cherishes it" (Ephesians 5:29). Let's face it: We love ourselves. We don't have to learn how to do that; it comes naturally to us right from the crib.

When Jesus said, "Love your neighbor as yourself" (Matthew 19:19), He was essentially saying, "You *already* love yourself. That's obvious! So just love your neighbor in the same way. And love God even more!"

It is not a sin to love and care for yourself. But it is a sin when you love and care for yourself more than you love God. That is when you begin to slip into worshipping and idolizing yourself. For many people, their god is facing them in the mirror every single morning.

Other people worship money or possessions.

Apple recently released its latest and greatest version of the iPad. (And of course, it is already out of date.) Basically, an iPad is just a big iPod — an iPod on steroids! There is no doubt that it's a cool device, and it's fun to play with. But maybe people are getting just a little carried away with the whole phenomenon. When the iPad was first released, the *Wall Street Journal* wrote, "Last time there was this much excitement about a tablet, it had some commandments written on it."[9] Another hailed this new product as "the messiah machine." Another article asked, "Can the Jesus tablet deliver a miracle?"

Excuse me, but did I miss something here? Will an electronic tablet grant forgiveness of my sins? Will the newest smart phone change my life or show me the way to heaven? I think some of these tech heads need to get a life (preferably an eternal one).

We get all excited about the latest new gadget and all its capabilities, and I love that stuff too. But today's cutting-edge technology is tomorrow's doorstop. We should beware of making idols out of these things. And that goes for any of our most treasured possessions. Be very careful that these things don't become more important to us than God Himself.

Some people are into physical fitness and bodybuilding. They worship every day at the First Church of the Perfect Physique and just can't get enough exercise or running or weightlifting or whatever. It becomes addicting, and they get obsessed with it.

Paul wrote, "Physical training is good, but training for godliness is much better, promising benefits in this life and in the life to come" (1 Timothy 4:8, NLT). In other words, there is some value and merit in getting exercise and staying in shape, but it can't be compared to spiritual fitness and pursuing spiritual goals. Don't let concern over your physical appearance become an obsession and an idol to you.

Scripture also mentions sexual lust in this regard. Paul wrote to the Colossians, "Consider yourselves dead to worldly contacts: have nothing to do with sexual immorality, dirty-mindedness, uncontrolled passion, evil desire, and the lust for other people's goods, which amounts to idolatry" (Colossians 3:5, PH).

Other people, of course, chase money, thinking about making it (and worrying about losing it) through many of the waking hours of their day.

The Bible says, "For the love of money is a root of all kinds of evil" (1 Timothy 6:10). Note that it *doesn't say,* as some quote it, "Money is the root of all evil." Money isn't the problem. It is the *love* of money that is the problem.

Some people worship celebrities. They get excited about a certain rock star, movie star, or sports icon. Others might even idolize some spiritual leader, putting him or her on a high pedestal. People (including pastors and spiritual leaders), however, eventually will disappoint you. I've had people in our church say to me, "Greg, we wish you could come over to our house for dinner. The church is so big, and we want to get to know you better."

But it may be best if I *didn't* come over for dinner. I'd probably disappoint you, and you would end up saying, "You know, I really liked Greg until he came over for dinner. But then he kept doing this one thing that really bothered me!"

What I am saying is that we have a tendency to make idols out of people. And then when they do something human, we say, "I can't believe he did that! I can't believe she said that!" And just what is it that you can't believe—that humans are humans? The fact is that none of us were built for pedestals. Pedestals belong to the Lord.

Worship the Lord God. Serve Him only. He will never disappoint you. He will never let you down—not in a million years.

Sometimes certain people in our lives keep us from God. We have a relationship that pulls us away from Him, and after a while, we realize, *If I really want to follow the Lord, I could lose my relationship with this person.* Yes, you could. And it might be a choice that you have to make.

Is someone dragging you down spiritually right now? Jesus said,

> "He who loves father or mother more than Me is not worthy of Me. And he who loves son or daughter more than Me is not worthy of Me. And he who does not take his cross and follow after Me is not worthy of Me. He who finds his life will lose it, and he who loses his life for My sake will find it." (Matthew 10:37-39)

That's another way of saying, "You shall have no other gods before Me."

The truth, of course, is that these gods we create in our minds aren't really gods at all. They're just false images that can't do anything for us. Here is my big question: Will this god—this person or thing you have placed ahead of Jesus Christ—save you in that final day? Will that god give you the strength you need in your moment of crisis? Will that god forgive your sins?

The answer is no. No false god can do those things for you. You need to turn to the true and living God who loves you.

THE PURPOSE OF THE LAW

No one can keep the Ten Commandments perfectly. The Bible tells the story of a wealthy young man who came to Jesus and asked, "Good Teacher, what good thing shall I do that I may have eternal life?" (Matthew 19:16).

Jesus replied, "If you want to enter into life, keep the commandments . . . 'You shall not murder,' 'You shall not commit adultery,' 'You shall not steal,' 'You shall not bear false witness,' 'Honor your father and your mother,' and, 'You shall love your neighbor as yourself'" (verses 17-19).

And this young man replied, "All these things I have kept from my youth. What do I still lack?" (verse 20).

The book of Mark says that Jesus looked at him and loved him. But the Lord also knew the truth: *No one* has kept all the commandments since childhood. Jesus had quoted the Law to him to show him his *need*. He needed a Savior. He needed Jesus in his life.

The commandments weren't given to make us righteous; they were given to show us that we are *not* righteous. Romans 3:19 says, "We know that whatever the law says, it says to those that are under the law, that every mouth may be stopped, and all the world may become guilty before God."

The Law shuts our mouth and opens our eyes. It condemns, but does not convert. It challenges us, but does not change us. It points the finger, but can't give mercy. It leaves us without excuse . . . and it drives us to Jesus, who has the answer we are looking for.

The Law is like a moral mirror, and we don't always like what we see. When you see yourself in the mirror (especially in the morning), it isn't always a pleasant sight, is it? And if you happen to have one of those magnifying mirrors, it can be just plain scary.

Imagine that you are out to lunch with some friends, and everyone keeps smiling at you and laughing at everything you say. You think to yourself, *Man, I didn't think I was that witty.* Then you go into the restroom, check yourself in the mirror, and find out why they were laughing. You had an encrusted noodle, coated with marinara sauce, on your face the entire time.

Well, that's embarrassing. So you become very upset—at the mirror! You say, "I don't like this thing. I feel like taking a brick and breaking it to pieces. It makes me feel bad about myself. I hate mirrors!"

But it's no use to get angry at the mirror, is it? Get mad at yourself for not using a napkin. All the mirror did was reveal the truth to you.

In a similar way, I sometimes look at the Law and say, "I don't like the Law." Why? Because I don't like what I see there when I fall short. The Law's whole purpose, however, is to send us to Jesus, the one who can help, save, redeem, cleanse, and heal. When He died on the cross, the Scripture tells us in Colossians 2:13-14 that "he forgave all our sins. He canceled the record of the charges against us and took it away by nailing it to the cross" (NLT).

I've broken the Law again and again, and I feel accused and condemned. But then I come to Jesus, who forgives my sin and wraps me in His own righteousness.

Yes, in the Ten Commandments I find absolute truth. But I also find standards that I can never live up to in my own ability. That is why I need Jesus to change my life and heart, which gives me the desire to obey God's commands out of love and devotion—instead of mere duty.

HOW TO LOVE GOD

What is love?

Imagine you are an alien, newly arrived on Earth from Mars in your spaceship and wanting to do a little research on human love. Where would you start? You might begin by borrowing someone's computer or iPad and doing a survey of love songs that have been in the movies and played on the radio over the last forty or fifty years.

You would definitely come up with some interesting definitions.

What do we know about love from such songs? For starters, we know, "What the world needs now is love, sweet love." Okay, we could begin there. But what is love? Of course we know that "love is a many-splendored thing." And we've also heard that "love is the answer." Led Zeppelin reminded us that "we need a whole lotta love." And then Phil Collins told us that "you can't hurry love." Why can't you hurry love? Because, as another song describes it, "that's the way love goes."

So, before you climb back in your spaceship to head home to Mars, you might try to summarize what you've learned: The world needs love—sweet love—right now. It is the answer, it is many-splendored, and we need a whole lot of it. But you can't hurry it, because that's the way it goes.

A colorful definition, perhaps, but I'm not sure how helpful it would be. So what in the world is love, anyway?

As you might expect, the real answer is in the Bible.

The Bible says that God is love.

THE GREATEST DEFINITION

The most definitive statement we have on love may be in the familiar words of John 3:16: "For God so loved the world that He gave His only begotten Son, that whoever believes in Him should not perish but have everlasting life."

In 1 Corinthians 13, we may have the greatest description of love. Here it is in a modern paraphrase:

> Love never gives up.
> Love cares more for others than for self.
> Love doesn't want what it doesn't have.
> Love doesn't strut,
> Doesn't have a swelled head,
> Doesn't force itself on others,
> Isn't always "me first,"
> Doesn't fly off the handle,
> Doesn't keep score of the sins of others,
> Doesn't revel when others grovel,
> Takes pleasure in the flowering of truth,
> Puts up with anything,
> Trusts God always,
> Always looks for the best,
> Never looks back,
> But keeps going to the end. (verses 4-7, MSG)

Whatever attributes we might identify with the word *love,* it all begins with God. He is the source, the wellspring, and the headwaters of all genuine love: "We love Him because He first loved us" (1 John 4:19). In other words, we know what love is, because He demonstrated it right before our eyes.

How should we respond to such love? We ought to love Him back.

We can talk all day and sing songs all night about love and how much we love God. But the Bible tells us that the best way to show our love for the Lord isn't in what we *say,* but in what we *do.* In John 14:15, Jesus said, "If you love Me, keep My commandments."

In the pages of this book, we have been considering what it means to think and live biblically. We're starting with the Ten Commandments, because in them, we have a clear set of absolutes to live by.

As we noted in the last chapter, Jesus summed up the Ten Commandments when He declared,

> " 'You must love the LORD your God with all your heart, all your soul, and all your mind.' This is the first and greatest commandment. A second is equally important: 'Love your neighbor as yourself.' The entire law and all the demands of the prophets are based on these two commandments." (Matthew 22:37-40, NLT)

In other words, if we give ourselves to accomplishing these two things, our hearts will be beating with the heart of God in the Ten Commandments. We will worship Him — and love Him — in the right way.

Commandment Two:
Worship the Right God . . . in the Right Way

"You shall not make for yourself a carved image." (Exodus 20:4)

The first commandment, which we looked at in the last chapter, has to do with worshipping the right God. The second commandment tells us to worship this right God in the right way.

In the first command, the Lord tells us that we must have no other gods before Him. In the second command, He directs us to worship Him the way He wants to be worshipped. In other words, *how* we worship matters as much as *whom* we worship.

Here is how Moses heard it on Mount Sinai in the presence of God:

> "You shall not make for yourself a carved image — any likeness of anything that is in heaven above, or that is in the earth beneath, or that is in the water under the earth; you shall not bow down to them nor serve them. For I, the LORD your God, am a jealous God, visiting the iniquity of the fathers upon the children to the third and fourth generations of those who hate Me, but showing mercy to thousands, to those who love Me and keep My commandments." (Exodus 20:4-6)

What does this whole business about carved images and likenesses mean to us today? Is it wrong, for instance, to have a decorative cross on your wall? Is it wrong to have a painting or a drawing of Jesus?

To begin with, no one has any idea what Jesus really looked like, of course. I guarantee that He didn't look as He is so often portrayed, with long blond hair parted down the middle, like some hippie dude. The fact is, the Bible doesn't give us a physical description of Jesus, which is noteworthy in itself.

But is it wrong to have even an artistic rendering of Christ? What if we have a little statue of an angel, or wear a cross around our necks, or something like that? Is this the same thing as having a "carved image"?

No, it's not.

God isn't against art or artistic expression — especially as these things reflect and honor the beauty of His creation. God gave us this creative ability and the desire to use it. When we read about the ark of the covenant in Scripture, we see that God instructed His people to create exquisite images of cherubim, sculpted in gold, with wings outstretched over the mercy seat. And in the temple itself, God gave directions for the most gifted to create carvings of lions and bulls and cherubim. So the Bible isn't criticizing the making of figures or objects. But it *does* warn us not to use such things as an aid to worship.

Jesus tells us that "God is Spirit, and those who worship Him must worship in spirit and truth" (John 4:24).

It is good to worship God in spirit, and there is a place for emotion in our worship too.

Think of the way we watch a really good football championship game (there have been a few of them). When it's suspenseful and surprising, there are a lot of excited people, and understandably so. In the stands, we see people yelling, screaming, hugging, and slapping hands. They come to the stadium draped with their team colors and sporting painted faces. What do we say when we see that kind of behavior? With a shrug of the shoulders we might say, "Yeah, that's a true fan for you."

By contrast, what do we think when we see someone getting a little excited during worship, raising their hands, praising God, or moving around a little? We might think to ourselves, *What a fanatic! That is so out of place.*

Is it? Is there a place for emotion in worship? Yes, there is. We need to worship God in spirit.

But Jesus said that we must also worship Him in truth. There is a right way to worship the right God, and He isn't pleased when we feel that we need images or icons or statues to help us in our worship.

TURN AWAY FROM ANY FALSE IMAGE

Here is another thing to consider: God is not only against *material* images that misrepresent Him; He is also opposed to false *mental* images. We say things like, "Well, God to me is like a nurturing mother, or a loving father, or like a flower, or like the sun in the sky." Or maybe, "I think of God like transparent tape; you can't see Him, but you know He's there."

And what happens? We subtly shift our attention and adoration from the true and living God to a grossly inadequate mental image in our brains.

In the previous chapter, we talked about people who say, "I believe in a God of love, not a God of judgment. I believe in a God of forgiveness, not a God who would send a person to hell." But here is the problem with that: They are inventing their own god. When they think and speak that way, they are putting another god, a false image, before the real God.

You can't edit God. You can't make God into your image of Him. Instead, you must allow Him to make you into *His* image.

So that is what this second command is talking about

when it says that you shall have no other gods before Him.

And what is the reason for that? Why can't I have another god before Him? Why can't I have a carved image I worship on the side? Because the Bible says that our God is a *jealous* God.

But what does that mean? When you and I think of jealousy, we equate it with pettiness or selfishness and see it as a vice, not a virtue. But that is not what God means when He says that He is a jealous God.

Maybe it would aid our understanding if we changed the spelling of *jealous* by dropping the *j* and inserting a *z* in its place. Our God is a *zealous* God.

He is zealous in His love for you, and He wants you to be zealous in your love for Him. God loves you and wants an exclusive relationship with you.

It makes sense, doesn't it? Doesn't a wife want her husband to be faithful to her? Doesn't a husband want his wife to be loyal to him as well? Doesn't a parent look out for his or her children and care about their welfare? Of course they do. If you saw your child running into the street with a car approaching, you would run as fast as you could into that street to pull your child out of danger, even at the risk of your own life. And that would seem perfectly normal to you. Would that make you a jealous parent? No, it would make you a parent who is zealous to protect the life of your child.

God was effectively saying, "I want your complete love. I don't want you to bow down before other gods."

AN AMAZING EXAMPLE

From earliest times, however, we human beings have had a tendency to create and chase after false gods. The book of

Exodus offers a vivid illustration of this, while Moses was on Mount Sinai in the very act of receiving the Ten Commandments from the finger of God.

Back in camp, while Moses was away, his brother Aaron was in charge. (And I use that term loosely.) Aaron, who was never a strong leader like his brother Moses, gave in to the people's demand for an idol. Crowding around him, they basically said, "Hey, where is this Moses guy who led us out of Egypt? We don't know where he's gone or if he's ever coming back. What are we supposed to do?"

Immediately caving, Aaron said, "Break off the golden earrings which are in the ears of your wives, your sons, and your daughters, and bring them to me" (Exodus 32:2). And so all of the men, women, and children brought their gold items to Aaron, who melted them down and made an image of a golden calf. He put it up before them and said, "This is your god, O Israel, that brought you out of the land of Egypt!" (verse 4).

The people loved it! At last, a god they could see and touch and carry around. The Israelites began dancing around the idol, bowing down to it, and having a party.

But there is one extra twist in the story. Right before they began to worship this idol, Aaron said, "Tomorrow is a feast to the LORD" (verse 5). Translation? "We will worship the Lord through the golden calf."

Meanwhile, up on Mount Sinai, the Lord told Moses that he had better get back down to the camp again, because the people were doing the very thing that He told them not to do. So Moses descended from the mountain, with Joshua walking out ahead of him. When Joshua heard the noise and commotion down in the camp, he said, "There is a noise of war in the camp" (verse 17).

And Moses effectively said, "No, son. There's no war. That's a big *party* going on down there." And when they came in sight of the camp, they saw the Israelites dancing and carrying on before Aaron's calf of gold. Later, when Moses demanded an explanation from his brother, Aaron offered what must be the lamest excuse in all of human history. He said,

> "Don't get so upset, my lord. . . . You yourself know how evil these people are. They said to me, 'Make us gods who will lead us. We don't know what happened to this fellow Moses, who brought us here from the land of Egypt.' So I told them, 'Whoever has gold jewelry, take it off.' When they brought it to me, I simply threw it into the fire — and out came this calf!" (Exodus 32:22-24, NLT)

But here's the point. How did the people rationalize their behavior in bowing down before an idol? They *blended* it with legitimate worship of the Lord and said, "This calf? Oh, it's for the Lord. Tomorrow we'll have a big festival to the Lord."

That sort of thing won't fly with God.

Sometimes in our lives, we may be doing all kinds of ungodly things, but we still remember to say grace before a meal or even attend church and go through the motions of worship. We somehow think that by performing the external formalities of following the Lord, it will give us some kind of benefit or covering in His eyes.

But it won't. It never will. God wants us to change our hearts and our behavior. He says, "If you love me, keep my commands" (John 14:15, NIV).

Aaron and the Israelites tried to cover over what they were doing by telling themselves that the calf was simply a representation of the Lord. The fact is, they could call it whatever they liked, but it was flat-out idolatry. The Lord doesn't want any such representation of Himself.

A person who really knows God, who has experienced a new birth in Christ and is living in fellowship with Him, should never need an image or some other representation as a help for prayer. Something isn't right if you feel you need to do that.

Why is this a problem? It gives us a false concept of what God is really like. If the image is false, then the thought of God is also false, and it will produce a character that is false.

Speaking of idols, the psalmist says it like this:

> They have mouths, but cannot speak,
>   eyes, but cannot see.
> They have ears, but cannot hear,
>   noses, but cannot smell.
> They have hands, but cannot feel,
>   feet, but cannot walk,
>   nor can they utter a sound with their throats.
> *Those who make them will be like them,*
>   *and so will all who trust in them.* (Psalm 115:5-8, NIV,
>   emphasis added)

A man becomes like the thing he worships. And if you put something in the place of God, you eventually will become like that thing.

What is the endgame here? What is our ultimate goal? It is to become like Jesus.

Commandment Three:
Don't Take the Lord's Name in Vain

"You shall not take the name of the LORD your God in vain."
(Exodus 20:7)

This is done more often than you might think. One of the most obvious ways is through profanity. We've all heard people use the name of Jesus to punctuate a point: "Jesus Christ!"

Sometimes I'll reply to the person who says that, "Be careful. He might answer you sometime."

The interesting thing to me is that people never do that with the names of other gods, religious leaders, or gurus. You don't hear someone who is upset say, "Oh, Buddha!"

Or, "Joseph Smith!"

If they hit their thumb with a hammer, they don't yell, "Aw, Hare Krishna!"

Why do they use the name of Jesus Christ? Even people who are avowed atheists will blurt out His name when they're upset or wanting to make an emphatic point. In fact, some atheists utter the name of Jesus more than Christians do, but not in the right way. It's "Jesus!" this and "Christ!" that.

Why? Why is that?

I believe that in their heart of hearts, even agnostics and atheists understand there is power in that holy name. And that is why they use it. Yes, they are certainly taking the Lord's precious name in vain and violating the third commandment. But in a backhanded sort of way, they are acknowledging the existence of God. Why invoke the name of a God you don't believe in? Why say the name of someone whose existence you adamantly deny? Why use His name? You know there is power in that name.

We are reminded in Philippians 2,

> Therefore God also has highly exalted Him and given Him the name which is above every name, that at the name of Jesus every knee should bow, of those in heaven, and of those on earth, and of those under the earth, and that every tongue should confess that Jesus Christ is Lord, to the glory of God the Father. (verses 9-11)

The name of Jesus has power.

If you don't believe that, just say it somewhere, anywhere there are people around. Just speak the name out loud: "Jesus!" See the kind of reaction you get. Sometimes it will become still. Heads will turn.

The truth is, in our culture you can freely discuss so-called spirituality and religion with no fear of censure. People won't blink an eye. You can even talk about Christianity if you want to, in a general sort of way. But when you say the name *Jesus*, and talk about Him as a living Lord and Savior, something happens. People do double takes. They look at you as if to say, *What? Did he actually just say the name, Jesus Christ? Did she just speak of Jesus as a real and living person? What kind of fanatic is this?* People pay attention to the name of Jesus whether or not they want to, whether or not they intend to, because it's like no other name that ever was or ever will be. The book of Acts tells us, "There is no other name under heaven given to mankind by which we must be saved" (4:12, NIV).

God doesn't want His followers to ever take His name in vain, but to revere and honor His name. Psalm 113:2-3 says,

Blessed be the name of the LORD
From this time forth and forevermore!
From the rising of the sun to its going down
The LORD's name is to be praised.

He wants us to invoke that holy name in our hour of need as well. Proverbs 18:10 says, "The name of the LORD is a strong tower; the righteous run to it and are safe."

Job knew the power of that name when tragedy hit. He cried out, "I came naked from my mother's womb, and I will be naked when I leave. The LORD gave me what I had, and the LORD has taken it away. Praise the name of the LORD!" (Job 1:21, NLT).

Up on Mount Carmel, the prophet Elijah knew the power of the name of the Lord as he faced off with the prophets of Baal. They called on their god from morning to night, to no avail. Then Elijah called upon the name of the true and living God, and fire fell from heaven (see 1 Kings 18).

Moses said, "For I proclaim the name of the LORD: Ascribe greatness to our God" (Deuteronomy 32:3). There is power in that name. God pays attention when we speak His name.

Have you ever noticed that when someone speaks your name, you hear it, even if you're across the room? Someone mentions your name in a conversation, and your ears perk up. You know your name. You are interested in what is being said about you. In the same way, our God knows His name when we speak it. He pays attention, and He looks in our direction. In view of this, we must be very, very careful about the way we use or speak His name. It is holy.

CARELESS HABITS

In what other ways do we take the Lord's name in vain?

Maybe you have heard people say, "I swear to God, this is true. I swear it's true." Why do people say that? Probably because they are liars, and they feel they need to take an oath to get you to believe them. They will say, "Listen, I know I've stretched the truth before, but this I swear—I swear to God. . . ."

Stop that kind of talk. It doesn't make a truth-teller out of a liar, and it is using God's name in vain. If you consistently make it a practice to tell the truth, then you don't have to swear by anything.

In Matthew 5:37, Jesus said it like this: "Just say a simple, 'Yes, I will,' or 'No, I won't.' Anything beyond this is from the evil one" (NLT).

How else do we take His name in vain? We do this when we say things like "Oh, my God" or "Oh, God!" It is one thing to cry out His name when you're in crisis: "Oh, God, help me!" But when you see a cool car driving down the street and say, "Oh, my God," that is misusing His name. You have no need to call on the Lord.

I would even take this down to texting "OMG!" on your cell phone. People know what you mean. You mean, "Oh, my God!"

My little granddaughter busted me on this the other day. I don't say, "Oh, my God," but I do occasionally say, "Oh, my gosh!" When I said it, little Stella quickly looked up at me and said, "You are not supposed to say that."

Rebuked by a three-year-old!

Another way the Lord's name is used in vain is when we use it for personal gain. We've all seen this happen. People put a Christian label on certain items to entice believers to buy the Christian version rather than the secular version. You see all kinds of tacky things with the name of Jesus or a Bible verse on them: doggy T-shirts, Frisbees, pens and pencils, mints, and gum. I even saw a Christian popcorn bowl advertised recently, with Philippians 4:13 emblazoned on the side. I've seen "walk-the-walk" Christian flip-flops, with Scripture on them. I've seen end-times-survivalist Bible covers in olive green, with GPS units enclosed. And have you seen the "Jesus reigns" golf umbrella? (I'm not making this up!) It seems to me that people are misusing the Lord's name to sell their products.

When we speak of using the Lord's name "in vain," that means to use it in an empty, idle, insincere, or frivolous way. We've all done it. I know I have. But it doesn't honor the Lord, and it doesn't please Him.

Another way we do this is to use His name in a cliché that we don't really mean. Some people say, "Praise the Lord!" in every sentence until it loses all its meaning and becomes little more than a verbal habit: "I'm going to go get a hamburger, praise the Lord!"

Do they mean that every time they say it? If they do, that's great. But if they are just saying empty words, then it is a misuse of His holy name.

Or how about "God bless you"? We throw that one around, don't we? *God bless you. Bless you. God bless.* Sometimes we say it to get rid of people, don't we? They're in the middle of a long story, and when they take a breath, we'll say, "God bless you. Gotta go now." In other words, the conversation is over, and we're out of there.

I'm not saying that we should never say, "God bless you" or "Praise the Lord." I'm simply saying that if you speak the name of God or Jesus, then do so intentionally and with purpose, and not in an empty or frivolous way. It is the name above all names, and the Lord pays attention to His name.

Perhaps the most subtle form in which this law is broken is through sheer hypocrisy. I'm speaking of the man or woman who talks openly about the Lord but really has no intention of keeping His commandments. Jesus said, "But why do you call Me 'Lord, Lord,' and not do the things which I say?" (Luke 6:46).

This may surprise you, but I think hypocrisy in the church is far worse than profanity in the street. Don't get me wrong; I hate seeing and hearing the name of God and the name of Jesus dragged through the mud in books and movies and music and out in the street. But there is something worse: It is singing praise to the name of Jesus in church on Sunday and then living the rest of the week in open contradiction to what He says.

"Are you saying I have to be perfect, Greg?"

No. Every one of us falls into hypocrisy from time to time, including me. We all fall short. The Bible says that we do. But I'm not talking about a Christian who occasionally stumbles. I'm talking about a pretender who masquerades as a believer. A hypocrite is an actor; that is the literal definition of the word. It speaks of someone who pretends to be someone and something they are not. In other words, they play a part.

When this happens in an assembly of believers, it is more offensive to God than anything. Jesus said,

"Many will say to Me in that day, 'Lord, Lord, have we not prophesied in Your name, cast out demons in Your name, and done many wonders in Your name?' And then I will declare to them, 'I never knew you; depart from Me, you who practice lawlessness!'" (Matthew 7:22-23)

Commandment Four: The Principle of Rest
"Remember the Sabbath day, to keep it holy." (Exodus 20:8)

This commandment has produced more confusion, misunderstanding, and hard feelings than probably any other.

Let me get one thing out of the way right up front: The Sabbath is Saturday. It always has been and always will be. When God had finished creating all things in six days, He set apart the seventh day as a day of rest and instituted this Sabbath rest as a law in the Ten Commandments.

But here is the question: Are Christians living under the New Covenant to still keep the Sabbath the way it was originally set up for the Jewish people, or has the emphasis changed?

I suggest the latter is the case. Saturday is still the Sabbath, but the key lies in how we view it today. It is interesting to me that this is the only one of the Ten Commandments *not* repeated in the New Testament. All the rest are repeated in the New Testament—and some are made even more stringent. In the Sermon on the Mount, for instance, Jesus said, "You have heard that it was said to those of old, 'You shall not murder, and whoever murders will be in danger of the judgment.' But I say to you that whoever is angry with his brother without a cause shall be in danger of the judgment" (Matthew 5:21-22).

Then again the Lord said, "You have heard that it was said to those of old, 'You shall not commit adultery.' But I say to you that whoever looks at a woman to lust for her has already committed adultery with her in his heart" (verses 27-28).

So Jesus actually took those two commandments to the next level. In fact, that is exactly what Jesus came to do. He did not come to do away with the Law and the Prophets, but to fulfill them.

When Jesus Himself, God in human form, walked this earth, He was accused of breaking the Sabbath because He healed a man on the Sabbath. He replied, in essence, "You guys have got it all wrong with all of the extra restrictions and laws you have added to the Law about the Sabbath. You've missed the point!" He said, "The Sabbath was made to meet the needs of people, and not people to meet the requirements of the Sabbath" (Mark 2:27, NLT).

The Sabbath was made for man. It is a day of rest, and it isn't repeated anywhere in the New Testament. Jesus never taught anyone to keep the Sabbath and neither did the apostles. In fact, they began meeting on the first day of the week, Sunday, because Jesus rose on Sunday. Under the Old Covenant, the Jews would gather in the temple or synagogue to worship on the Sabbath. But now under the New Covenant, because our Lord rose on the first day of the week, Sunday is the day we set apart.

But Sunday does not become the Sabbath day. Sabbath is Sabbath. Sunday is Sunday. Nevertheless, Sunday is a day set apart to worship the Lord.

Scripture even criticizes those who make a big deal out of the Sabbath when it comes to Christians. In Colossians 2:16, Paul wrote, "Therefore do not let anyone judge you by what you eat or drink, or with regard to a religious festival, a New Moon celebration or a Sabbath day" (NIV).

Why? The apostle answered that question in the very next verse: "These are a shadow of the things that were to come; the reality, however, is found in Christ" (verse 17, NIV).

In a similar way, we don't sacrifice animals anymore as part of our worship. Why don't we do that? Jesus is the Lamb of God who *fulfills* those Old Testament types. It's the same situation with the Sabbath. The Sabbath has been fulfilled in a relationship with Christ, where we enter into the rest of His finished work, accomplished for us on the cross.

Animal sacrifices and the Sabbath were whispers and shadows of greater things to come.

When my granddaughter, Stella, and I are playing together, we will sometimes chase our own shadows or jump on them. But you can't hug a shadow. And who would want to? Why hug a shadow when you can hug the real person from whom the shadow comes? Animal sacrifices and the Sabbath were shadows of the Lord, who has come to fulfill all of these things.

The author of the book of Hebrews pulled it all together when he wrote, "So there is a special rest [or Sabbath] still waiting for the people of God. For all who have entered into God's rest have rested from their labors, just as God did after creating the world" (4:9-10, NLT).

I bring this up because, at some point, you might find yourself in a conversation like this:

"What day do you go to church?"

"I go to church on Sunday."

"Oh . . . you don't go on the Sabbath?"

"Well, no."

"Do you realize that you're breaking the fourth commandment by not worshipping the Lord on the Sabbath day? That day is holy."

But the truth is, I worship the Lord on Monday, Tuesday, Wednesday, Thursday, Friday, Saturday, and Sunday. *Every* day is holy to the Lord. *Every* day is a day to enter into His rest. Don't let anyone tell you that you have to keep the Sabbath day to be a true follower of Jesus. It is a distortion of Scripture.

"COME UNTO ME"

If that is what the Sabbath *is not*, then what is it? Is there any principle here for us? Yes, there is, because I believe we do need a day of rest. Have you noticed how many people seem to be in a hurry? (You certainly would if you lived in Southern California and needed to traverse the freeway system every day.) We are the only nation in the world with a mountain called Rushmore. Many of us have schedules that are packed with layer upon layer of activities, appointments, and obligations—and they're sometimes spread all over town.

Some people call it multitasking.

I call it too busy.

We're talking to one person and texting someone else at the same time—all while scanning the news or checking the stock market on our iPad. In the process, we're really not giving any of these things (or people) our full attention or doing anything as well as we ought to.

The Sabbath principle would call us to step back from all the activities, quiet our hearts and minds, and seek the Lord. As Psalm 46:10 puts it, "Be still, and know that I am God."

Even Jesus took time off. The gospel of Mark gives us this account:

> The apostles gathered around Jesus and reported to
> him all they had done and taught. Then, because so

many people were coming and going that they did not even have a chance to eat, he said to them, "Come with me by yourselves to a quiet place and get some rest." (6:30-31, NIV)

Our bodies are busy every single day. Did you know that in the next 24 hours, your body is going to work very hard? Your heart will beat 103,689 times. Your blood will travel 168,000 miles. You will breathe 23,000 times. You will inhale 438 cubic feet of air. You will consume 3.5 pounds of food. (I can eat that much in one good burrito!) You will drink 2.9 quarts of liquid. You will speak 4,800 words. You will move 750 muscles. And you will exercise 7 million brain cells. Whew! No wonder you feel tired!

It is a very, very good thing to say, "On Sunday morning—the very first day of the week—we're going to gather with other believers, worship the Lord, get into the Word, have fellowship with one another, and just take this time to get spiritually recharged."

That is a good thing. It is a gift from God. And when we enjoy that rest and reconnect with the Lord in a deeper way, we're benefiting from the Sabbath principle that God has given us in His Word.

The ultimate fulfillment for every believer is to simply rest in the work that God wants to do for each one of us. Jesus said, "Come to Me, all you who labor and are heavy-laden and overburdened, and I will cause you to rest. [I will ease and relieve and refresh your souls]" (Matthew 11:28, AMP).

The really wonderful thing about being a Christian is that I don't have to do a bunch of things to earn God's approval. Why? Because God's approval was accomplished at the cross, where Jesus met all the righteous requirements and demands of a holy Father. All other religions say, "Do this," "Do that," "Do, do, do."

Christianity says, "Done."

When Jesus cried out, "It is finished!" from the cross, He used the Greek word *tetevlestai*. In other words, the task was completed, that was the end of it. It was a common word back in that culture. If you were building a chair and you finally finished, you would step back from your work and say, "*Tetevlestai*. It's done." You might say the same thing at the end of a long work day or when the food came out of the oven.

But when Jesus used that phrase at Calvary, accomplishing our redemption, it took on a whole new meaning. *It's done! It's satisfied! The price is paid! The transaction is completed!* I don't have to accomplish a long list of requirements to be loved and accepted by God. Instead, I do things *for* God, knowing in the deepest part of my being that I am already loved and accepted by Him.

God loves me, and in response to that great love, I want to find a way to love Him back—not just in what I say or what I sing, but in every area of my life.

It really isn't rocket science. If we love Him, we will keep His commandments.

HOT-BUTTON ISSUES

The Ten Commandments have us covered in our most important relationships. They have us covered in our vertical relationship with God; that is what the first four are all about, as we've just noted. But they also cover us in our horizontal relationships with people.

In this chapter, we'll look more closely at that second group of six.

Commandment Five:
"Honor Your Father and Mother"

"Honor your father and your mother, that your days may be long upon the land which the LORD your God is giving you."
(Exodus 20:12)

Before a word is spoken about how to treat others in our lives, God starts with the family. It's a paradox, I know, but I don't think anything can bring greater pleasure—or greater pain—than our family. Kids have problems with parents; parents have struggles with kids.

Sometimes you will hear people say (by way of excusing

some fault or failing of their own), "Well, you know, I came from a dysfunctional family."

I always want to reply, "Oh, really? Welcome to the club. Welcome to humanity." My question is, who *doesn't* have a dysfunctional family? I came from a dysfunctional family, and I am currently the head of a dysfunctional family.

But God enables me to be the man, the husband, the father, and the grandfather that He wants me to be as I rely on Him day by day. So I don't worry too much about being dysfunctional.

The family is so important. Our very existence as a society depends on the success of the family. It has been said, "A family can survive without a nation, but a nation cannot survive without the family."

Maybe that's why Satan has launched an unprecedented attack against the family in our nation today. In fact, the Bible tells us that one of the signs of the last days will be a breakdown in the family—and a disrespect for parents in particular.

In 2 Timothy 3:2, the apostle wrote, "Men will be lovers of themselves, lovers of money, boasters, proud, blasphemers, disobedient to parents." That may be the direction of our culture, but God has a countercultural word for us: "Honor your father and mother."

Notice something specific here. This commandment says, "Honor your *father* and your *mother*," and it doesn't give any other combinations. It doesn't say, "Honor your father and your father," "Honor your mother and your other mother," or "Honor your mother and her live-in lover." God's template for the family is one father and one mother, and we tamper with that pattern at our own peril.

We're all aware of the movement afoot today to redefine

marriage and family. The media and modern culture are pushing with all their considerable influence to legitimize same-sex marriage. We've always had homosexuality as part of the culture, but we have never had such a concerted, concentrated, well-funded movement to legitimize and promote homosexuality as we have today.

Don't be fooled: This is not a merely political issue; this is a moral issue and a biblical issue. This is a clear-cut issue in Scripture, and you are either looking at it from a biblical worldview or you are not. As for the Bible itself, there is no room for equivocation. Homosexuality is neither God's intention nor God's order. Period.

In the Garden of Eden, the Creator brought a man and a woman together. It was Adam and Eve, not Adam and Steve. No, God is not anti-gay; God is anti-sin, no matter how it is expressed. But the bottom line is that He loves all people and wants all people to come to repentance and enter into a relationship with Him.

Someone will say, "Okay, Greg, I guess you're a homophobe."

I've come to really hate that word *phobic*. If you speak out on anything or have an opinion on anything, you're accused of some kind of phobia. If you are critical of drunks, you're drunkaphobic. If you criticize cats, you're cataphobic. Me? I'm a sinaphobic. I want to please God and steer clear of sin in my life.

Let me make a clear and simple statement here: You are not born gay, and alcoholism is not a disease. "Oh," some will say. "That is so insensitive, so mean, so harsh, so judgmental."

It is also *so biblical*.

You are not born gay; you are born a sinner. Yes, as a person born with a sinful nature, you might be attracted to members of the same sex. Certainly that can happen. And as a person who is born a sinner, you might be more prone to issues of addiction. Some people become addicts if they even touch alcohol or drugs. So I will agree that certain people, born in sin, may be more vulnerable than others in certain areas.

But I have a stronger statement to make than that.

All of these sins—*all* of these addictions or vulnerabilities—can be overcome by the power of the Holy Spirit. I have met people who were addicts who no longer are, and they are now under the control of the Holy Spirit. I have met people who were homosexuals, and they are now living a heterosexual lifestyle.

Again, no one was born gay. But we were all born sinners in need of a Savior who can change us and help us to live the life He has called us to live.

Here's what the Bible says:

> Or do you not know that wrongdoers will not inherit the kingdom of God? Do not be deceived: Neither the sexually immoral nor idolaters nor adulterers nor men who have sex with men nor thieves nor the greedy nor drunkards nor slanderers nor swindlers will inherit the kingdom of God. And that is what some of you were. But you were washed, you were sanctified, you were justified in the name of the Lord Jesus Christ and by the Spirit of our God. (1 Corinthians 6:9-11, NIV)

The Bible is neither vague, contradictory, nor confusing when it comes to the issue of homosexuality. Romans 1:22-27 lays out the biblical position plainly and with great clarity.

God's order for the family is one man and one woman, a husband and a wife who are faithful to each other for a lifetime. *That* is marriage, and we need to give it the honor and respect it deserves.

If you came from a family where your mom and dad stayed together and raised you as a Christian, then you need to really thank them — and the Lord.

I grew up in a home of divorce where we moved around a lot, and people would soon find out that I didn't have a dad. That was considered scandalous back in the 1950s and early 1960s. When other kids would find out that my mom was divorced and I didn't have a dad, they would look at me like I had just arrived from Mars.

Now it's considered curious if you *do* have a mom and a dad who live together and love each other.

Sometimes someone will ask Cathe and me how long we have been married, and we will say, "Thirty-eight years." When we say that, it's like their jaw drops to the ground. For starters, my wife looks like she is thirty-eight. Nevertheless, as the years go by, our marriage becomes more and more of a testament to the power and faithfulness of God in our lives.

The fifth commandment is for all who have living parents, whether we are little children or grown adults. "Regard (treat with honor, due obedience, and courtesy) your father and mother, that your days may be long in the land the Lord your God gives you" (Exodus 20:12, AMP).

Speaking directly to children still in the home, the Bible says, "Children, obey your parents in all things, for this is well pleasing to the Lord" (Colossians 3:20). Or as the Phillips translation puts it, "As for you children, obey your parents in everything, for this is the right and Christian thing to do."

Yes, I know, this can seem difficult at times.

Sometimes kids will look at their parents and think they don't know what they are talking about. *How could you say that to me? Why won't you let me do this thing? What is wrong with you?*

Mark Twain once wrote, "When I was a boy of fourteen, my father was so ignorant I could hardly stand to have the old man around. But when I got to be twenty-one, I was astonished at how much he had learned in seven years."[1]

It reminds me of a magazine article I read years ago that described how a child sees his father as the years go by.

At age four, the child says, "My daddy can do anything."

At seven, he says, "My daddy knows a lot. A whole lot."

At eight, he says, "My father doesn't know quite everything."

At twelve, "Oh well, naturally my dad doesn't know about that, either."

At fourteen, "Dad is so out of date."

At twenty-one, "Dad is so lame."

At twenty-five, "Dad knows a little bit about it, but not too much."

At thirty, "Let's find out what Dad thinks about that."

At thirty-five, "Before we decide, let's get Dad's idea first."

At fifty, "I wonder what my dad would have thought about that."

And at sixty, "You know what? My dad knew literally everything."

You might ask the question, "What if my parents aren't Christians? Should I still honor them?" The answer is yes, you should. In fact, that may be the way that you win them to the Lord.

It is often true that the hardest people to reach are members of your own family—your mom, dad, brother, sister, and extended family. Even Jesus didn't reach His whole family before His death and resurrection—and who was a better example than Jesus Christ? He never did anything wrong.

Can you imagine being one of Jesus' siblings and having Mary lecture you? "Why can't you be more like Jesus? Look at how your brother behaves. Look at how respectful He is. Look at how hard He works. Be more like Jesus."

"But Mom, He is like *perfect*."

But the fact is, Jesus' siblings and Mary didn't see the light until after the resurrection (see John 7:3-5).

The point is, honor your father and mother if they don't believe in the Lord. Obviously, if your parents ask you to do something that is unbiblical, you aren't required to do that. If your parents were to say, "We forbid you to believe in Jesus Christ," then it would be permissible under those circumstances to disobey them, because sometimes one law supersedes another.

It is like when the apostles were forbidden by the Jewish authorities to speak or teach in the name of Jesus. They replied, "Whether it's right in God's eyes to listen to you rather than to God, you decide. As for us, there's no question —we can't keep quiet about what we've seen and heard" (Acts 4:19-20, MSG).

God is your ultimate authority, but under most circumstances, you are to obey your parents and honor them as much as you can.

Commandment Six: "You Shall Not Murder"

"You shall not murder." (Exodus 20:13)

We live in a violent and murderous culture today, with over 2 million people a year becoming victims of violent crimes.

In the old King James English, the sixth commandment reads, "Thou shalt not kill," but a better translation of this verse is, "You shall not murder."

This commandment obviously forbids the taking of another human life for no justifiable reason. But be careful here: The Bible does *not* condemn all killing. A careful reading of Numbers 35 reveals there is a difference between killing and murder.

Obviously, all murder is killing, but not all killing is necessarily murder. There are times when death is permissible, though not desirable. You are permitted to defend yourself and your family. When Jesus sent His disciples out to preach the gospel, He told them to take a sword with them. Why should they take a sword? For shish kebab? No, it was for the purpose of defending themselves. They had every right to defend themselves, as do you.

When we try to stop a person who is bent on destroying innocent lives—as with a shooter or a terrorist—taking that life is justifiable. I've heard people try to use an argument of moral equivalency and say, "Oh no, *any* killing is wrong. And if we kill murderers or terrorists, that makes us as evil as they are."

How ridiculous.

Was the United States wrong to stop the Nazis from eradicating the Jewish people from the face of the planet in World War II? Was that a just cause? Yes, it was. War is never desirable, and neither is the deadly force a police officer may be compelled to use. But there are times when we simply do what we have to do to defend human life.

God has established laws by which to govern a culture, and those who break those laws will face repercussions. (And they know it.) God has even established the police and the military according to Scripture. Paul made that very clear in Romans 13:

> Everyone must submit to governing authorities. For all authority comes from God, and those in positions of authority have been placed there by God. So anyone who rebels against authority is rebelling against what God has instituted, and they will be punished. For the authorities do not strike fear in people who are doing right, but in those who are doing wrong. Would you like to live without fear of the authorities? Do what is right, and they will honor you. The authorities are God's servants, sent for your good. But if you are doing wrong, of course you should be afraid, for they have the power to punish you. They are God's servants, sent for the very purpose of punishing those who do what is wrong. (verses 1-4, NLT)

When you're breaking the law, you hate the police, and you're paranoid every time you see a cop. "Oh no, it's the man . . . the fuzz . . . the pigs . . . the heat."

The fact is, if you're obeying the laws and doing what is right, you don't have to worry or feel that little shiver of fear when you see a police vehicle.

I've spent a lot of time with police officers and currently

serve as chaplain for the local police department. As a result, I've done a number of ride-alongs with the officers. When you're out in a public place with a police officer in uniform, it's funny to see how people react. You walk into a coffee shop, and everyone steals little glances at you—then they quickly look away.

Why do they do that? Because the police officer represents the law, and he or she has been placed in that position by God. The sight of that badge and the weapon stir up a sensation of either healthy respect or out-and-out fear.

It's the same with the military. That uniform means something. Does that mean police officers and military personnel always do the right thing? No. Does that mean these are institutions established by the Lord Himself? The answer is yes.

What does it mean to not murder? The word *murder* could be translated "to dash in pieces." Understand this: The word used in Exodus 20 for "you shall not murder" never describes the death of an animal. Nor does it describe the death of an opponent in war. Nor does it describe death by capital punishment.

I believe in capital punishment, and I believe that the Bible teaches it (but I know there are good people on both sides of that debate). Genesis 9:6 says, "If anyone takes a human life, that person's life will also be taken by human hands. For God made human beings in his own image" (NLT). This is a command of God that predates Moses and the Ten Commandments.

Now we are assuming, of course, that the person would be proven guilty beyond any doubt whatsoever before being executed. But the ironic thing is how you will see people outside a prison, praying, singing hymns, and holding a candlelight vigil for a person who has murdered a child or slaughtered an entire family. They hold up signs that say, "Thou shalt not kill." But that is not what the Bible says. It says, "You shall not murder," and if you do, you should pay for that act with your life.

Here is what seems so strange to me: I have met people who are passionately against capital punishment, but support abortion. What sense does that make? They want to destroy the innocent and spare the guilty? I think it should be the other way around: spare the innocent preborn baby, and punish those who willfully shed innocent blood.

ABORTION

Sometimes people will preface their comments on abortion by saying, "I realize this is a controversial subject."

Really? Controversial to whom?

"Well, you know, even theologians debate when life begins."

Seriously? Which theologians are those? Certainly they are not theologians who believe in the Bible. And if they don't believe in the Bible, then why should we pay any attention to what they say? What do their comments have to do with the real world?

As for the Bible, it isn't hesitant or unclear at all on the subject. Life begins at conception. End of story. Listen to David's words as he spoke of being in the womb:

> You made all the delicate, inner parts of my body
> and knit me together in my mother's womb.
> Thank you for making me so wonderfully complex!
> Your workmanship is marvelous — how well I know it.

You watched me as I was being formed in utter seclusion,
>   as I was woven together in the dark of the womb.
You saw me before I was born.
>   Every day of my life was recorded in your book.
Every moment was laid out
>   before a single day had passed. (Psalm 139:13-16,
>   NLT)

This passage shows clearly that God has a plan for each and every boy or girl, even before birth. Over in Jeremiah 1:5, the Lord told the prophet: "I knew you before I formed you in your mother's womb. Before you were born I set you apart and appointed you as my prophet to the nations" (NLT).

Notice that God said, "*I* formed you in your mother's womb."

Every child is created by God and should be given a chance to live. God does not say, "I waited until you were born to have a plan for you, because you weren't human yet. You were just a mass of tissue."

No, God had a plan before the child was out of the womb.

Max Lucado wrote, "You were deliberately planned, specifically gifted, and lovingly positioned on this earth by the Master Craftsman."[2]

Looking at my own life, I was conceived out of wedlock. I wasn't planned, and in one sense, I wasn't meant to be. But I'm so grateful that my mother didn't get an abortion. She carried me to term and allowed me to live out my life and to serve the Lord.

Every child has a right to live.

"But what about a mother's rights, Greg?"

The mother's right is to protect her child. There are no

illegitimate children. Every child is legitimate in the eyes of God, no matter how they were conceived.

In spite of these obvious truths, abortion is commonly used today as a form of birth control. Since the passing of *Roe v. Wade* in the early 1970s, more than 53 million babies have been aborted. I wonder if one of those babies might have grown up to find the cure for cancer . . . or if one of those babies would have been the president of the United States . . . or if one of those babies would have been a great preacher . . . or if one of those babies would have done something to help our world. But we will never know, because they were silenced. Stopped. Abortion has grown into a multimillion-dollar industry in the U.S., and it takes in billions worldwide.

And here is something that is rarely discussed. When young women obtain an abortion, many of them experience a much higher depression and suicide rate than women who did not make this terrible choice.

Abortion is not the answer. If you have conceived a child, then marry the father if possible and raise the child. If you can't do that, then raise the child as a single mother. And if you can't do that, then carry the child to term and give him or her up for adoption.

You hear all kinds of terms used to dehumanize preborn babies. We hear them called fetuses, embryos, globs of cells, uterine contents, products of conception, or even "potential human beings."

That last one cracks me up. What *else* would a child become? A horse? A cow? How absurd. A preborn child is a human being, not a potential human being. What's more, he or she is a human being with vast and incredible potential, created in the image of God Himself.

"But, Greg, what if the mother's life is in danger? Is that an acceptable risk?"

In response to that question, let me ask another. What if, as a mother, you saw your child running across the street with a car rapidly approaching. Would you, as a mom, put your life in danger to snatch that little one out of the path of the oncoming car?

Any mom or dad worthy of that title would not hesitate. They would rush into the street instinctively to save their son or daughter. Of course they would! The child's life is in danger, and a parent lays down their life for the child, not the other way around. The parent would do whatever it would take to save that life.

Yes, the doctor may tell you as a mother that your life might be endangered by carrying a child to term. But what if the doctors tell you that, and then you go ahead and have the baby anyway—and come through it alive and well? That is what happened with NFL quarterback Tim Tebow. Tim's parents were Christian missionaries in the Philippines in 1987 when Pam, Tim's mother, contracted amoebic dysentery, the leading cause of death in the country. She was pregnant with Tim, her fifth child, and she became very ill and dehydrated. At that time and place, the Tebows didn't have access to the best medical care, and a doctor told her to abort the baby. He explained that the powerful medication she would need to cure her of amoebic dysentery would kill the child.

Pam and her husband prayed, and they made the decision to carry the baby to term. The boy survived—and so did his mother. And as the years have gone by, both have recognized that this was a gift from God.

Tim is now a strapping six-foot-three, 235-pound

quarterback for the Denver Broncos. While at the University of Florida, he won the Heisman Trophy for the best college football player in the nation. Not only that, but Tim has been a bold witness for Jesus Christ and speaks up for his faith.

Didn't he have a right to live?

I recognize that someone reading this chapter might be saying, "Greg, you've made me very uncomfortable, because I've had an abortion. So what about me? Have I killed an innocent human being?"

To be truthful, yes, you have. And you need to turn to the Lord for forgiveness and restoration. The same God who gives us His laws and standards also has provided a way for us to be forgiven and cleansed when we violate the standards. Praise His name!

David wrote in the Psalms, "If you, LORD, kept a record of sins, LORD, who could stand? But with you there is forgiveness, so that we can, with reverence, serve you" (130:3-4, NIV).

He doesn't offer you karma; He offers you forgiveness. In the New Testament we read, "If we confess our sins, He is faithful and just to forgive us our sins and to cleanse us from all unrighteousness" (1 John 1:9).

The fact is that we all need this forgiveness, because we have all broken these commandments in some way, shape, or form. As a case in point, Jesus took this "you shall not murder" command and brought it to a whole new level in His Sermon on the Mount.

He said, "You have heard that it was said to those of old, 'You shall not murder, and whoever murders will be in danger of the judgment.' But I say to you that whoever is angry with his brother without a cause shall be in danger of the judgment" (Matthew 5:21-22).

Have you ever hated anyone? Have you ever hated anyone so intensely that you wished they were dead? The Bible says, "Anyone who hates another brother or sister is really a murderer at heart" (1 John 3:15, NLT).

Hating is a sin before God, just as murder is a sin before God. So we might congratulate ourselves for having never taken the life of another human being, but have we held murderous hatred in our hearts?

Murder and hatred have no place in our lives. The Bible tells us in Ephesians 4:31-32, "Get rid of all bitterness, rage, anger, harsh words, and slander, as well as all types of evil behavior. Instead, be kind to each other, tenderhearted, forgiving one another, just as God through Christ has forgiven you" (NLT).

The Bible teaches that we are to love, not hate, our enemies. We are to love them and forgive them, just as God has loved and forgiven you and me.

We are all sinners. We have all broken God's commandments, and we all need forgiveness, grace, mercy, and help.

The good news is that Jesus freely and graciously offers that help if we will come to Him.

MORE ABSOLUTE TRUTH

A little boy who heard a message from his Sunday school teacher about the Ten Commandments got a little confused about the seventh commandment. So he decided to ask his dad about it on their way home from church.

"Daddy," he said, "what does the Sunday school teacher mean when she said, 'Thou shall not commit agriculture?'"

The father knew exactly what his boy was asking about and refrained from smiling. He knew that the teacher was referring to the commandment that says, "You shall not commit adultery."

"Well, let's see, son," he said. "If we're talking about agriculture, I guess that means you're not supposed to plow the other man's field."

That is a pretty good answer.

In this chapter, we'll be looking more closely at the seventh commandment.

Commandment Seven:
"You Shall Not Commit Adultery"

"You shall not commit adultery." (Exodus 20:14)

Committing adultery is having sex with someone besides your spouse. It is speaking of immorality in general, not merely the specific act of unfaithfulness on the part of a marital partner.

Remember, these are God's top ten commands. The Bible identifies many issues that concern Him, but these are the ten things God chose to break out and say, "It is terribly important for you to understand and obey these commandments. If you violate them, it will be spiritually harmful and destructive in your life."

Sexual purity is one of those things—one of the specific commands God inscribed in stone with His own finger.

Adultery is when you have sex with someone besides your spouse; fornication is when you have sex before marriage. Both are condemned in Scripture—and for good reason.

Can you even imagine how different our world would be today if everyone in our culture kept this seventh commandment alone? Prostitution would disappear overnight. AIDS and STDs would fade away like a bad dream. Imagine how many marriages and families still would be together. Imagine how many abortions never would happen. Imagine how many tears never would have to be shed.

Sadly, our secular culture has taken this topic of sex and sexuality and poured its own meaning into what it is and what it isn't, virtually taking control of the subject and redefining how we view it.

It is time for the church of Jesus Christ to take the subject of sex back again and set it in the context of a wonderful gift from the Creator that needs to be handled with respect and great care.

Without embarrassment, we need to say what is good about sex and declare its beauty and wonder within the bounds of marriage. In fact, if it were not for sex, we wouldn't be having this conversation, because none of us would be here. God Himself designed and created human sexuality, and there doesn't need to be any shame or embarrassment connected to it, if it is done in God's way, with God's guidelines.

What is God's way?

In a marriage relationship.

"Well, what about just living together?"

No, that is not God's way.

"What about trying things out, just to see if we're compatible in this area?"

No, that is not God's way.

Think about it like this. A river is one of the great wonders of God's creation. A river brings life, refreshment, recreation, and commerce to a city. It is a thing of beauty, joy, and great utility . . . within its banks. But when a river starts flowing outside its banks, it becomes an instrument of death, destruction, sorrow, and unbelievable devastation.

So it is with the gift of sex. Within the "banks" God has established in His Word, sex and sexuality is an unparalleled force for life, strength, and beauty. Outside those banks, however, it is a natural disaster, destroying life and leaving mud and chaos in its wake.

God's way for sex is within a marriage commitment between one man and one woman, with no other variation of that. When a man and woman pledge their love to one another and are united in marriage, God blesses their sexual union within the protection of that lifelong relationship.

Does it surprise you to hear that God wants to *bless* sex between a husband and wife? It's true. Did you know that was even possible? He can truly bless it. You don't have to feel guilty or bad about it. You can feel quite good about it, as a matter of fact. In the book of Proverbs we read,

> Drink water from your own cistern,
> running water from your own well.
> Should your springs overflow in the streets,
> your streams of water in the public squares?
> Let them be yours alone,
> never to be shared with strangers.
> May your fountain be blessed,
> and may you rejoice in the wife of your youth.
> A loving doe, a graceful deer —
> may her breasts satisfy you always,
> may you ever be intoxicated with her love. (Proverbs
> 5:15-19, NIV)

That sounds to me like God has a pretty good opinion of married sex. And yet if His order is violated in these things, it can result in incomparable spiritual destruction.

Sometimes people will say the Christian view on sex is that it is only for procreation and childbearing. I'm not sure where people come up with statements like that. Clearly, sex is the process through which childbearing takes place. But at the same time, something powerful takes place when two people come together sexually that goes beyond the mere physical union.

Sex can be pleasurable and fulfilling, and God made it that way. In fact, we are told in 1 Timothy that we are to put our hope in God "who richly provides us with everything for our enjoyment" (6:17, NIV). And guess what? That includes sexual pleasure in marriage.

If you don't believe me, read Song of Solomon. While the book certainly can be seen as an allegory of our relationship with the Lord, it also can be read and appreciated at face value. It is a love story between a man and a woman who find fulfillment and pleasure in a sexual union.

Sex really isn't the issue. The issue is the *place* of sex. In marriage it is blessed, enjoyable, and fulfilling. Outside of marriage it is harmful, damaging, degrading, and unbelievably destructive. We are told in Hebrews 13:4, "Marriage should be honored by all, and the marriage bed kept pure" (NIV). That is why there can be no such thing as a one-night stand.

Sexual infidelity never can be regarded as something inconsequential or trivial. "Oh, it was just a little fling. It didn't mean anything." Yes, it did. It meant a lot. Sex isn't some casual toy; it is a gift from God to be saved for the person with whom you are joined in marriage. When you engage in sexual contact with another person, you become one with that individual.

In 1 Corinthians, Paul wrote:

Don't you realize that your bodies are actually parts of Christ? Should a man take his body, which is part of Christ, and join it to a prostitute? Never! And don't you realize that if a man joins himself to a prostitute, he becomes one body with her? For the Scriptures say, "The two are united into one." But the person who is joined to the Lord is one spirit with him.

Run from sexual sin! No other sin so clearly affects

> the body as this one does. For sexual immorality is a sin against your own body. (6:15-18, NLT)

Someone might say, "Come on, Greg. Having sex doesn't hurt anyone."

Really? I think sexual sin hurts a lot of people. It damages them spiritually—and emotionally too. A University of Tennessee study among young women discovered a direct correlation between illicit sexual behavior and serious emotional problems.

It doesn't hurt anyone? What about teenage pregnancies? Every year, 1 million teens become pregnant, and many of those pregnancies never make it to term. In fact, one out of every five abortions is performed on a woman under the age of twenty. These same statistics show that 400,000 of the 1.6 million abortions occurring annually are performed on teenage mothers.

It doesn't hurt anyone? What about the mother who, for the rest of her life, carries the shame and regret of taking her baby's life?

It doesn't hurt anyone? What about the baby who is never given the privilege of living out his or her life? I believe that God, in His grace, welcomes every one of those aborted children into heaven. But sadly, they are denied the opportunity to live out their lives and discover their gifts and potential in our world. Who knows what some of these children could have accomplished had they been allowed the privilege of life? Who can imagine the difference they might have made?

That is why the Bible warns against sexual sin, because it *does* hurt, and it brings mind-boggling spiritual and emotional devastation.

Jesus, of course, took this to another level in the Sermon on the Mount. We might congratulate ourselves, saying, "Well, I'm not an adulterer. He's talking about someone else here, because I would never do that."

Conceding that point, let me ask you this: Have you ever looked on a woman with lust in your heart? Have you ever looked at a man with lust in your heart?

The answer, by the way, is yes, you have. We all have. So here is the bottom line: Jesus said, "You have heard that it was said to those of old, 'You shall not commit adultery.' But I say to you that whoever looks at a woman to lust for her has already committed adultery with her in his heart" (Matthew 5:27-28).

Granted, it is worse to commit adultery than to look lustfully. But at the same time, looking lustfully is a violation of this commandment as well. By the way, the word Jesus used here for *look* doesn't refer to a casual glance. The Greek term refers to the continuous act of looking. In this usage, the emphasis isn't on an incidental or involuntary look, but rather on an intentional and repeated gazing.

In our twisted culture today, it is pretty hard to avoid images that could stir up lust. You don't even have to go out looking for them. You could be standing in line at the supermarket and suddenly find yourself looking at an image on a magazine cover. Or you are driving down the street, and there it is on a billboard.

You say, "I wish I hadn't seen what I just saw," but there's not much you can do about it. There is a big difference between sort of seeing and going out of the way to look at this sort of thing.

Obviously, one of the ways you could violate this

particular commandment of the Lord is through pornography. Not so very long ago, it wasn't very easy to access pornography. But nowadays, wickedness is just a mouse click away. Click . . . click . . . click . . . and you open up a Pandora's box of perversion.

According to an Internet filter review that analyzes and rates Web content filters, revenues of pornography exceed those of all professional football, baseball, and basketball franchises combined. There are 4.2 million porn sites, which amount to about 12 percent of all websites in the world, displaying over 372 million pornographic pages. Pornographic search engine requests total 68 million a day.

That is why we need to guard our minds—and put safeguards in place where we can. An Internet filter is a good idea—especially when small children are around. But children or no children, we want to be very, very careful of what we allow ourselves to view, because we don't want to commit adultery.

Here are six quick reasons why.

1. You do incredible damage to your spouse. I have already pointed out the oneness that takes place between a man and a woman who are unified sexually. But when you have sexual relations with someone besides your spouse, you violate that oneness. That is why the Lord actually gave a release clause to a marriage when there had been sexual unfaithfulness. It is a very, very big deal to God, and it should be a big deal to us as well.

Having said that, let me also say this: Adultery is not only grounds for divorce, but it is also grounds for *forgiveness.* And I would hope that such forgiveness would take place in a marriage that has been marred by unfaithfulness. Even with forgiveness, however, it takes a long, long time to rebuild a trust factor in a marriage once that trust has been violated.

2. *You do incredible damage to yourself.* In the case of adultery, it usually isn't just a one-night stand; it is usually an ongoing relationship. People end up in adulterous affairs most often with coworkers, men and women who are in close proximity on a regular basis. This so-called "affair" involves habitual deception, incredible duplicity, lie upon lie, and the deliberate hardening of their hearts.

When you are in an adulterous relationship, you are in a backslidden state. Yes, you may go to church every Sunday, read your devotions every morning, and pray regularly (though I seriously doubt a person who is involved in adultery would do those things). Nevertheless, you are in a backslidden state and out of fellowship with the Lord, because somehow in your mind, you have learned to live with a terrible lie in your life.

What you probably have done is compartmentalized this sin in your life. You have said to yourself, "I know this attitude or these actions in my life are wrong, but I'm not thinking about that now. I'm with my family and my Christian friends, and everything is good."

So you have that adulterous relationship or that pornography addiction tucked away in a closet in your life—out of sight, out of view, and neatly divided from the rest of your life. But that is not the way life works. What you keep in the closet eventually comes out of the closet. What you keep hidden away in a secret compartment eventually begins leaching poison into the rest of your life. As a result, your hypocrisy begins to damage your soul and your heart—and that damage eventually extends to your most precious relationships.

3. *You do incredible damage to your children.* When

you commit adultery, you undermine your sacred position as spiritual leader in your home, shattering your spouse's and your children's trust in you into a thousand shards and splinters. You may imagine that your family has forgiven you, but life is still unfolding. The chickens may come home to roost ten years from today, when your children engage in the same activity that you did. And then, when you wave your finger at them and tell them that what they are doing is wrong, they will say, "*You* did it, didn't you?"

To his great grief and regret, David saw his own sins repeated in the lives of his children. He had committed adultery with another man's wife and then tried to cover it up by basically murdering the woman's husband.

Was he forgiven? Yes, he was.

But as the pages of the calendar turned and the years slipped by, he saw his own kids fall into sexual sin, violence, and even murder.

4. You do great damage to the church. Scripture teaches that when one member of the body of Christ suffers, we all suffer. As Christians, we are all interconnected, and when one of the members of our fellowship is honored or experiences victory, we all bask in the joy and honor of that victory. Similarly, when a brother or sister in Christ falls away from the Lord and becomes entrapped in some sin, we all feel the pain and the shame of that defeat.

5. You do great damage to your witness and the cause of Christ. Nonbelievers will call you out for your hypocrisy, and it will be a hit you'll have to take. After David fell into sin with Bathsheba, the prophet Nathan told him, "By this deed you have given great occasion to the enemies of the LORD to blaspheme" (2 Samuel 12:14).

6. You sin against the Lord Himself. This is sometimes the last thing we think about—when it should be the first. The book of Genesis describes young Joseph, the son of Jacob, as a handsome, well-built young man. Even though he had become a slave in Egypt, he had risen to a position of prominence and authority because of God's blessing and protection. But he also had to deal with Mrs. Potiphar, the lustful and headstrong lady of the house, who was determined to corrupt Joseph and get him into bed with her.

She kept hitting on this young man, day in and day out. No doubt she was attractive and shameless, using every opportunity to draw his gaze. Yet he continually resisted her advances.

Finally, when she had him almost cornered one day, he said, "How then can I do this great wickedness, and sin against God?" (Genesis 39:9). He wasn't resisting this woman simply because he feared for his job or the wrath of his master. What he feared was sinning against a God who loved him and had blessed him.

I've had people who were involved in adultery say to me, "If I sin against God, He will forgive me." Perhaps He will, if they truly repent from their hearts and turn away from their sin. But they also should know this: Their sin grieves the Spirit of God, and that is no small matter (see Ephesians 4:30).

Commandment Eight: "You Shall Not Steal"
"You shall not steal." (Exodus 20:15)

Stealing is widespread in our culture today. We've become almost accustomed to locking up everything and keeping our eyes on our possessions. Think of how we drive up to a gas station and give our credit card to some guy who is sitting there behind bulletproof glass. That ought to be a clue that something isn't right in our nation. And the sign behind him says, "No money in safe." In other words, "Please don't shoot me."

We all have car alarms. I don't know if anyone really pays attention when a car alarm goes off anymore, but we all have them. Many of us put up those little signs on our front lawns that say we have a security system—whether or not we really do. We also put up signs warning people of our ferocious guard dog—which may, in reality, be a Chihuahua who trembles at his own shadow.

Newsweek did a cover story called "The Thrill of Theft," pointing out that $13 billion of merchandise is stolen every year in our country. In fact, one retailer who manages a jewelry and accessories store in a mall in L.A. said they now use shoplifting as a guide to taste. She told the reporter, "We know what's hot among teens by seeing what they steal."[1]

According to a University of Florida survey, however, retail stores lose more to employee theft than to shoplifting —most of which goes unreported. An employee screening company, Guardsmart, estimates in-house thievery at $120 billion a year.

A recent poll asked a wide cross-section of people, "Why do you *not* steal?"

The number-one answer? "I might get caught."

Number two: "The person I stole from might try to get even."

Number three: "I might not need the item."

Do you see anything missing in these answers? How about, "I don't steal because it would be wrong."

Or maybe, "I don't steal because it would be a sin against God." Those sorts of answers don't even seem to be on the radar today. Incredible!

Fortunately, many of the people who do steal are, well, let's just say they are a few clowns short of a circus. Take the true story of Natron Fubble, who tried to rob a Miami deli. The owner, however, foiled the robbery by breaking Fubble's nose with a giant salami. (I'm not making this stuff up.) Fubble fled the owner's wrath by climbing into the open trunk of the nearest parked car and closing the lid. The car, however, belonged to an undercover police team, which was trailing a different criminal. After five days, the officers heard Fubble whimpering in the trunk, extracted him, and arrested him, broken nose and all.

In New Hampshire, a teenager robbed the local convenience store, getting away with nothing more than a pocketful of change. What he didn't realize, however, was that both of his pockets had holes in them. All the police had to do was follow a trail of quarters and dimes directly to the thief's home.

Here is what God says about stealing: "Anyone who has been stealing must steal no longer, but must work, doing something useful with their own hands, that they may have something to share with those in need" (Ephesians 4:28, NIV). Out of this brief passage, we can identify three simple principles about how to live our lives as Christians.

1. If you have stolen, steal no longer. Don't ever take anything that belongs to another individual, business, or government. It is wrong before God, and His eyes miss nothing! And if you have taken something, if at all possible, give it back. That is called making restitution.

Remember the story of Zacchaeus in Luke 19? He lived in Jericho and collected taxes from his fellow Jews for the Roman government. Back in those days, such people were despised for lining their own pockets with the revenue they collected from their own countrymen.

Then one day Jesus was passing through town, making His way along the street, surrounded by a great crowd and a buzz of excitement. Zacchaeus wanted to check out what was going on, but he was too short to see over the heads of all the people. So he got the idea of shinnying up a tree to get a bird's-eye view of this strange Rabbi everyone had been talking about.

But the little man got the surprise of his life when Jesus walked right underneath his tree, looked up at him, called him by name, and said, "Zacchaeus, make haste and come down, for today I must stay at your house" (verse 5).

Excited beyond words, Zacchaeus ran home and prepared his house and a meal for this distinguished guest. After disappearing behind closed doors for a while, the two later reemerged . . . and Zacchaeus was a changed man.

He stood up (maybe on a stool, so people could see him) and declared, "Look, Lord, I give half of my goods to the poor; and if I have taken anything from anyone by false accusation, I restore fourfold" (verse 8).

That is restitution, and it was evidence of a changed heart and life. Even though most of the people in the crowd were still skeptical, Jesus declared, "Today salvation has come to this house" (verse 9).

So if you have stolen, give it back.

2. *Do something useful.* Ephesians 4:28 says, "Let him who stole steal no longer, but rather let him labor, working with his hands what is good, that he may have something to give him who has need."

Many people today are out for every government benefit

or freebie they can get their hands on, but this verse encourages us to work with our own hands for everything we have. Just moments after humanity's fall, the Lord pronounced this judgment: "You'll get your food the hard way, planting and tilling and harvesting, sweating in the fields from dawn to dusk" (Genesis 3:18-19, MSG).

In 2 Thessalonians 3:11-12, the apostle wrote, "We hear that some of you are living idle lives, refusing to work and meddling in other people's business. We command such people and urge them in the name of the Lord Jesus Christ to settle down and work to earn their own living" (NLT).

Here's a newsflash: The world does not owe you a living. Your parents don't owe you a living. The government doesn't owe you a living. You need to find a job and do it with all your strength. Get out there in the marketplace and work hard for what you have.

3. Share what you have. Ephesians 4:28 ends with this phrase: "That he may have something to give him who has need." Sharing is the opposite of stealing. God wants us to help others who find themselves in needy situations. To accomplish that, we need to hold down a job and earn a steady income.

One little footnote to this matter of stealing: The book of Malachi tells us that it is possible to rob from God. In Malachi 3:8, we read, "Will a man rob God? Yet you have robbed Me . . . in tithes and offerings."

The Bible teaches that everything you have comes from God, and you are to take a percentage of your income and give it to the Lord for the work of His kingdom. When we neglect or fail to do that, we are, in effect, robbing God of what is rightfully His.

Commandment Nine: "You Shall Not Bear False Witness Against Your Neighbor"

"You shall not bear false witness against your neighbor."
(Exodus 20:16)

Simply put, don't tell lies. Don't tell white ones and don't tell black ones. Don't tell convenient ones and don't tell blatant ones. Just tell the truth, and you'll never have to look over your shoulder to see whether it is sneaking up on you.

Strictly speaking, this commandment was originally focused on perjuring oneself in a judicial trial. In principle, however, it applies to all lying in general.

God hates lying. In Proverbs 6:16-19, the Bible lists seven things that God hates, that are an abomination to Him, and two of the seven pertain to lying. In verse 17, it says the Lord hates "a lying tongue." And in verse 19, it also says He hates "a false witness who speaks lies."

Why does God hate lying so much? First of all, it is completely antithetical to His character—the polar opposite of who He is. In John 14:6, Jesus identified Himself with these words: "I am the way, the truth, and the life." In Hebrews 6:18, we are told that "it is impossible for God to lie." It is not, nor ever has been, part of His persona or nature. Besides that, it is Satan who is completely identified with lying. Jesus said, "He [the devil] was a murderer from the beginning. He has always hated the truth, because there is no truth in him. When he lies, it is consistent with his character; for he is a liar and the father of lies" (John 8:44, NLT).

The bottom line? When we are engaged in habitual lying and deception, we are behaving like a child of the devil.

And we may tell more lies than we think. For instance,

when someone calls your home and you don't want to talk to that person, do you ever say to your spouse or your child, "Tell them I'm not at home"?

That is a lie for the sake of your convenience.

Or if someone asks you about something you had promised to do, you might reply, "Oh, yeah . . . I guess I forgot." But you didn't forget; you just didn't get around to doing it.

That is a lie for the sake of saving face.

Or maybe in conversation you flatter someone and say, "Oh, it's so good to see you," when it isn't. Or, "I love your outfit," when you don't. Or we may even say, "I will be praying for you for sure," when we really have no intention of praying for that person at all. Those are lies, and even though they may seem small, they displease the Lord.

Another way we lie is through gossip and backbiting. Proverbs 20:19 says, "A gossip goes around telling secrets, so don't hang around with chatterers" (NLT).

As a pastor, I am sometimes asked to keep something in confidence. When someone says to me, "Please don't share this with anyone else," I try, to the best of my ability, to keep it private. We probably all know people, however, with whom we could never share anything in confidence. If you shared something with them this morning, it would be on CNN tonight. Actually, if you say, "Please don't share this," it makes it even more tempting for them to blab it all over.

Why? It is because we human beings love a juicy tidbit of information. Gossip is attractive to us. It slides down easily. It's a dainty little morsel that secretly delights us, even though we say, "Oh, that's too bad" or "We should pray for her." In our old nature, we love to hear gossip and dispense it.

Either way, it may not be true. It may an exaggeration, a

distortion, or an outright lie that will greatly damage someone's reputation. And God hates it.

Yes, gossip may contain truth. It even works better that way. But it is often truth mixed with a lie, served up with a spin. People love to take those bits of information and add a little something to them to make them look or sound a certain way.

It is time to just call this what it is: a lie. And God hates it.

Another way we lie is through flattery, one of the most subtle forms of deceit. One definition of flattery is saying things to a certain person's face you would never say behind his or her back. (Contrast that to backbiting. Backbiting is saying behind a person's back what you would never say to his or her face.)

"You're so smart." "You're so clever." "You haven't aged a day!" You look great!" If we're saying things like this simply to gain someone's favor or to make a sale or to gain a commitment, then it is lying. If you don't really mean it, then don't say it. Don't fill up the airspace with empty or deceptive words.

Another way we lie is through exaggeration, which is very easy to do. To impress our listeners, we make something sound bigger or more difficult or more surprising than it really was.

Keeping our silence can be a lie too. How could saying nothing be a lie? It might be on one of those occasions when you hear something said about someone that you know isn't accurate or true, or when you hear someone state a so-called "fact" that isn't a fact at all. You find yourself wanting to flatter the person speaking by agreeing with him or her instead of gently and humbly setting the record straight. In that case, it becomes slander by silence—complicity by passivity.

The apostle James gave great advice when he wrote, "Let every man be swift to hear, slow to speak" (James 1:19). Don't pass along falsehood, and when you can't help it, don't encourage it or receive it either.

If there is one thing God hates, it's a lie.

Commandment Ten: "You Shall Not Covet"
"You shall not covet." (Exodus 20:17)

This is a tricky one. All of the other commandments we have considered are outward. Not worshipping another deity, not taking the Lord's name in vain, not murdering, not stealing, not committing adultery—these are outward things.

Coveting is different. In fact, the apostle Paul implied that while he was able (to a large degree) to keep the other commandments, he really struggled with commandment number ten. Why? Because it is an action of the heart (see Romans 7:7-8), and you may not even realize you are actually doing it. Even so, it is a big enough deal to God that He deliberately broke it out as one of the ten things He especially wants us to know, pay attention to, and obey.

What does it mean to covet? Here is what it *doesn't* mean. It doesn't mean that it is wrong to see something you like and wish that you had it. That is not necessarily coveting. You might be walking through the mall with your friend, see a nice outfit in one of the store displays, and say to her, "Oh, wow! That is a cute outfit. I would like to get that."

There is a difference between coveting and just admiring. It isn't wrong to admire something. It isn't even wrong to want something.

Just what is coveting then, and how is it different from

wanting or admiring? Let's look again at the full statement of this command in Exodus 20:17:

> "You shall not covet your neighbor's house; you shall not covet your neighbor's wife, nor his male servant, nor his female servant, nor his ox, nor his donkey, nor anything that is your neighbor's."

I don't know if you have coveted anyone's ox or donkey lately. But it may very well be that you have coveted something else that belongs to a neighbor, friend, coworker, or family member. Notice that coveting is in the context of something that belongs to someone else. That is the key.

The New Testament uses the Greek word *lust* when translating the Hebrew term rendered in our Bibles as *covet.* To covet something is to lust for it. It is the idea of "panting after" something, like a dog panting after his food in the morning.

How does coveting work? The eyes look at an object, the mind admires it, the will seeks to possess it, and the body follows through with the action.

It is not coveting when your friend buys a car, and the next day you go out and buy the same car with the same color and the same options. That is not coveting, that is copying. Your friend may not appreciate your buying a car identical to his, but he still has his car.

Coveting is the idea of wanting something that belongs to someone else—and making plans to take it away from that person no matter what. It is when you think to yourself, *I don't care what price I have to pay. I don't care what harm comes from it. I want what you have, and—one way or another—I'm going to get it.*

Coveting destroys lives and families. If you covet someone else's husband or wife, it will blow apart their marriage and yours. It can even happen in ministry, where a pastor or Christian leader covets someone else's gifts, talents, finances, facilities, or congregation. *Why is their ministry more effective than my ministry? Why do they have all of those gifts? I'm going to undermine them so that I will look better.*

You can see how this sin can infiltrate so many areas of life. In the Old Testament, Elisha's servant, Gehazi, coveted something, and he was stricken with leprosy as a result (see 2 Kings 5). Adam and Eve could not resist the forbidden fruit and ate of it (see Genesis 3), and we are still paying the price for that.

WHY THESE COMMANDMENTS?

Have you ever coveted? Have you ever looked at a woman or a man to lust after them? Have you ever stolen? Have you ever lied? Have you ever taken the Lord's name in vain?

Of course you have. We all have broken these commandments.

The fact is, these commandments were never given to make us righteous. They are absolute truth and reveal the holy standards of a holy God who can never be shaken.

What are these commandments for? The commandments were given to send us into the open arms of Jesus. Every one of us breaks these commandments in some way, shape, or form.

"Well," you might say, "I think I've really only broken one."

That's enough to make you a lawbreaker. The Bible says, "For the person who keeps all of the laws except one is as guilty as a person who has broken all of God's laws" (James 2:10, NLT).

In John 8, the Bible gives us the story of a woman who was caught (probably deliberately entrapped) in the act of adultery. She was brought before Jesus and thrown down in a heap at His feet. Her arm was probably bruised, mascara running, lipstick smeared. Her facial features must have twisted in fear.

Her accusers said to Jesus, "The law of Moses says to stone her. What do you say?" (verse 5, NLT).

Here was this poor woman, so filled with shame that she didn't even want to look up. Death was in the air all around her . . . but so was Life.

The question arises, of course, where was the other party in this act of adultery? She didn't do this solo. What happened to the guy? They probably let him go. In fact, he may have even been one of her accusers. We don't know. But do we know the Scriptures say, "This they said, testing Him" (verse 6).

This wasn't at all about dealing justly with a sin. This was about putting Jesus on the horns of a dilemma. This was about setting a trap for Christ.

As He quickly assessed the situation, the Bible tells that Jesus "stooped down and wrote on the ground" (verse 6). But what was He writing? After making those marks in the dirt, He stood up, squared His shoulders, and said, "He who is without sin among you, let him throw a stone at her first" (verse 7).

Then He stooped down and wrote again, and the Bible says, they "went out one by one, beginning with the oldest even to the last" (verse 9).

What did He write? Whatever it was, it was powerful. He

was writing in the sand, just as His Father wrote the Ten Commandments in stone. It is my opinion that Jesus wrote commandment numbers in the sand—one, two, three—in a way they would recognize.

What else was He writing? Might He have been writing down the names or initials of people among those accusers who had broken those commandments? Whatever He wrote, the would-be judges got the message and slipped off one by one, from the eldest to the youngest. They, too, had broken the commandments, and they knew it.

> And Jesus was left alone, and the woman standing in the midst. When Jesus had raised Himself up and saw no one but the woman, He said to her, "Woman, where are those accusers of yours? Has no one condemned you?"
>
> She said, "No one, Lord."
>
> And Jesus said to her, "Neither do I condemn you; go and sin no more." (verses 9-12)

The Law brings us—drives us—into the arms of Jesus for help, mercy, forgiveness, and provision.

He is our only hope.

HOW TO BE HAPPY

appiness is a warm puppy."

For cartoonist Charles M. Schulz, that pretty much said it all.

Taking the subject in a different direction, Albert Schweitzer declared, "Happiness is nothing more than good health and a bad memory."

Comedian George Burns said, "Happiness is having a large, loving, caring, close-knit family . . . in another city."

Frank Sinatra opined, "A man doesn't know what true happiness is until he is married. By then it's too late."

According to Oscar Wilde, "Some cause happiness wherever they go; others, whenever they go."

In a 1963 pop tune, singer Jimmy Soul belted out the words, "If you wanna be happy for the rest of your life, never make a pretty woman your wife." It doesn't make any sense at all to me, but that was his particular philosophy. (As far as I know, it was his last song on the hit parade.)

What exactly is happiness, and where do you find it?

We might begin the discussion with where you *won't* find it.

You won't find it in this crazy culture in which we live today. To put it biblically, you won't find it in this world. Why? Happiness in our world, happiness in our culture, basically depends on good things happening. If circumstances are going reasonably well, then we might call ourselves happy. If circumstances start to go south, however, happiness evaporates like water on a hot sidewalk.

Is happiness getting what we want?

That didn't work out too well for forty-nine-year-old Juan Rodriguez, who won $149 million in the lottery. For the former parking lot attendant, all that money only brought him a boatload of trouble. Since winning the mega-millions jackpot two days after filing for bankruptcy, Rodriguez had been besieged by a swarm of friends and relatives seeking handouts—not to mention reporters seeking interviews. Days before he won the lotto, Rodriguez had reconciled with Iris, his wife of seventeen years, who had kicked him out of their house after yet another fight about money woes. The couple was all smiles at a lottery press conference. But, the article continues, ten days after he won the lottery, his Iris filed for divorce, demanding half the jackpot—and effectively freezing *all* of the money.[1]

Certainly, there are some things money can buy. But there are just as many that it can't buy. For instance, money can buy you a bed, but it can't buy you a good night's sleep. It can buy you books, but it can't buy you brains. It can buy you a house—a very nice house—but it can't buy you a home. It can buy you medicine, but it can't buy you health. It can buy you amusement, but it can't buy you happiness. And in the words of Paul, John, George, and Ringo, money can't buy you love.

So how can we be truly happy people? Believe it or not,

there have been a number of polls taken and quite a bit of research done on the subject.

Here is what some of the researchers have come up with. Surveys by Gallup, the National Opinion Research Center, and the Pew Organization conclude that spiritually committed people are twice as likely to report being very happy than the least religiously committed people.

But let's take that a step further. Godly people, in fact, are happy people. According to the Bible, if we seek to know God and discover His plan for our lives, then we actually will find the happiness that has eluded us for so long. It is not from seeking the happiness, but from seeking Him, the Lord.

The Bible says, "Happy are the people whose God is the LORD!" (Psalm 144:15). The truth is, God formed and created us to turn to Him, finding our fulfillment, contentment, and happiness in relationship with Him.

C. S. Lewis put it this way:

> God designed the human machine to run on Himself. He Himself is the fuel our spirits were designed to burn, or the food our spirits were designed to feed on. There is no other. That is why it is just no good asking God to make us happy in our way without bothering about religion. God cannot give us a happiness and peace apart from Himself, because it is not there. There is no such thing.[2]

So the idea is to seek God, and happiness will come.

Henry Ward Beecher said, "The strength and happiness of a man consists in finding out the way in which God is going and going in that way too."

So yes, God truly does want us to be happy.

But here's the twist: His definition of happiness may be a little bit different than ours. Thankfully, He reveals His definition of happiness in the greatest sermon ever preached, The Sermon on the Mount, recorded in Matthew 5, 6, and 7. This is Jesus Christ, God in the flesh, giving us His worldview, showing us how to survive—and thrive—in this crazy, upside-down culture. At the very beginning of His Sermon on the Mount, Jesus tells us what happiness is and how to find it.

BLESSED = HAPPY

"Blessed are the poor in spirit,
>   For theirs is the kingdom of heaven.
Blessed are those who mourn,
>   For they shall be comforted.
Blessed are the meek,
>   For they shall inherit the earth.
Blessed are those who hunger and thirst for
>   righteousness,
>   For they shall be filled.
Blessed are the merciful,
>   For they shall obtain mercy.
Blessed are the pure in heart,
>   For they shall see God.
Blessed are the peacemakers,
>   For they shall be called sons of God.
Blessed are those who are persecuted for
>   righteousness' sake,
>   For theirs is the kingdom of heaven." (Matthew 5:3-10)

These eight beatitudes form the beginning of the Sermon on the Mount. The first four deal with your relationship with God, and the final four deal with your relationship with people. Why do we call them "beatitudes"?

Very simply, it is because these are attitudes that should be.

This is the way we ought to be living. You might even call them the "Be Happy Attitudes." The word *blessed* appears again and again in this passage, and it's a word that is interchangeable with *happy*. Our chapter title—"How to Be Happy"—might just as easily have been called "How to Be Blessed."

Blessed. As Christians we use the words *blessed* and *blessing* quite often—and most of the time we mean it. It also has been hijacked by our culture. You'll hear people talk about blessings in their lives. But the nonbeliever has no idea what a real blessing is, because only the child of God truly knows what it is to be blessed.

It's worth noting that Jesus both began and concluded His earthly ministry with blessing people. When people brought their babies and little ones to Jesus, He took them into His arms and blessed them. After His death and resurrection, He walked alongside two devastated, discouraged disciples on the road to Emmaus, and He blessed them. And then when His ministry on earth was completed, He ascended into the air, blessing His disciples.

Jesus loved to bless people. And He still does.

But what does it mean to be blessed? The word used for blessing in this passage is the Greek term *makarios*. It's a word that means to be happy or blissful.

The Greeks called the island of Cyprus "the happy isle." They believed that because of its geographical location, perfect climate, and fertile soil, anyone who lived on the island of

Cyprus had it made in the shade. That is where this expression originated. *Makarios* portrayed a self-contained happiness. Everything you needed to be happy was right there on that beautiful island.

So how do we apply this to our lives? What does it mean? We can't all move to that island, can we? No, but what we draw from *makarios* is the idea of a happiness that is independent of our circumstances. It is a self-contained happiness. It means that regardless of what might be happening to you externally, you can be a truly happy person internally—a genuinely blessed person.

If, as you read these words, life is sailing along smoothly for you, if the bills are paid, your health is reasonably good, your career is moving forward, and there are no major conflicts at home, then you might say, "I am a blessed man" or "I am a blessed woman."

Yes, you are.

But what if things aren't going that well for you? What if there are concerns or problems in your life that seem to be pressing in on you? Maybe you have some new health concerns, you're dealing with pain, or your marriage has hit some rough water.

You are *still* blessed.

Why? It is because of your relationship with God. *He* is your island. The apostle Paul said, "For I have learned to be content whatever the circumstances" (Philippians 4:11, NIV).

When you and I, as believers, speak of being happy, blissful, or blessed, we're operating from a different definition than that of the culture in which we live.

If we were to rewrite the Beatitudes for the twenty-first century, they would be vastly different from what we just read in Matthew 5. Modern beatitudes might sound something like this:

> Blessed are the beautiful, for they shall be admired.
> Blessed are the wealthy, for they have it all.
> Blessed are the popular, for they shall be loved.
> Blessed are the famous, for they will be followed. (On Twitter, probably.)

But no, Jesus started off the real Beatitudes with a bombshell that most likely doesn't make a lick of sense to our contemporary culture.

Poor in Spirit

"Blessed are the poor in spirit, for theirs is the kingdom of heaven." (Matthew 5:3)

Let's first of all understand what this statement *doesn't* mean. Some have falsely interpreted this verse to say, "Blessed are the poor." But that is not what Jesus said. Yes, you certainly can be poor and still be blessed, as the apostle Paul and thousands of others could attest. But this verse doesn't teach that concept.

In fact, the Bible doesn't anywhere commend poverty. Nor does it condemn wealth. Being poor in spirit has nothing to do with your bank account or 401(k). The word *poor* is from a verb meaning to shrink, cower, or cringe, as beggars often did in that day. This is speaking of a person who is destitute and completely dependent on others for help. Again, however, Jesus is not speaking in financial terms here. He is speaking of people who see themselves as they really are before God. They are lost, hopeless, and helpless. The truth is, apart from Jesus

Christ and His provision of grace, *everyone* is spiritually destitute or poor in spirit, regardless of education, wealth, accomplishments, or even religious knowledge. To be poor in spirit means to acknowledge your spiritual bankruptcy and your total need of God.

Maybe you haven't been able to bring yourself to do this. Maybe you imagine that, after all, you have something to bring to the table.

No, you don't. You don't bring anything to the table. You are depraved, you are a sinner, and you are in desperate need of a Savior. It is His grace and His mercy being offered to you.

A person who is poor in spirit sees that. But it is difficult for some people to accept. In fact, some never do, and they never gain the kingdom of heaven.

Sometimes this is more difficult for men than it is for women (although it's true of both genders). A man might say, "Wait a minute. I'm not stupid. I have intelligence. I have strength, or experience, or discernment, or accomplishments, or good works, or whatever."

No, you are poor in spirit.

I like to reflect back on the story of that proud old Syrian army general, Naaman, in the Old Testament. He was a man who was close to his king, a highly decorated military officer, and a leader among men. He was powerful, influential, and admired. Oh, and one other thing: He had leprosy.

When you were a leper back in those days, it was a death sentence. There was no treatment or medication for this horrific disease. If you contracted it, you knew you were going to die a terrible, disfiguring death.

Naaman knew this about himself, even if the people of Syria didn't know. But it wasn't something this great general was able to forget, even for a moment.

Then, from a captured Israelite slave girl, he heard about a prophet in Israel named Elisha, who prayed for people to be healed. So General Naaman made the journey to visit the prophet. He probably had a really cool chariot, painted in camouflage and as big as a Hummer. Besides that, he had an entourage of Syrian soldiers marching beside him. I can imagine him in gleaming armor, with all his medals and battle ribbons glistening in the sunlight—the mighty General Naaman!

He showed up at the prophet's door, and I don't imagine Elisha's house being anything fancy. One of the Syrian servants probably knocked at the door, and Elisha's servant opened it, announcing in an excited voice, "General Naaman is here!"

But Elisha knew very well who was outside and why he had come. And he didn't even come to the door. He simply sent a message to the general who was waiting outside on his chariot: "Go and wash yourself seven times in the Jordan River. Then your skin will be restored, and you will be healed of your leprosy" (2 Kings 5:10, NLT).

With that, the servant shut the door, leaving Naaman outside, fuming with frustration, disappointment, and anger.

One popular Bible paraphrase records his reaction like this:

Naaman lost his temper. He turned on his heel saying, "I thought he'd personally come out and meet me, call on the name of GOD, wave his hand over the diseased spot, and get rid of the disease. The Damascus rivers, Abana and Pharpar, are cleaner by far than any of the rivers in Israel. Why not bathe in them? I'd at least get clean." He stomped off, mad as a hornet. (2 Kings 5:11-12, MSG)

As he was turning back, one of his servants put an arm on his shoulder and basically said, "General, sir, what do you have to lose? Is what the prophet said so difficult? Why don't you give it a go?"

Oh, but he didn't want to give it a go. Why? Because he didn't want to reveal his diseased skin to watching eyes! Beneath all that gleaming armor, people would be able to see his real condition: He had leprosy.

Nevertheless, he swallowed his pride and decided to obey the Lord's instructions. He climbed out of that beautiful chariot, removed his helmet, stripped off his breastplate, and began to reveal to his men what he already knew about himself: *I have leprosy. I am a diseased man in desperate need of help beyond myself.* It probably was a shock to them to see their leader in this condition. Would this business of dipping in the Jordan River really make any difference?

Naaman went down once and came up, wet but unchanged. He went down a second time, with the same result, and a third, fourth, fifth, and sixth time. Nothing changed until he dipped himself the seventh time, and he came up completely healed, with skin as fresh and new as a child's.

He had seen himself as he truly was: a diseased man with a death sentence over his head, desperately in need of help. It is the same for each one of us. If you want to be a happy person, then you have to see yourself for what and whom you truly are: a sinner in need of a Savior.

It was Spurgeon who said, "The way to rise in the kingdom is to sink in ourselves."

Again, to quote C. S. Lewis, "The real test of being in the presence of God is, that you either forget about yourself altogether or see yourself as a small, dirty object. It is better to forget about yourself altogether."[3]

What? We don't hear that kind of message thundering from America's pulpits today, do we? No, we hear how we all can be champions and highly successful. We don't want to think of ourselves as "a small, dirty object," spiritually destitute, or poor in spirit.

Jesus, however, tells us that if we want to be truly happy —blissful, blessed—we have to first see ourselves as we truly are so that we can repent and reconcile with a God who loves us.

"Blessed are the poor in spirit, for theirs is the kingdom of heaven."

When the Bible speaks of the kingdom of heaven here, it is speaking of something more than that wonderful future destination God has promised us when we leave this world and go into His presence. It is also speaking of the present experience of the believer who is living under the rule and reign of Jesus Christ. The Bible says, "For the kingdom of God is . . . righteousness and peace and joy in the Holy Spirit" (Romans 14:17).

Blessed are the men and women who see themselves as they really are. They will have heaven in the future, and the rule and reign of Christ in the present.

Those Who Mourn
"Blessed are those who mourn, for they shall be comforted."
(Matthew 5:4)

What is the Bible saying here? It's saying that happy people are unhappy people. You read that right. Another way to translate this verse would be, "Happy are the unhappy."

The Greek term used for *mourn* in this verse is the most severe of all nine Greek words used for grief in Scripture and is reserved for mourning the dead. Even so, this verse certainly applies in principle to all who mourn.

Are you mourning today? I've been mourning a long time, after losing my son Christopher in 2008. When you lose someone that close to you, you mourn and you don't get over it like people so many people want you to — especially if it was a loved one, especially if it was a child. You never plan for such a thing, so yes, I mourn every single day. But even as I affirm the truth of that statement, I also affirm the truth of the Lord's statement: "Blessed are those who mourn, for they shall be comforted."

There is a blessedness, or happiness, in mourning.

How so? It is found in a number of ways. For one thing, you gain a new perspective on life. You see things differently. Some of the things that seemed so important to you before aren't nearly so important to you now. And by the same token, some of the things that didn't seem important to you before become very important in your life now.

You find yourself longing for heaven more than before. Prior to Christopher's passing, I thought about heaven from time to time and found comfort in those thoughts. But after he left for heaven, it became a lot more tangible to me than it was before. I think more specifically about heaven now, because someone so close to me is living there — right at this very moment.

When you mourn, you begin to understand what really matters in life and what doesn't. You also begin to see this world for what it is and what it isn't. You recognize in a more profound way that this world isn't the end-all, but something you will leave behind—and perhaps sooner than you might imagine.

You find yourself drawing close to God because, quite frankly, there is nowhere else to go. No human being has the answers you're looking for. There is nothing or no one who can help you in your mourning. But the Lord is there, and He is enough—more than enough.

If you remember the comic strip *Peanuts,* Charlie Brown was always saying, "Good grief!" But there is a sense in which it truly exists. There *is* good in grief or mourning.

Weeping can be good and has its place. It doesn't have to be suppressed. We all have things that we cry about, even if only in private. Sometimes women may think that men really don't have much emotion, but that is not true. Men do have emotions, but we hold those emotions in check more than women do. Why? Many of us have grown up believing that it is unmanly to cry.

As a man living in this culture, I certainly understand that reluctance. On the other hand, I read in Scripture that the Lord Jesus wept—right out in public. He wept at the tomb of His friend Lazarus, and He wept over the city of Jerusalem as He approached it for the final time. Jesus was the manliest of men who ever walked the planet, and He wept.

You may be weeping over something in your life right now. Perhaps you have found yourself crying in your loneliness, in your discouragement, or over feelings of rejection.

Go ahead and cry. But know this: God cares. If it concerns you, then it concerns Him. What's more, not one of those tears falls unseen; God keeps track of every one of them. The Bible tells us in Psalm 56:8, "You keep track of all my sorrows.

You have collected all my tears in your bottle. You have recorded each one in your book" (NLT).

Isn't that great news? We also read that "The LORD is close to the brokenhearted; he rescues those whose spirits are crushed" (Psalm 34:18, NLT). Another translation says, "If your heart is broken, you'll find GOD right there; if you're kicked in the gut, he'll help you catch your breath" (MSG).

Yes, blessed are those who mourn, because the comfort of the Lord is wonderful. Jesus will be there to bring His supernatural comfort to you in your lowest times. I know this is true, because He has done that for me and for countless others who have turned to Him in a time of sorrow.

So what are we mourning over? The passage we have been looking at speaks contextually about mourning over our spiritual state, or our standing before God. The problem today is that people are laughing when they ought to be crying; people are celebrating when they ought to be grieving over their distance from a holy God who loves them.

The book of James says, "Grieve, mourn and wail. Change your laughter to mourning and your joy to gloom. Humble yourselves before the Lord" (4:9-10, NIV).

The problem with our culture today is that many people are laughing and joking when they ought to be looking at their lives and saying, "Oh, I can't believe the state I'm in. I feel so far from God, and I need Him!"

The book of Ecclesiastes records King Solomon's epic binge with drinking, sex, and materialism. At the end of it, when his head cleared a little, he wrote, "I said to myself, 'Come now, be merry; enjoy yourself to the full.' But I found that this, too, was futile. For it is silly to be laughing all the time; what good does it do?" (2:1-2, TLB).

Have you ever watched a bunch of people drinking? Maybe you were in a restaurant and the party at the table next to you was ordering drinks. At first they were not talking too much, but after their first drink, they talked a little more. After their second drink, they were laughing over silly things. By the time they had downed their third or fourth drink, they were laughing like a bunch of hyenas. If you were to ask them the next morning, "What in the world were you laughing about last night?" they might reply, "I really don't know, but my head sure hurts."

There is a place for laughter. We have a lot of laughter in our home and in our church and with our friends. But there is also a place for sorrow. And the Bible says that people who see their own spiritual poverty and take action to seek God and turn from their sins will be greatly comforted. True sorrow will lead to incredible joy, but without that sorrow there will be no joy. As the apostle Paul wrote, "Godly sorrow brings repentance that leads to salvation and leaves no regret" (2 Corinthians 7:10, NIV).

Sometimes you and I may be sorry over the repercussions or consequences of what we have done. Maybe you're driving on some highway, breaking the speed limit, and suddenly see the flashing blue lights of a state trooper coming up behind you. Are you sorry? Oh, yes! By why are you sorry? Is it because you broke the law, or because you got busted?

That is the way it is with us sometimes. We're sorry for the repercussions of what we've done, but not sorry about the act itself—and not sorry enough to stop doing it. Again, the Bible says, "Godly sorrow brings repentance." And that means you are sorry enough to stop, change your direction, and go in a different way.

Blessed are the unhappy, for they shall be happy—not with the tepid, shallow happiness of happenings, but with the joy that comes from Jesus. Psalm 32 says, "What happiness for those whose guilt has been forgiven! What joys when sins are covered over! What relief for those who have confessed their sins and God has cleared their record" (verses 1-2, TLB).

But without sorrow over sin, without mourning over a life separated from the life of God, there will be no true happiness. Without that mourning, there can be no lasting joy.

The Meek

"Blessed are the meek, for they shall inherit the earth."
(Matthew 5:5)

Now that I have seen myself for who I really am and realized that I'm spiritually bankrupt, I have to lay down my pride. I can't be proud of my spiritual condition. As a result, I am meek.

What is meekness? First of all, it is *not* weakness. When a weak guy is at the beach and some bully comes up and kicks sand in his face, he doesn't fight back. It is not because he is meek, but because he is scared spitless and doesn't want to be pulverized. In contrast, a truly meek man is a guy who has multiple black belts in mixed martial arts and chooses not to beat the bully to a pulp. He is the one who says, "I'm going to restrain myself here. I'm not going to do to this jerk what I *could* do to this jerk."

In New Testament times, the Greek word for *meek* was used to describe the process of reining in a stallion. You have a bit in his mouth, and you're holding onto the reins, controlling the great power of that animal. And if he chooses to submit to your authority, then he is meek. That is meekness; it is power under constraint.

Jesus said, "Happy are the meek." But we don't celebrate meekness in our culture. Instead, we celebrate asserting oneself. We celebrate getting things from other people or even taking advantage of other people.

How different this is from what the Bible teaches. The biblical worldview says that last is first. Giving is receiving. Dying is living. Losing is finding. Least is greatest. Meekness is strength. The overall message we receive from the Beatitudes is that living by God's truth, not by what the world says, will bring happiness and blessing into our days.

In the book of Genesis, Joseph was a startling illustration of meekness, or power under constraint. After he came to power as second-in-command over all of Egypt, he had the ability and the opportunity to kill his brothers who had sold him into slavery. Instead, he forgave them, met their needs, and took care of them. How was he able to do that? It was a God-given perspective that helped him come to this realization about his brothers: "But as for you, you meant evil against me; but God meant it for good, in order to bring it about as it is this day, to save many people alive" (Genesis 50:20).

When was the last time you saw a movie that celebrated the virtue of meekness? Can you think of one? Can you remember a movie hero who was greatly wronged but meekly restrained himself?

No, you and I don't really care about seeing a movie like that. We like payback-themed movies, where the evil guy gets what he deserves in the end, and the hero gets his sweet revenge. That is what entertains us, and that is what our culture celebrates. But the Bible celebrates meekness.

The greatest example of meekness of all time, of course, is Jesus Himself. Here was Almighty God walking among us in flesh, and yet look at the abuse He took—without hitting back.

Have you ever been hit in the face? I mean, really struck with a fist, squarely in your face? It is not like it is in the Westerns. In those big saloon brawls, some guy gets smashed in the face and gets right back up, smiles a little, spits out a couple of teeth, and gets back into the fight. But it is not fun to be hit in the face. It hurts. It is shocking and traumatizing.

Imagine your beard being ripped from your face and then having people spit on you. Sometimes being spit on is more offensive than being hit. But that is what they did to Jesus. They hit Him multiple times, yanked His beard out of His face, and spit on Him. And all of that, of course, was before they opened up His back with thirty-nine lashes of a cat-o'-nine-tails. It is amazing that He even survived the whipping. Then He had to carry that four-hundred-pound cross through the streets of Jerusalem.

He was a man's man. And He was meek.

At one point, He told his followers, "Don't you realize that I could ask my Father for thousands of angels to protect us, and he would send them instantly?" (Matthew 26:53, NLT).

But He didn't call those angelic warriors to save Himself. He yielded to the abuse, to the cross, and to death in order to pay the price for our salvation. He restrained His unimaginable power for a better end. He had you and me in mind all along.

Blessed are the meek, for they shall inherit the earth. Ultimately, God will reward the man or woman who walks before Him in meekness.

Hungry for Righteousness

"Blessed are those who hunger and thirst for righteousness, for they shall be filled." (Matthew 5:6)

A happy person passionately desires a righteous life.

To follow the progression in the Beatitudes, I have seen myself as I truly am — as God sees me — and I have mourned over my condition. The result is that I now walk in meekness before God.

And guess what that sort of life leads to? Now I have a new hunger and a new thirst — for God Himself.

Have you ever been really hungry? I probably overdramatize my hunger, because my stomach is like a clock. As soon as it's 10:00, I'm hungry for lunch. And then I am just waiting. 10:05 . . . 10:10 . . . 10:20 . . . 10:30. Finally, by 11:00, I feel like I'm closing in on it. By 11:20, I'm thinking it could be time for an early lunch — definitely by 11:30. At 11:45, I'm glancing at my watch every few seconds. By 12:00, I'm thinking, "Let's get this on!"

I may even say, "I'm starving."

My wife will say, "Greg, you are *not* starving."

"But it feels like I am!"

"Well, you're not. You have plenty of reserve to get you through the next few minutes."

She's right, of course. I'm not really starving, and there is no danger I will suddenly keel over from malnutrition. But I *am* hungry, and when I feel those hunger pangs, it's difficult for me to think of anything else.

Or maybe you have found yourself in a situation where you were really thirsty — perhaps even a little dehydrated. Remember what that felt like? Remember visualizing how good a glass of cold, clear water would taste—or maybe an ice-cold bottle of cola?

Sometimes in our church we will sing a worship song about being desperate for God and lost without Him. And that is what this beatitude describes.

So the question is, are you hungry for God? Are you thirsty—really thirsty—for spiritual things? This is what the psalmist was describing in Psalm 42:1-2: "As the deer pants for the water brooks, so pants my soul for You, O God. My soul thirsts for God, for the living God."

What would it look like in your life if you truly were hungry and thirsty for God? When you are getting ready for work or school in the morning (or whatever it is you do during the day), are you making any time to be in the Word of God and talk to your heavenly Father? Are you *that* hungry for Him? Or, can you easily wait for sometime later in the day—or tomorrow?

A happy person is someone who hungers and thirsts for righteousness. He or she wants to be right with God and walk with God. It is the person who *longs* for these things. That is where true happiness originates in our lives, not from the cheap, temporary things of this world.

When the prodigal son was hungry, he went to feed on the food that the pigs ate. But when he was *starving,* he turned to his father. Do you starve for a holy life? Do you hunger for God's best for you? If you do, then you will be taking practical steps to find it and obtain it.

To put it all together, if you want to be a happy person, then you need to be poor in spirit, which means that you need to see yourself as you really are and this world for what it really is. It will never satisfy you. Nor is the answer "within you," as some would suggest. No, the answer isn't within you; the problem is within you and within me.

We are sinners in need of a Savior, which causes us to mourn for our sin and be sorry for our condition. How sorry? Sorry enough to stop what we are doing and turn to Jesus Christ for forgiveness and relief.

Then, as you believe and trust in Jesus, your life begins to change. Your outlook changes, your attitude toward life changes, and you turn away from arrogance and become a meek person, a person with your strengths and emotions under His control. You realize that you are a forgiven person, not *better* than others but *better off* than others, because of your relationship with the living God.

Finally, you will find a new hunger and a new thirst in the deepest part of your life. You hunger for God. You thirst to know Him better.

And as you begin to live in these new realities, guess what? Happiness slips into your life while you're not looking and takes up residence. Just like Jesus said it would.

THE PURSUIT OF HAPPINESS

Why are we on this earth? What is the purpose of our existence?

Some would say, "We're here to pursue happiness." And by the way, that is not unique to our time. More than two thousand years ago, the Greek philosopher Aristotle said, "Happiness is the meaning and the purpose of life, the whole aim and end of human existence."

As Americans, the importance of happiness is even embedded in our Declaration of Independence. That founding document states, among other things, that as Americans we are endowed with certain inalienable rights, including life, liberty, and *the pursuit of happiness.*

It continues to be a hot topic to this day. You don't have to research the subject very deeply before learning that many studies have been done on happiness, and some college courses even delve into the topic.

But all of that looking for happiness under the microscope hasn't seemed to actually produce much happiness. As philosopher Eric Hoffer noted, "The search for happiness is one of the chief sources of unhappiness."

Hoffer has a valid point. If you want to be a happy person, then don't dedicate your life to the pursuit of happiness. If you do, it is almost certain that you will never find it.

No matter how many examples we witness to the contrary, many of us still think that great wealth or fame—if we could only somehow attain it—would finally bring us the happiness we desire. Actor and comedian Jim Carrey, who has had his share of both wealth and fame, sadly disagrees with that conclusion. He was quoted as saying, "I hope everybody could get rich and famous and will have everything they ever dreamed, so they will know that it's not the answer."[1]

USA Today did an article on happiness and said that the happiest people on earth are Scandinavians.[2] Why? I don't know. Go figure. (Maybe sunshine and warm temperatures are overrated.)

We can do something about applying most of these things to our lives. We can try to surround ourselves with family and friends and seek to be grateful for all we have. (I don't know about the Scandinavian part.) Nevertheless, even the happiness of Scandinavians mostly depends on happenings. As with people the world over, they are happy when events in their lives go well, and their happiness evaporates when circumstances turn against them.

As we saw in the last chapter, the Bible speaks in detail about the subject of happiness, but defines it in an altogether different way than our culture. When we read the word *happiness* in the Bible, it speaks of something self-contained. In other words, you can have it regardless of your circumstances. The happiness the Bible advocates does not come from what you have; it comes from whom you know. It comes from the Lord Himself.

THE FINAL FOUR

In the last chapter, we looked at the first four beatitudes — the statements of Jesus about how we can be happy in this life. In this chapter, we will consider the final four. This isn't rocket science; these are simple, bite-sized truths. If Jesus walked among us today and had a Twitter account, He might tweet these things, because each one is less than one hundred characters.

But how wonderful to have such a description from our Creator and Lord Himself! In these simple statements, we find the keys to lasting happiness in a wildly unhappy, cynical world.

I might also point out that these beatitudes are in sequence. There is an order to them, with each appearing in its appropriate place and not haphazardly.

Let's consider our final four statements on the subject of being blessed, in Matthew 5:7-10:

> "Blessed are the merciful,
>   For they shall obtain mercy.
> Blessed are the pure in heart,
>   For they shall see God.
> Blessed are the peacemakers,
>   For they shall be called sons of God.
> Blessed are those who are persecuted for
>   righteousness' sake,
>   For theirs is the kingdom of heaven."

In these final four attitudes-that-should-be, Jesus shifted gears from what happy people *are* to what blessed, or happy, people *do*. The first four statements dealt more with our relationship with God; these last four deal with our relationship with others. As Martyn Lloyd-Jones once said, "A Christian *is* something before He does anything; and we have to *be* Christian before we can act as Christians."[3]

A Happy Person Will Be a Merciful Person

"Blessed are the merciful, for they shall obtain mercy."
(Matthew 5:7)

In Matthew 5:3-6, I see myself as I really am, and as I mourn over my needy spiritual condition, I seek to walk in meekness before the Lord. As I do, my hunger and thirst for Him grow more intense by the day, and I deeply desire to live a righteous life.

I become a merciful person, because I recognize how much mercy has been extended to me. I realize more and more that I'm just one beggar telling another beggar where to find bread.

Jesus tells us that happy, blessed people are merciful people. In the time and culture when He spoke these words, mercy wasn't held in high regard. The Romans didn't care for mercy at all, and saw it as a weakness rather than a virtue. One of the Roman philosophers of the day said that mercy was "a disease of the soul."

The Romans glorified justice, courage, discipline, and power. As the gladiators faced death in the arena, they would say to one another, "Strength and honor." That was the Roman way. It was the way of force, conquest, and iron discipline.

Mercy? What good was it? In fact, during those days, the

Roman law gave fathers the right to kill their own children after they were born if, for some reason, they didn't want the baby. They couldn't do sonograms in those days to determine the sex of a child or to see what physical state he or she may be in. So if the father wanted a son but had a daughter instead, he would give a thumbs-up if he decided the child would live. If he gave a thumbs-down, the child immediately would be drowned. That was the mentality of the day.

The sad fact is that we don't value mercy much in today's culture either.

What is mercy? Mercy isn't just something we *feel*; it is something we *do*. In Matthew 6:3, the word used for *mercy* is translated "alms" or "aid to the needy." If you are merciful, then you will help a person in need and rescue the person in misery. Mercy implies a sense of pity, coupled with a desire to relieve the suffering.

It's not enough to simply say, "I feel your pain." That is not mercy. Mercy is meeting a need, not just feeling it. It is pity in action. So if you see a person without food, you give them food. If you see a person who is lonely, you bring them comfort. So if we see a problem and say, "Oh, that's so sad. It breaks my heart," we might be showing pity. But if we go on to say, "I'm going to do something about that," then we are showing mercy.

If, for instance, you hear about the desperate condition of people in Haiti, with many still homeless, destitute, and vulnerable, even several years after that nation's terrible earthquake, and if you think about what those people are going through and feel saddened by that, then you are showing some pity in your life. That is good—to a point. At least you are looking beyond yourself and your own wants and needs for a moment.

If, however, you hear about those needs in Haiti and feel moved to send some money to a Christian relief agency like Samaritan's Purse, which is working to build shelters for the Haitians and improve sanitation for them, then you will have gone beyond mere pity. You will be showing mercy, and that makes you a blessed person.

The merciful person gets out of his or her chair to actually do something about a needy situation. And Jesus said, "Blessed are the merciful, for they shall obtain mercy."

The more righteous a man is, the more merciful he will be. The more sinful a man is, the more harsh and critical he will be. Merciful people aren't quick to condemn, criticize, or come down on others who seem to be stepping out of line. On the contrary, a godly man or woman will seek to help struggling individuals rather than condemning them or cutting them down with critical remarks.

Here is what we need to realize: If we know anything of God's forgiveness in our lives, then we should be forgiving other people. Forgiven people are forgiving people. And if you're not a forgiving person, then I have to question how much you know about God's forgiveness that has been extended toward you.

You may say, "It's fine for you to say that, Greg. But you don't understand how much that person hurt me."

You're right, I don't. But to refuse forgiveness to someone is like drinking rat poison and then waiting for the rat to die. In other words, it makes no sense. When we refuse to forgive, guess who suffers? Is it the person who hurt us? No. We are the ones who suffer.

If I am not merciful toward others in my life, I have to ask if I know anything of God's mercy extended toward me.

Thomas Adams said, "He that demands mercy, and shows none, ruins the bridge over which he himself is to pass."

A Happy Person Will Be a Holy Person
"Blessed are the pure in heart, for they shall see God."
(Matthew 5:8)

Maybe you read those words and just shake your head. You say, "Pure in heart? Who could ever be pure in heart?"

Here is the answer. *You* can. But you have to understand what this statement means. By "pure in heart," Jesus is *not* saying that you never can have impurity or inconsistency in your heart or your thoughts. If that were true, we all would be disqualified. None of us ever would see God! The Bible clearly teaches, "The heart is deceitful above all things, and desperately wicked" (Jeremiah 17:9).

So how do I obtain the happiness that Jesus promises in these beatitudes? Here's how it works, following the sequence of the verses. First of all, I come to the realization that my heart truly is deceptive and desperately wicked. That is my spiritual condition, and I see myself for what I really am. I mourn over the condition of my heart and life, and with the psalmist I pray, "Create in me a clean heart, O God. Renew a loyal spirit within me" (Psalm 51:10, NLT).

Lord, give me a new heart.

In our culture, we often refer to the heart as the center of emotion and the mind as the center of intellect. So we will say things like, "My mind says one thing, but my heart says another." What we mean is that our logic tells us one thing, but in our emotions we feel something else.

But that is not how the Hebrews saw the heart. In Hebrew

culture, the heart referred to everything—it was the very center of the personality, mind, and thoughts as well as the emotions. Proverbs 23:7 says, "As he thinks within himself, so he is" (NASB). In other words, the heart is the center of who you are. This means that you and I should be pure with all of our being.

But what does it mean to be pure? Does it mean to be flawless? No. A good translation of *pure* would be "focused" or "single-minded."

In the King James Version of the Sermon on the Mount, Jesus says that if our eye is "single," our "whole body shall be full of light." But if our eye is "evil"—an eye that sees with double vision—our body will be "full of darkness" (Matthew 6:22-23).

To be single, or pure, means to have a single-minded devotion to Jesus. In other words, you don't have a divided heart. That is why the psalmist said, "Unite my heart to fear Your name" (Psalm 86:11).

To be pure, then, means seeking a holy life, because that is the secret to happiness. If you want to be happy, then seek to be holy. Don't chase after happiness; chase after holiness.

Martyn Lloyd-Jones once wrote, "Seek for happiness, and you will never find it, seek righteousness and you will discover you are happy."[4]

A Happy Person Will Be a Peacemaker

"Blessed are the peacemakers, for they shall be called sons of God." (Matthew 5:9)

Of all the beatitudes, this one is the most likely to meet with the approval of almost everyone who reads it. Both Christians and non-Christians like this thought, because we all want peace in the world.

But this statement of Christ really doesn't advocate working for global peace, as honorable as it may be to do that. The Christian is for peace, but not for peace at any cost. There will be times when we have to draw the line and stand up for what is right, even when the results of that stand aren't peaceful.

Prior to World War II, the Allied powers could have said, "We want peace," and simply let Hitler have his way, exterminating the entire Jewish population of Europe. But there came a point where we said, "This is wrong. This has to stop," and we entered into a war. There is such a thing as a just war. It is never desirable, yet it is something that must be undertaken sometimes.

In this context, let it suffice to say that our Lord's statement in Matthew 5:9 is not speaking of political peace or peace between nations. Instead, it is speaking of those who bring the gospel of peace to their world, offering people the opportunity to enter into a relationship with the Prince of Peace, the Lord Jesus Christ. Romans 10:15 says, "How beautiful are the feet of those who preach the gospel of peace, who bring glad tidings of good things!"

In a nutshell, then, we are men and women who have realized our spiritual poverty, sought and found the mercy of God, and now hunger and thirst for Him as never before. As a result, we tell others what we have experienced in our walk with God . . . and we become true peacemakers. Having said that, let me forewarn you a little.

Peacemakers are often troublemakers. That may sound contradictory to you. In fact, it probably will if you think of a peacemaker as an individual with a big peace symbol on his or her shirt—and maybe a few love beads. "Peace and love, man. Chill, dude."

That is not a peacemaker; that is just a hippie. If you are a real peacemaker, then you also may be a troublemaker. Why? You know that as long as people are at war with God, you may very well have to make them sad before you can make them happy. You may have to confront them with the reality of their spiritual state before the Lord, and they may not like that. Peacemaking, then, isn't passive. Sometimes it first has to be proactive.

Who was a greater peacemaker than Jesus Himself, the Prince of Peace? So how did they treat Him? They crucified Him. The point is that if you are a determined peacemaker, you won't be able to dodge occasional persecution, because it comes with the territory.

Happy People Will Be Persecuted

"Blessed are those who are persecuted for righteousness' sake, for theirs is the kingdom of heaven. Blessed are you when they revile and persecute you, and say all kinds of evil against you falsely for My sake. Rejoice and be exceedingly glad, for great is your reward in heaven, for so they persecuted the prophets who were before you." (Matthew 5:10-12)

This is neither the most popular nor the most frequently quoted of the beatitudes. Nevertheless, you can count on this: If you live a consistently godly life, you will be persecuted. It's not a matter of *if*; it's a matter of *when* and *how much*.

We all love the promises of God, and we like to claim the Bible's promises for healing, help, provision, and protection. But when was the last time you claimed this promise: "All who desire to live godly in Christ Jesus will suffer persecution" (2 Timothy 3:12)?

Who likes to be persecuted? Who wants to feel the pressure, pain, and intimidation of a world system that is violently opposed to Jesus?

Nevertheless, Jesus says that you are blessed—happy—if you are persecuted for the sake of His name. Notice that in this particular beatitude, He uses the word *blessed* twice. In all the others, the word *blessed* is used only once. It seems as though He is emphasizing a generous, double-sized blessing for those who are persecuted. *Happy, happy are those persecuted for Me.*

Why are we persecuted? Righteousness, by its very nature, is confrontational—even when you are not preaching. I'm not saying that you have to be loud, obnoxious, or get into a person's face. But here is the reality: The very fact that you believe in and love Jesus really will upset some people. Have you noticed that? They are bothered by the fact that you believe the Bible and call Jesus your Lord.

Why does that bother them? In John 3:20, Jesus told Nicodemus, "For everyone practicing evil hates the light and does not come to the light, lest his deeds should be exposed."

That is the reason for their animosity. People don't want their evil deeds exposed. People don't want to admit they are sinners. People don't want to be reminded that they will find themselves accountable someday to a holy God. And you, as a representative of Christ on earth, remind them of these things by your very presence.

You know what it's like. People find out you are a Christian, and they begin treating you differently. It is not because of something you necessarily said or did, but just because you profess faith in Christ. They change their attitude toward you when they realize that you are a representative of God on earth.

If all of this seems strange to you, then imagine how difficult it is for me when people find out that I'm a preacher!

"So what do you do for a living?"

"I'm a pastor."

"Oh . . . you mean a preacher?"

"Yes."

There are times when I might as well have said, "I'm an ax murderer." Or worse, "I'm a telemarketer, and I have your phone number! When do you eat dinner? Because that is when I like to call!"

Preacher or not, the reality is that if you are going to follow Jesus, then you will face persecution at some point. To the degree that you have fulfilled the first seven beatitudes, you will experience the eighth. In other words, if you really are poor in spirit, sorry for your condition, meek, hungering and thirsting after righteousness, and a diligent peacemaker, then you will be persecuted.

So here is my question: Are you being persecuted? If not, then why not? Scripture says that all who desire to live godly in Christ Jesus will suffer persecution.

Before we move on, I want you to take note of *why* we will be persecuted. Jesus said, "Blessed are those who are persecuted for righteousness' sake." Then again, He said, "Blessed are you when they revile and persecute you, and say all kinds of evil against you falsely for My sake." Notice He did *not* say, "Blessed are you when you are persecuted for being *self-*righteous." Nor did He say, "Blessed are you when you are persecuted for being obnoxious." (Or tactless. Or tiresome. Or condescending. Or moronic. Or idiotic.)

The sad truth is that there are some, shall I say, *unwise* believers out there who do and say some strange, bizarre, and obnoxious things. Why do they have to be unnecessarily offensive? Why do they have to be disrespectful or discourteous or insulting? Isn't the objective of sharing our faith to build a bridge to another person rather than to blow it up with ten tons of TNT?

It's a fact: Some believers, well-meaning though they may be, will face persecution because they are rude, tactless, or even mean. I don't see any benefit of being persecuted for being a jerk. But there is a double blessing promised when you endure heartache and hardship for humbly acknowledging your love and devotion to the Lord Jesus Christ.

What does it mean to be persecuted? The word *persecute* could be translated "to be chased, to be driven away, to be pursued." Sometimes that persecution turns violent, and there have been people — even in our own nation — who have been physically assaulted for their faith.

In Islamic nations or communist regimes, of course, Christians are harassed, jailed, discriminated against, and sometimes even martyred for their faith.

Sometimes it may be much more subtle than that. It might be the loss of a job, the loss of some friends, or maybe being the brunt of someone's jokes. Whatever form it takes, the Bible tells us that a godly life and some form of persecution simply go together.

So what should you do when you are persecuted? According to Jesus, "Rejoice and be exceedingly glad" (Matthew 5:12). Jump and skip with happy excitement. Look up to God and say, "Thank You, Lord, that I have been allowed the privilege to face this as Your representative."

Verse 12 goes on to say, "Great is your reward in heaven, for so they persecuted the prophets who were before you." Not only does persecution draw us closer to Jesus and, as a result, further away from a world system that is hostile to Him, but it also guarantees a reward. God allows persecution for His own special purposes.

Maybe you are being persecuted right now. Maybe it is at school, on the job, or even at home. Perhaps you have a spouse who doesn't believe, who is hostile to the faith, and he or she will mock you or put you down for believing in Jesus. Maybe it is a coworker who sits next to you at work and always has one hundred sharply pointed questions for you every Monday morning. Maybe your teacher or professor tries to intimidate you or humiliate you for your faith in the Lord and your belief in Scripture.

At times, you may have found yourself praying, "God, please get me out of this situation. Remove this person. Get me away from this." But God may be allowing the harassment for a reason, to help you become stronger spiritually or learn to lean even harder on Him for help and wisdom.

I read that a certain company was having problems shipping cod from the East Coast to the West Coast, because the fish quickly spoiled in transit. They tried freezing it, but that seemed to reduce the texture of the fish to mush. They tried sending the fish alive in tanks, but they would die before they arrived.

Then someone got the idea of shipping the fish alive, but with one difference. They included in the tanks of the live cod their mortal enemy, the catfish. And when the fish arrived at the end of their transcontinental journey, they were alive and well, because they had spent the entire trip fleeing the catfish.

Could it be that God has put a catfish in your tank too? Maybe it is the person who mocks you, harasses you, belittles you, or makes life difficult for you. You say in your frustration, "Why does God allow this?" He might allow it to keep you on your toes spiritually. He might allow it to keep you digging into the Bible for answers. He might allow it to encourage you to spend time on your knees, seeking His help, His wisdom, and His encouragement.

TWO GOOD RESULTS OF PERSECUTION

I see at least two beneficial results from being persecuted for our faith.

First, we are reminded that we are children of God. Jesus said, "For so they persecuted the prophets who were before you" (Matthew 5:12). It serves as a reminder that I am child of God, that I'm following a grand tradition, and that I'm in very, very illustrious company.

Second, it causes me to cling more tightly to Jesus and be reminded that this world is not my home. Has a catfish been chasing you lately? God can use it in your life. If you are living a godly lifestyle, then you will experience this pressure somewhere along life's path.

No one said that being a Christian was going to be easy. And if someone did say that, they were wrong. When it comes to being a follower of Jesus, wimps need not apply. But if you want to be a man or woman of God, this is what Jesus says about living out this life in the real world. And it is worth it. A million times over. Our faith in Jesus Christ is worth living for and worth dying for, if it comes to that.

But before we become too grim or set our jaws too firmly,

remember the context of this discussion. Jesus is talking about happiness. Jesus is talking about how to live a blessed and blissful life. And as we pursue Him first in our lives, happiness will come tiptoeing in the back door as a by-product.

You won't find happiness by chasing after it as an end in itself, but if you pursue the Lord with all your heart and make knowing Him and walking with Him your number-one priority, then you will be a happy person—according to the best definition of that word.

It won't be a shallow happiness.

It won't be a happiness that gets dinged up or faded by circumstances.

It will be a happiness that lasts forever.

MAKE A DIFFERENCE

few years ago I came home after an evening service at the church in the middle of one of those crazy California rolling blackouts.

The power was down, the phone was down, the Internet was down, and the streetlights were dark.

As I approached my front door, all I had to light my way was the illumination from my cell phone—and it had a low battery. Even so, enough light emanated from that little device for me to find my way around.

Here's what I discovered: When it is very, very dark, even a little light goes a long way.

As I write these words, it is with the knowledge that we live in a very dark time, culturally. But a little light still will go a long way.

We have an entire generation of young people today who seem to be morally and spiritually adrift. *USA Today* did a cover story not long ago about the millennial generation, born between 1980 and 1991. The extensive research revealed that most millennials today don't pray, don't read the Bible, and don't go to church. One expert was quoted as saying, "If the trends continue, the Millennial generation will see churches closing as quickly as GM dealerships."[1]

Part of the fault can be attributed to my generation, the baby boomers. We are the generation that effectively started what we know today as the youth culture. We are obsessed with staying young forever, and many of us can't let go. It's kind of sad, really.

The Eagles, a 1970s band, has been on a revival tour, and in one of their concerts, band member Glenn Frey said, "Welcome to the Eagles assisted living tour." That is not too far from the mark! Their big hit "Heartache Tonight" probably has been changed to "Heartburn Tonight." In our generation, we have gone from acid rock to acid reflux.

Suffice it to say that this generation has a hard time letting go. The tragic fact is that we have been so obsessed with ourselves that we have forgotten to raise our children in the way of the Lord. We have been so busy rebelling from our own upbringing that we have raised a generation that doesn't seem to have any moral bearings whatsoever.

That is why a biblical worldview is so desperately needed today—by millennials and boomers alike.

THE CHRISTIAN AND CULTURE

Is our world getting better and growing toward the light, or is it getting worse and slipping into deeper darkness? What should our position as believers in this world be? Should we withdraw or engage? Should we isolate or infiltrate?

Jesus gave the answer to those and other questions in His Sermon on the Mount:

"You are the salt of the earth; but if the salt loses its flavor, how shall it be seasoned? It is then good for nothing but to be thrown out and trampled underfoot by men. You are the light of the world. A city that is set on a hill cannot be hidden. Nor do they light a lamp and put it under a basket, but on a lampstand, and it gives light to all who are in the house. Let your light so shine before men, that they may see your good works and glorify your Father in heaven." (Matthew 5:13-16)

Jesus used two word pictures in quick succession in this passage: salt and light. Why salt and light? Because the world is dark, and the world is corrupt. In its darkness, the world needs light; in its corruption, the world needs salt as a preservative.

So what is the biblical worldview on our culture? Are things getting better? Is humanity improving the world?

The Bible is really clear on this one. The biblical worldview on culture is that it is dark and getting darker, day by day, week by week, year by year. It is not going to get better; it is going to get worse. We live in a world that is headed for the judgment of God.

Despite the fact that humanity has increased in scientific, medical, historical, educational, psychological, and technological knowledge to an astounding degree, it has not in any way, shape, or form changed its own basic nature or improved society.

Our confidence may have increased, but our peace of mind has diminished. We have multiplied our accomplishments, but our sense of purpose and meaning in the world has all but disappeared. Instead of improving the moral and spiritual quality of life in our world, humanity's discoveries and accomplishments—marvelous and amazing as they may be—have simply provided new ways to show ourselves for what we really are: depraved, sinful, and wicked.

For all of our innovation and technological advancement, humanity has discovered new ways to corrupt and destroy itself. We go from war to greater war, from immorality to greater immorality, and from perversion to greater perversion. The spiral is downward, not upward.

Back in the nineteenth century, many possessed a buoyant optimism about the future of the human race. People believed that humanity would one day create the equivalent of a heaven on earth. Mark Twain described that period of history as the Gilded Age, and other writers spoke of the dawn of a new millennium.

In that day, shipbuilding was the counterpart to today's space race. After years of planning and careful construction, shipbuilders launched the largest and most luxurious cruise ship ever built. You know the name don't you? The *Titanic*.

Her captain, Edward J. Smith, had declared, "I cannot imagine any condition which would cause [the] ship to founder. I cannot conceive of any vital disaster happening to this vessel. Modern shipbuilding has gone beyond that."[2] Another fool actually said, "God himself couldn't sink this ship."

Famous last words? The leading technology of the day went to the bottom of the sea on her maiden voyage after striking an iceberg. The *Titanic* became a metaphor for the human ego, thinking that by its own ability, humanity could bring about utopia on earth.

In short order after that, two horrific World Wars put an end to the euphoric writings about humanity's building a heaven on earth.

The Bible leaves no doubt: Conditions on our planet will go from bad to worse as the years go by.

IS WITHDRAWAL THE ANSWER?

Some Christians reading this will say to themselves, "If the world is really going to hell in a handbasket, then maybe we should separate ourselves from all that depravity and decay, and build our own Christian culture within a culture."

But that is not a biblical worldview either.

The Bible calls on us to touch and influence the culture around us, rather than hiding away like the monks and nuns of the Middle Ages who locked themselves behind the walls of monasteries and convents.

It is virtually impossible to remove yourself and your children from the culture of our day. You may try, but your culture will find you.

In his book *Culture Shift*, Al Mohler said, "We use language, wear clothing, and engage as consumers in a world of continuous cultural invasion. The culture is a vast network of institutions, laws, customs, and language that is a constant part of our lives, like it or not."[3]

So you might try to withdraw to a Christian subculture, but that is not what Scripture calls us to do. The objective of believers is not to isolate but to infiltrate, not to evade but to invade. We are to impact our culture without being compromised by it.

Is it a tricky balance? Without question. But listen to the words of Jesus in John 17:

"I have given them your word. And the world hates them because they do not belong to the world, just as I do not belong to the world. I'm not asking you to take them out of the world, but to keep them safe from the evil one. They do not belong to this world any more than I do. Make them holy by your truth; teach them your word, which is truth. Just as you sent me into the world, I am sending them into the world." (verses 14-18, NLT)

Did you catch that? Jesus said He is sending us *into* the world. He wants us to infiltrate, invade, impact, and engage, without losing our identity as children of God.

While urging us to make a difference in our world, the Bible clearly warns against becoming *conformed* to this world. The apostle Paul wrote to the Romans, "Don't let the world around you squeeze you into its own mould, but let God re-make you so that your whole attitude of mind is changed" (Romans 12:2, PH).

The apostle John wrote, "Do not love this world nor the things it offers you, for when you love the world, you do not have the love of the Father in you" (1 John 2:15, NLT).

And yet, Jesus sent us into this world. So how does this work? Paul shed some light on this delicate balance in 1 Corinthians 5:9-10. He said,

When I wrote to you before, I told you not to associate with people who indulge in sexual sin. But I wasn't talking about unbelievers who indulge in sexual sin, or are greedy, or cheat people, or worship idols. You would have to leave this world to avoid people like that." (NLT)

So we will be rubbing shoulders every day of our lives with men and women who hold to a radically different worldview than our own. And the idea is that we want to influence them rather than having them influence us.

But we have to be careful. As we seek to invade our culture with the Good News, we must recognize where we are. We are in a hostile environment. We are behind enemy lines. By and large, the people of today's culture won't always be supportive, receptive, or appreciative of what we have to say. But that's okay. God calls on us to do it anyway.

And all of this brings us to an important question.

HOW DO WE IMPACT OUR CULTURE TODAY?

We must speak in a language they can understand. Sometimes as believers, we can become frustrated because it doesn't seem like people are listening to us, and we say, "I don't know why my efforts at evangelism aren't more effective!"

Maybe it is because we sound as though we came from a different planet.

Think about the nonbeliever who is approached on the street by a zealous Christian evangelist. He hears words like these: "Hey, you! You nonbeliever over there. Yeah, I mean you, you uncircumcised Philistine! Here's the problem with you. You're sinful, wicked, and bound for hell. You are unregenerate and need to repent, believe, and then be justified, live a sanctified life, join the body of Christ, and be washed in the blood."

And the unbeliever is scratching his head and saying, "Excuse me? What in the world did you just say?"

There is nothing wrong with biblical terminology. Just don't imagine that it will necessarily make sense to a biblically illiterate culture. Obviously, if you travel to another nation where they speak another language, you either will have to speak to people through an interpreter, or learn the language yourself. In the same way, if we want to engage this biblically illiterate culture, we will have to speak in a way they understand and that makes sense to them. Otherwise, why waste our time—and theirs?

We can't assume they will understand any of our cliché-ridden biblical language or Christian-culture code words. Once they hear you say they "need to be washed in the blood," they will freak out, and that will be the end of the conversation.

We need to explain these things to people and break down the terms a little. Even when I am preaching the gospel in our Harvest Crusades, I don't assume that my listeners understand what I mean when I say something like, "You need to ask Christ to come into your life."

What does that really mean? We have to define our terms as we go and speak in a language that others will understand.

Paul was a master at this. In 1 Corinthians 9:22 he wrote, "I try to find common ground with everyone, doing everything I can to save some" (NLT). Or, as another translation puts it,

Even though I am free of the demands and expectations of everyone, I have voluntarily become a servant to any and all in order to reach a wide range of people: religious, nonreligious, meticulous moralists, loose-living immoralists, the defeated, the demoralized— whoever. I didn't take on their way of life. I kept my bearings in Christ—but I entered their world and tried to experience things from their point of view. (verses 19-22, MSG)

The greatest example of this was Jesus Himself. In the gospel of John, we see Him engage the woman at the well, a "loose-living immoralist." This was a woman who had been married and divorced five times and was currently living with a man who wasn't her husband. Yet Jesus didn't condemn her or blow her out of the water. Instead, He built a bridge to her, appealed to her inner spiritual thirst, and then brought the solution she needed.

The objective of evangelism is always to build a relational bridge, not torch one.

Jesus also sat down with Nicodemus, the religious man who could be described as "the meticulous moralist." This was a man who lived by the rules—all of them. But the one thing that Nicodemus (in John 3) and the woman at the well (in John 4) had in common was their need for Jesus. Whether moral or immoral, they both had hungry hearts, and they both were without God in their lives. Jesus adapted to each situation and brought the gospel to them.

Again, as Paul said in Colossians 4: "Let your conversation be always full of grace, seasoned with salt, so that you may know how to answer everyone" (verse 6, NIV).

Please remember, the goal is never to win an argument; it is to win a soul. And in order to do so, we must speak in a language that our listeners will understand.

We must use every means possible. The first-century church made good use of the Roman road system, traveling to all parts of the empire with the Good News.

After the mighty Roman armies had vanquished much of the world and ruled through a military-enforced peace known as the *Pax Romana*, the conquerors built a sophisticated system of roads and bridges. Through these roads, the Romans would export goods and dispatch messages to the many provinces under their far-flung rule. The early church walked down these roads, bringing the gospel to the four corners of the earth.

Today we have our own superhighway, an information superhighway that we call the Internet. And by this means, we can take the message to more people today than ever before in human history. Almost every message I preach these days ends up on the Internet and may be read, listened to, or watched by people all over the globe. In the twentieth century, we made good use of radio, television, and printed media. But now there is new media, including the Internet, podcasts, webcasts, blogs, Twitter, and social networks.

Should we use these methods? Let me ask you this: If the Romans opened a new road to a city, would the first-century Christians have walked down that road with the gospel? Of course they would. And we need to use every road and every means possible to get the gospel out to as many people as we can.

We need to bring the gospel to them. Here's a sobering question: What if we have marvelous, new high-tech delivery systems in place, but we don't have a message to deliver? Contemporary philosopher Marshall McLuhan once declared that "the medium is the message." But that is not true, is it? The gospel is the message, and it must not be diluted, no matter what medium is used to send it forth.

Sometimes in our attempts to cross over to contemporary culture with the gospel, we fail to bring the cross over! Some churches are a little too preoccupied with being cool and relevant and have forgotten how important it is to continually confront people with the claims of Jesus Christ.

If we miss that, we miss everything.

The cross of Christ is the only hope for our culture, our nation, and our world. It is the only hope for the individual nonbeliever. And, just like always, some people will respond favorably to that message, while others will respond unfavorably.

Paul put it this way in his second letter to the believers in Corinth:

> Now he uses us to spread the knowledge of Christ everywhere, like a sweet perfume. Our lives are a Christ-like fragrance rising up to God. But this fragrance is perceived differently by those who are being saved and by those who are perishing. To those who are perishing, we are a dreadful smell of death and doom. But to those who are being saved, we are a life-giving perfume. (2:14-16, NLT)

Isn't that true?

Some people like to wear a lot of cologne or perfume. They haven't heard the phrase "less is more," and it gets just a tad overpowering at times.

My main problem with cologne or perfume is that I'm allergic to it. If someone in my presence happens to be wearing a lot of it, I'll start sneezing. So what is fragrant to one isn't always fragrant to another.

Another illustration might be garlic. Does anything smell better when you walk into a kitchen and someone is making spaghetti sauce with garlic? But does anything smell *worse* than the breath of the person who just ate that spaghetti? Brutal!

In the same way, Paul tells us that when we bring the

message of the gospel, some immediately sense it as a fragrant perfume. To others, it is offensive and repugnant.

Either way, whatever the response, we still have to bring this message.

Before we can effectively tell the message, we have to first live the message. Nothing is worse than a hypocritical Christian.

Every Christian will fall short in his or her life. But there is a huge difference between a believer who struggles but seeks to live a godly life, and the person who claims to be a believer yet blatantly disregards what the Bible says. This is an individual who deliberately chooses to live a lifestyle out of God's plan and still wants to talk about Jesus to people.

I have a request for that kind of person: Please do us all a favor and shut up. If you are going to live a lifestyle contrary to what the Bible teaches, then please *don't* talk about Jesus.

The world desperately needs an authentic presentation of the gospel message. It doesn't need another phony one. There are enough of those to go around.

One of the key texts in the Sermon on the Mount is Matthew 6:8, where Jesus said, "Do not be like them." In other words, "Don't be like this world. Don't be like them. Be different and make a difference."

SO HOW ARE WE TO LIVE AS BELIEVERS?

We are to be salt. Again, in Matthew 5:13 we read, "You are the salt of the earth; but if the salt loses its flavor, how shall it be seasoned? It is then good for nothing but to be thrown out and trampled underfoot by men."

When we hear of salt today, it doesn't mean a lot to us, because we don't think of salt as a valuable commodity. It is relatively inexpensive and not a big deal. You can find it free in a lot of places. But back in biblical times, salt was a much bigger deal. In fact, few things were more valuable. The Romans actually used it as a form of currency, and Roman soldiers would sometimes be paid in salt. (Hence the expression "He's not worth his salt.")

Salt has several purposes. Salt had another major purpose in addition to being a flavor enhancer in foods. It also was used as a preservative. Not having refrigeration or ice machines, people in that day would rub salt in the meat to keep it from the process of putrefaction. They would sometimes take the meat, slice it into slender strips, and dip it into a saline solution, thereby enabling their families to eat that meat at a later date. Otherwise it would be spoiled and lost.

Knowing this, Jesus looked at His disciples and said, "*You are the salt of the earth*" (emphasis added). People of that day immediately would have understood Him to be saying, "You are a preserving factor in the culture today."

And that is what we are as believers in our own culture. It is the Christian who stands up for what is right. It is the Christian who speaks out against what is wrong. It is the Christian who is always at the front line of every effort around the world to help hurting people, regardless of their faith. That is what Christians do. That is what Christians are. We are the salt of the earth.

On a personal level, as a representative of Jesus, you change the dynamics of a room. It's true. Maybe one of your coworkers is telling a dirty joke, and he is just getting to the punch line: "And so the guy says . . ." Then you come walking in, and the joke stops. The joke teller says, "Umm, we'll get back to that a little bit later."

Everything changes because you are there, and that is a good thing. Maybe someone around you curses—then looks around and sees you there. And he or she says, "Oh . . . sorry about that."

Don't be embarrassed by that. It's a good thing. There is a little tension in the room at that moment, because that person sees you as a representative of Jesus Christ. It's not because you're arrogant, sanctimonious, or holier-than-thou. No, it's because you're a man of God. You're a woman of virtue. And they know it. Your very presence makes a difference.

But you are just doing your job. You are just being salt.

Consider this: When the Lord calls His church home at the time of the Rapture, it will take only seven years for the world to degenerate to a place of complete depravity and wickedness, with people worshipping the Antichrist and the devil himself. Salt stops the spread of corruption, and it is doing so in the world to this very day.

Another thing that salt does is create thirst. If you have eaten something really salty—like a big box of popcorn at the movies—you will suddenly find yourself craving a big drink of something cold.

Salt stimulates thirst. And when you are walking with Jesus, guess what? Your life, your walk with Him, your happiness in Christ actually will stimulate a thirst for God in others.

Maybe you have experienced something similar yourself. Have you ever been around a believer who loves the Lord so much that just being around that person makes you want to be more godly? There is just something about his or her lifestyle, attitude, and very presence in a room, and you find yourself thinking, *I want to be more like that. . . . I want a marriage more like that. . . . I want to walk with God like that. . . . I want to worship like that. . . . I want to be someone who shares my faith like that. . . . I want to do it the way that Christian does it.*

That person is doing his or her job as a Christian, as a salty believer stimulating a thirst for Jesus Christ in others.

The greatest tribute a nonbeliever can pay to you as a believer is to approach you and say, "Why are you the way that you are? I see the way that you love your wife or husband. I see the way you smile in the face of adversity, and I want what you have."

What an incredible compliment that is.

But know this: We can't be an influence for purity in the world if we ourselves are compromised in our purity. We can't sting the world's conscience if we go against our own. We can't stimulate a spiritual thirst in others if we have lost our own. We can't be used by God to stop the corruption of sin in others if it has corrupted us. If so, we are flavorless salt, which, according to Jesus, is good for nothing.

Look at Matthew 5:13: "If the salt loses its saltiness, how can it be made salty again? It is no longer good for anything, except to be thrown out and trampled underfoot" (NIV). Those are solemn and heavy words. It is a strong warning to keep your edge, to keep your saltiness as a believer.

A Christian should have flavor. Zest. Zing. Edge. Christians aren't supposed to be bland, tasteless, laid-back, going along with everything. They are to be salty. They are to stop the spread of evil. They are to stimulate thirst for Christ in others. They are to make a *difference.* Otherwise, they're like tepid coffee or flat cola.

The world doesn't need uncarbonated Christians or decaf disciples. In other words, what good are you to the kingdom of Christ if you aren't living the life that God has called you to live?

We are to be light. In addition to being salt, Jesus also said that we are to be light in our culture.

Why is that? When you are salt, you have a preserving effect, and your lifestyle and presence sting others. Having acted as salt, you follow up by functioning as light, showing the way to life. Having aroused the curiosity of nonbelievers by what you are and how you live, you earn the right to tell them why.

In Matthew 5:14-15, Jesus said, "You are the light of the world. A city that is set on a hill cannot be hidden. Nor do they light a lamp and put it under a basket, but on a lampstand, and it gives light to all who are in the house."

Taken together, the illustrations of salt and light paint a vivid picture. Salt is hidden and works secretly. Light is obvious and works in the open. Salt works from within, light from without. Salt represents the more indirect influence of the gospel, while light represents its direct communication. Salt works primarily through our lives, while light works primarily through what we say to others. Salt is largely negative. It can retard corruption, but it can't change corruption into incorruption. Light, however, is more positive, not only revealing what is wrong and false, but actually helping to produce what is good and true. Light exposes the darkness.

Have you ever lost something in your car at night? This happens to me quite often, because my car has a black interior, and I have a black wallet (that I always seem to be losing, along with other things). But when the light is on, I can see those lost things again.

When you are living for Jesus Christ, your very presence sometimes will irritate or offend others, simply because the light is shining out of you. You may try to cloak or hide it, but it leaks out. Really, you shouldn't even try to hide it. You are a city on a hill. Uncover that light, and let it shine for people to see.

Why don't certain people whom you care about come to Jesus Christ and receive His salvation? According to Christ Himself, here is the reason:

> "And this is the condemnation, that the light has come into the world, and men loved darkness rather than light, because their deeds were evil. For everyone practicing evil hates the light and does not come to the light, lest his deeds should be exposed." (John 3:19-20)

The reason people don't believe is because they don't want their sin to be exposed. They don't want to acknowledge their shortcomings. And the more godly the person might be who is sharing the message of salvation, the more this individual will shrink back and pull away.

Few things are more difficult to put up with than a good example. And when you just live out that example—in good times and bad—it really gets people's attention.

Light not only exposes what is hidden in the darkness, but it also shows the way out. Have you ever found yourself in an unfamiliar hotel room at night, perhaps trying to find the door? You grope for a lamp or a light switch to help you find your way—before you trip over something. In the same way, light shining from a believer's life not only reveals a nonbeliever's shortcomings, but it also shows them a way out, a way to hope and help and freedom—the way to Jesus Christ.

"YOU, AND YOU ALONE"

Take a moment to note a very important three-letter word in Matthew 5:13-14. It is spelled Y-O-U.

Jesus said, "*You* are the salt of the earth. . . . *You* are the light of the world" (emphasis added). Why is this important? Because in the original language, it could be translated, "You, and you alone, are the salt of the earth. You, and you alone, are the light of the world."

You, and you alone? Think about that for a moment.

What if every Christian in our country lived exactly like you? What kind of nation would we live in if every believer behaved just as you do? How many would be attracted to — or turned off by — the gospel? What kind of general opinion do you think people would have of Christianity if you were its sole representative?

What if all of the church were just like you? What if everybody worshipped as you worship? Would the church fall silent as we stood as observers, or would we be a singing, rejoicing church? What if all of the church prayed as diligently as you pray? Would we be a praying church? What if all of the church studied and knew the Word of God like you know it? Would we be a biblically literate or illiterate church?

What if all of the church gave as faithfully as you do? Would we have the resources we need, or would we have very little to work with? What if everyone shared the gospel as faithfully as you share the gospel? Would we have a world hearing about Jesus? Or would we have a world that knows very little about Him?

The truth is, you are a member of the living church of Jesus Christ in today's world. And in one sense, you, and you alone, are the salt of the earth. You, and you alone, are the light of the world. No, you may not be the only light in the world, but you may be the only light in *your* world. You may not be the only salt on the planet, but you may be the only salt in your school — or your workplace, or your carpool, or your exercise class.

The fact is that among your friends, family, coworkers, and neighbors, you may be the only representative of Jesus they will ever meet. As a result, they will evaluate the whole idea of Christianity on the basis of what they see in you. They will form an opinion about God based on what they see in you.

You say, "Whoa, that's a lot of pressure, Greg."

Yes, I know. But the pressure is from Jesus, who said, "You, and you alone . . ." Jesus was effectively saying that the only hope for changing a culture is the church and the individual believers who comprise that church.

Do you think our nation will turn around morally on its own? Do you think that politics will bring solutions to our tragic and intractable problems? Think again, friend. The world is dark and getting darker, and humanity can't fix this. Politics can't renew us. Neither can technology or philosophy. The only thing that could turn America around is a spiritual awakening — a revival.

Where does it begin, then? It begins with you, making a difference for Jesus Christ, being salt and light exactly where you are. Whether you realize it or not, you have a strategic and important part to play.

I once heard it said, "I am only one, but I am one. I cannot do everything, but I can do something. And what I can do, I ought to do. And what I ought to do, by the grace of God, I will do."

That is how you will make a difference in your world.

SELF-DEFENSE AND RETALIATION

I'm writing this chapter on Memorial Day, a day dedicated to those who served in the military and died in our nation's service. How we should thank God for every one of these men and women who have served our nation in the past and, at this very hour, defend our nation's interests in dangerous and faraway places.

Sometimes, however, the question might arise among some about how this military service or a career in law enforcement works with the teachings of Jesus in the Sermon on the Mount. Turning the other cheek? Not repaying evil for evil? Are these professions in contradiction with the teachings of Jesus? Should Christians all be pacifists? Should we never defend ourselves? How does this all work?

Let's begin with the worldview of the Lord Jesus, as it is revealed in the Sermon on the Mount. We study this passage because it is the official manifesto of the King of Kings and Lord of Lords. But I must add this: These teachings are for believers only, not for nonbelievers. The Sermon on the Mount isn't a set of principles by which to govern a society. These are the words of Jesus, given specifically to those who have chosen to follow Him.

SHOULD CHRISTIANS RESIST EVIL?

"You have heard that it was said, 'An eye for an eye and a tooth for a tooth.' But I tell you not to resist an evil person. But whoever slaps you on your right cheek, turn the other to him also. If anyone wants to sue you and take away your tunic, let him have your cloak also. And whoever compels you to go one mile, go with him two. Give to him who asks you, and from him who wants to borrow from you do not turn away.

"You have heard that it was said, 'You shall love your neighbor and hate your enemy.' But I say to you, love your enemies, bless those who curse you, do good to those who hate you, and pray for those who spitefully use you and persecute you, that you may be sons of your Father in heaven; for He makes His sun rise on the evil and on the good, and sends rain on the just and on the unjust." (Matthew 5:38-45)

These are very, very high standards. Turning the other cheek? Going the extra mile? Loving your enemies? Are these standards by which we govern society? And if so, how could we justify having a military or a police force?

In his book *What I Believe*, nineteenth-century Russian novelist Leo Tolstoy gave the conclusions he came to after reading and rereading the Sermon on the Mount. Tolstoy believed that criminals love good and hate evil, even as we do. He concluded that followers of Jesus Christ shouldn't be involved in the army, the police force, or courts of law.

One man who was dramatically influenced by Tolstoy's teachings was Gandhi. Gandhi believed that by practicing these teachings, you could bring about a perfect state in which punishment could end and prisons would be turned into schools.

It sounds good, doesn't it? Nevertheless, it is wrong. Tolstoy and Gandhi weren't promoting the teachings of Jesus Christ—only their own interpretation of them.

Quite frankly, the Sermon on the Mount never was intended as a set of principles by which we govern our society. If someone deliberately seeks to harm another, we don't want police officers turning the other cheek. If we are attacked by a foreign power that wants to enslave or destroy us, we don't want soldiers, sailors, and marines to walk the extra mile with these foes of our nation. No, there is a place for self-defense, and there is a place for standing your ground.

Here's the distinction: The biblical teaching of the Sermon on the Mount was given by Jesus for believers to live by. If you want to know how a society should be governed, that is found in verse 38, where Jesus said, "You have heard that it was said, 'An eye for an eye and a tooth for a tooth.'" Exodus 21 continues on with, "Hand for hand, foot for foot, burn for burn, wound for wound, stripe for stripe" (verses 24-25).

This was the Hebrew civic justice system. Our modern equivalent would be tit for tat. The purpose of this punishment, according to Deuteronomy 19:20, was so the rest of society would hear of it, be afraid of such measures, and never repeat that evil action again.

This never was carried out by the victim of the crime, but by the legal system. It was a merciful law, because it limited the judgment, matching the punishment to the offense.

Scripture—both Old Testament and New—clearly teaches that God Himself has established government, the military, and the use of force when necessary. In Romans 13 we read,

> Everyone must submit to governing authorities. For all authority comes from God, and those in positions of authority have been placed there by God. So anyone who rebels against authority is rebelling against what God has instituted, and they will be punished. For the authorities do not strike fear in people who are doing right, but in those who are doing wrong. Would you like to live without fear of the authorities? Do what is right, and they will honor you. The authorities are God's servants, sent for your good. (verses 1-4, NLT)

Then, speaking of the soldier or police officer as well, the apostle Paul went on to say,

> For the one in authority is God's servant for your good. But if you do wrong, be afraid, for rulers do not *bear the sword* for no reason. They are God's servants, agents of wrath to bring punishment on the wrongdoer. Therefore, it is necessary to submit to the authorities, not only because of possible punishment but also as a matter of conscience. (Romans 13:4-5, NIV, emphasis added)

A sword? Did we read that right? God's servant, God's agent of wrath, bears a sword? What is a sword used for? It is used to kill a person. A modern equivalent perhaps would be a gun. God delegates vengeance, or the enforcing of justice, to the government. Otherwise, evil people will dominate.

According to Scripture, then—and yes, New Testament Scripture—government, law enforcement, and the military all have their God-ordained place in this fallen world. In fact, the Bible even uses a soldier as a model of what a Christian ought to be. Paul spent a lot of time around Roman soldiers, and he analyzed their methods and their gear.

In Ephesians 6, he used the Roman soldier's armor as a metaphor for spiritual warfare, describing each piece of a Christian's body armor in detail. Would the Holy Spirit, the Author of Scripture, have chosen a dishonorable profession as an illustration for how a Christian ought to walk in this world? No, it's the other way around. God's use of the military metaphor in Ephesians 6 draws attention to the positive qualities of a well-equipped soldier and shows us parallels for our lives.

Soldiers need to be alert, awake, well-equipped, and ready for battle. So do followers of Christ.

Once again, in 2 Timothy 2:3-4, Paul wrote, "Endure suffering along with me, as a good soldier of Christ Jesus. Soldiers don't get tied up in the affairs of civilian life, for then they cannot please the officer who enlisted them" (NLT).

Back in the Gospels, some soldiers who had been touched by the message of John the Baptist approached him with a question. In view of John's teaching, the soldiers asked, "What should we do?"

Here is how John answered: "Don't extort money or make false accusations. And be content with your pay" (Luke 3:14, NLT). He could have said, "Find another job. Turn in your swords. Give up being in the military." But he didn't use the opportunity to say anything like that. In essence, he replied, "Just be good soldiers and do your job."

WAS JESUS A PACIFIST?

Why do I bring up these passages? Because some try to insist that the Bible teaches pacifism, and that Jesus Himself was the ultimate pacifist. But He wasn't. Nor was He a peace-and-love hippie or an antiwar activist. Those are inaccurate, unbiblical portrayals of our Lord.

Jesus administered justice when He drove those money-changers out of the temple—with a whip—overturning their tables, sending their coins and paperwork flying. He told His disciples of coming dangerous days when they might need swords. When Peter mentioned they already had two swords, Jesus replied, "It is enough" (Luke 22:38).

Why would they need swords? The swords were for self-defense.

God has indeed established human government to administer justice, and it is acceptable for Christian men and women to both defend themselves and exercise their rights under the law. Even the apostle Paul, when falsely charged and beaten by the authorities in Philippi, exercised his rights as a Roman citizen. The Bible isn't saying the Christian is supposed to be some kind of a doormat.

What, then, is that turning-the-other cheek business all about? This is the Lord's advice for a specific situation in which a believer is being persecuted. These aren't mechanical rules, but biblical principles for meeting the personal wrongs that come to those who follow Him. There are times, for the sake of the kingdom and for the salvation of a soul, we will take the hit. We will turn the other cheek. We will go the extra mile. The idea is to do whatever you can to reach a person with the gospel.

In Romans 12:17-19, Paul wrote,

> Do not repay anyone evil for evil. Be careful to do what is right in the eyes of everyone. If it is possible, as far as it depends on you, live at peace with everyone. Do not take revenge, my dear friends, but leave room for God's wrath, for it is written: "It is mine to avenge; I will repay," says the Lord. (NIV)

The idea here is that we do what we can to influence a person for Jesus. And in the process, we may have to endure some abuse, to the point of turning the other cheek to this individual rather than paying back insult for insult.

This isn't so much about someone who just walks up to you out of the blue and punches you in the face. This is more the idea of enduring an insult for the Lord's sake. Back in those days, a slap on the face was something more than just a physical blow; it was a highly offensive insult—a demeaning and contemptuous act of hostility. And Jesus was saying, "Sometimes you have to stand there and take it, without retaliating."

A modern equivalent might be someone spitting in your face. It doesn't physically hurt, but it is an insulting and offensive way to be treated.

Maybe it is that universal and well-known gesture that people offer you on the highway while you're driving. People are so quick to do this. You find yourself asking, "What in the world was that all about?" And then you want to do it back, or even worse. Jesus is saying, no, don't do that. Take the insult, and don't give it back.

Is this an easy principle to live by? Not at all! It can be very difficult. Even the great apostle Paul struggled with it. Once when he was speaking to the Jewish Sanhedrin, the high priest gave an order to one of the guards to hit Paul squarely in the mouth. In surprise and anger, Paul shouted to the priest, "God will strike you, you whitewashed wall!" When someone pointed out to him that he was addressing the high priest, he backed off and said, "I did not know, brethren, that he was the high priest" (Acts 23:3,5).

TAKE THE INSULT . . . FOR HIS SAKE

Here is the point: Even if it is difficult to endure the insults, mockery, or reckless charges of a nonbeliever whom you want to win to Christ, it is worth the effort! The one who is now mocking you or insulting you may be your brother or sister in Christ someday.

In Matthew 5:40, Jesus said, "If anyone wants to sue you and take away your tunic, let him have your cloak also." The tunic was an undergarment, and everyone had one. The cloak was an outer garment that served as a blanket at night. It was indispensible for living in Israel, especially in the cold evenings.

What Jesus was saying in principle was, "Go further than they ask. Don't just give them your tunic. Give them your cloak. Go the extra mile."

Back in those days, a Roman soldier had the right to ask any citizen to carry his armor for a Roman mile, which was just a little bit shorter than our mile. The armor, however, was very heavy. It was tiring to always be lugging around a breast-plate, helmet, shield, and sword. A weary Roman soldier had the right to pick someone at random and say, "Come here. Carry my armor," and he would have to do it.

Jesus said, "Okay, if they ask you to carry their armor, go ahead and take it for the regulation Roman mile—and then go for an extra mile." Maybe during that extra mile a follower of Jesus might be able to say, "Let me tell you about my faith. Let me tell you about someone who carries *me* every day of my life."

We can apply this principle at school or at work, where you make up your mind to do a little bit more than the bare minimum. Yes, I fully understand that your coworkers may not like that. They might say, "Hey, chill out a little. Don't work so hard all the time. You're making the rest of us look bad." Or, maybe they will say, "What are you trying to do? Butter up the boss?" What they don't understand is that the boss at work is not your ultimate employer; Jesus is your boss. We read in Ephesians, "Work hard and with gladness all the time, as though working for Christ, doing the will of God with all your hearts" (6:6, TLB).

You work hard and cheerfully because you belong to Christ. You go the extra mile because you belong to Christ. You put up with insults over your faith and your lifestyle because you belong to Christ. You are doing these things for the sake of the gospel, trying to win a hearing for your message, trying to turn your enemies into friends.

Enemies? A kind, others-oriented, sweet-spirited believer in Jesus will have enemies? Yes, you can count on that.

Why? It's very simple. Darkness doesn't like light. Jesus said in John 15, "If the world hates you, you know that it hated Me before it hated you. If you were of the world, the world would love its own. Yet because you are not of the world, but I chose you out of the world, therefore the world hates you" (verses 18-19).

So what do we do? Hate them back? Do unto them before they do unto us? No. Far from it. Jesus tells us to actually love our enemies. In Matthew 5:44 He said, "Love your enemies, bless those who curse you, do good to those who hate you, and pray for those who spitefully use you and persecute you."

Don't strike out in revenge. Don't give tit for tat. Don't return an obscene gesture for an obscene gesture. Love people who are unkind to you in a positive way. That will bring attention to Jesus.

Abraham Lincoln had it right when he said that the best way to destroy enemies is to make them friends.

Do you have some enemies right now? Try to win them over, not just as friends but as followers of Jesus Christ. When people see a Christian who is willing to forgive, willing to turn the other cheek, willing to go the extra mile, it blows them away. They may not like it, but they can't completely dismiss it either. They can't put it together or figure it out.

This was the attitude Abraham showed toward his nephew Lot when he offered the younger man the best parcel of land. It was the attitude that David had when he refused to strike back at King Saul or take vengeance on him, even though Saul had hounded David for years. It was the attitude Joseph displayed when he extended forgiveness to the very brothers who had meant to see him enslaved or dead. It was the attitude young Stephen had when he prayed for those who were in the very process of stoning him to death. He said, "Lord, do not charge them with this sin" (Acts 7:60).

We all need God's help to live by these principles. No one can live out the Sermon on the Mount—or the Ten Commandments, for that matter—in his or her own strength.

How do we do it? I think the apostle Paul put his finger on the best answer in the book of Galatians. In a modern translation, this is how he described his journey:

> What actually took place is this: I tried keeping rules and working my head off to please God, and it didn't work. So I quit being a "law man" so that I could be *God's* man. Christ's life showed me how, and enabled me to do it. I identified myself completely with him. Indeed, I have been crucified with Christ. My ego is no longer central. It is no longer important that I appear righteous before you or have your good opinion, and I am no longer driven to impress God. Christ lives in me. The life you see me living is not "mine," but it is lived by faith in the Son of God, who loved me and gave himself for me. (2:19-20, MSG)

That is the secret. For me to live out the principles of Jesus, Jesus Himself must live out His life through me.

SINGLENESS, MARRIAGE, AND DIVORCE

A pastor was invited to speak to a group of fourth graders on the topic of marriage. As the children took their seats in their little wooden chairs, the preacher smiled and said, "Kids, I want to talk to you about marriage today. I wonder if any of you could tell me what Jesus has to say about marriage."

Immediately one little boy waved his hand back and forth, so the pastor called on him.

"Okay, son," he said, "what does Jesus say about marriage?"

The little boy replied, "Father, forgive them, for they know not what they do."

There are a lot of miserable people out there who have not found their marriages to be what they had hoped or expected. Maybe that is why one disillusioned soul wrote: "Marriage is like a three-ring circus: engagement ring, wedding ring, and suffering." If that is a description of your marriage right now, I want you to know that it can change.

What does the Bible have to say about marriage and

divorce? What is the biblical worldview? I speak with some experience on this topic for two primary reasons.

First, I know a little bit about divorce. I haven't been divorced, but my mother was married and divorced seven times. I have seen divorce up close and personal, and it isn't pretty. In fact, it was that very thing that made me determined, when I found the right girl, to have a marriage that would work.

Second, by God's grace, my wife and I have been married now for thirty-eight years. So we thank God for that. She hates it when I say this, but she doesn't even look like *she* is thirty-eight, much less has been married for thirty-eight years.

When someone asks us, "How long have you two been married?" and we tell them, they look at us like we are from another planet. Is anyone married that long? Yes, and there are people out there who have been married even longer than us.

In this chapter, I want to talk about the Bible's view on marriage, because that is what this culture needs so desperately —not the commonly accepted, generic secular view, but a biblical worldview.

I hope you are not looking to celebrity culture for your cues on how to have a successful marriage. Actually, you don't have to go looking; you can see all you want to on the magazine covers at the checkout line in the grocery store. That is what keeps those magazines going—the hookups and break-ups, the heartaches and betrayals of all those celebrities. No, this secular culture has very little to say to us on this topic. But the Bible has a great deal to say about finding, building, sustaining, and protecting a successful marriage.

Why am I bringing up the topic of divorce as well? Because we've been delving into the Sermon on the Mount in Matthew 5, and this is one of the subjects Jesus dealt with head-on.

I personally find divorce so repugnant and hateful that I wish we could somehow strike the word from our vocabulary. But even that wouldn't change the reality of the human heart, apart from the transforming work of Christ.

Nevertheless, I do believe this: Wedlock should be a padlock. Once you take those vows before the Lord and make that commitment to that woman or that man, you need to stand by it for your entire lifetime. Yes, I realize there are times and circumstances when a marriage simply can't survive, and the Bible makes allowances for those instances. And that makes it all the more important to marry the right person at the start.

SINGLE . . . AND PATIENT FOR GOD'S BEST

If you are single, I believe God has someone handpicked just for you. You may not know that person yet, or then again, maybe you do.

I know it is difficult to be single, and I understand what it means to be lonely. You wonder, *When will that right person finally come along in my life? I'm not getting any younger.* Or, you may find yourself thinking, *If only I were married, I know I would be happy.* Of course, there are married people who are thinking, *If only I were still single, then I would be happy.* Some cynical person once compared marriage to flies on a screen door; those on the outside want to get in, and those on the inside want to get out.

It's true, however, that there are advantages to being married and to being single. (As far as I'm concerned, marriage wins, hands down.) But at the same time, when you are single, you have a certain freedom and mobility that you don't have when you are committed to a spouse in marriage. Listen to the words of the apostle Paul, from 1 Corinthians 7 in this modern paraphrase:

> When you're unmarried, you're free to concentrate on simply pleasing the Master. Marriage involves you in all the nuts and bolts of domestic life and in wanting to please your spouse, leading to so many more demands on your attention. The time and energy that married people spend on caring for and nurturing each other, the unmarried can spend in becoming whole and holy instruments of God. I'm trying to be helpful and make it as easy as possible for you, not make things harder. All I want is for you to be able to develop a way of life in which you can spend plenty of time together with the Master without a lot of distractions. (verses 32-35, MSG)

Paul isn't being critical of men and women who spend time nurturing their marriage. He isn't speaking ill of the time we spend strengthening that bond. The fact is, we should do those things. But he is saying that when you are single, you have the blessing of mobility and a greater ability to concentrate more of your affection and attention on the things of God.

Here's the key: Whether you are single or married, you need to be content where you are right now. Your contentment shouldn't come from a relationship with a person; rather, it should come from your relationship with God.

Let's face it. Imperfect people are imperfect people, and all people will disappoint you along the way — even the best people.

In his letter to the Philippians, Paul wrote, "I have learned in whatever state I am, to be content" (4:11). And in Hebrews we read, "Let your conduct be without covetousness; be content with such things as you have. For He Himself has said, 'I will never leave you nor forsake you'" (13:5).

If you are a woman, you have to realize—and I hate to break this to you—that no man in the world will meet the deepest needs of your life. And men, no woman will do that for you, either. I know little girls long for that prince to come riding in on a white horse. Or maybe she will find a frog she can turn into a handsome prince with a kiss. Unfortunately, it is also true that handsome princes can turn into frogs.

Bottom line, it is the Lord whom we need and long for. Marriage can be the closest thing to heaven on this earth, but only the Lord will meet the deepest needs of our hearts.

If you are single, then, what are you looking for in a guy or a girl? A survey was done among singles, and the most important qualities they looked for in a date were beauty, brains, and disposable cash. No one said anything about character, inner qualities, or spirituality. Those qualities weren't even on the radar.

It is great to be beautiful or handsome, but those attributes fade so quickly over time. I happen to believe my wife is more beautiful than she ever has been. However, what impresses me even more than her outer beauty is an inner loveliness that grows more radiant year after year.

Women, instead of waging that never-ending battle with the aging process, concentrate your energies on becoming women of virtue. Proverbs 31 says,

Who can find a virtuous and capable wife?
She is more precious than rubies.

> Her husband can trust her,
>> and she will greatly enrich his life.
> She brings him good, not harm,
>> all the days of her life. . . .
> Charm is deceptive, and beauty does not last;
>> but a woman who fears the LORD will be greatly
>>> praised. (verses 10-12,30, NLT)

We often think of the word *virtue* as a feminine word. Actually, the word *virtue* is translated many ways in Scripture, describing both men and women—and even an army. In Proverbs 31, it describes a woman who is strong and influential but also feminine.

The Bible tells us that girls and women should think more about their inner beauty than their outward appearance. That certainly isn't to say that a woman should disdain or neglect her appearance. But don't neglect your inner beauty either. Listen to the words of 1 Peter 3: "What matters is not your outer appearance—the styling of your hair, the jewelry you wear, the cut of your clothes—but your inner disposition" (verses 3-4, MSG).

How many young women today even give a passing thought to their inner person? By the way, when you are a godly woman, pretty on the inside as well as the outside, this is very attractive to men—Christian and non-Christian alike. Do you know why? They haven't seen anyone like you before. You stand out in their eyes. You catch their attention and curiosity.

Before I was a believer, a virtuous young Christian girl got my attention, and I actually went to a Bible study just to find out what she was into, because I knew she hung out with Christians. At the time, it was a great disappointment to me that she was a believer. (It seemed like such a waste of a cute girl.)

But then at that Bible study, something happened to me that I hadn't expected. I heard the gospel and gave my life to the Lord. That girl and I never did have a relationship; she was just a friend. But how the Lord used her in my life! I remember thinking, *There's something different about this girl. She has a glow about her when she walks into the room.*

By the way, girls need to be aware that guys will fake being a Christian or having an interest in the Lord just so they can get an attractive Christian girl to go out with them. They will turn on the Christian talk and pretend to be interested in spiritual things when they are not at all, really.

Why am I telling you this? Because the faster young women know what guys are really thinking about, the better off they will be. That is why fathers are so protective of their daughters. They know what is going on in that young man's mind.

Be very, very careful in this area, because one thing you never want to do is hook up with a nonbeliever. The Bible is very clear on this topic. In 2 Corinthians, we read this strong warning:

> Don't become partners with those who reject God. How can you make a partnership out of right and wrong? That's not partnership; that's war. Is light best friends with dark? Does Christ go strolling with the Devil? Do trust and mistrust hold hands? Who would think of setting up pagan idols in God's holy Temple? But that is exactly what we are, each of us a temple in whom God lives. (6:14-16, MSG)

Who can count how many young Christian women have been brought down in this way? Yes, it starts romantically. But it quickly becomes sexual, and invariably it is the believer who gets pulled down rather than the nonbeliever who gets pulled up.

There is no place for what some call "missionary dating," in which a young woman is so sure that she will bring her boyfriend to the Lord and change him into the kind of young man she really wants.

Just don't go there. It offers incredible hazards and never seems to work very well anyway. Men, look for a woman of God. Women, find a real man of God. In fact, look for someone who is more godly than you! Many people will claim to be Christians, but that doesn't prove a thing. It takes time to discover and get to know a truly godly person, and time is the single person's friend.

Don't be in a rush with this second most important decision of your life. Let that prospective relationship stand the test of time. And if God is really in it, it will. The Bible says, "Many waters cannot quench love, nor can the floods drown it" (Song of Solomon 8:7). And in 1 Corinthians 13:4 we're reminded that "love is patient" (NLT).

STRONG FOUNDATION

I've heard it said, "Love at first sight is nothing special. It's when two people have been looking at each other for years that it becomes a miracle." Every marriage gets tested. Every marriage gets challenged. My marriage with Cathe has been tested, just as your marriage has—or your future marriage will be. Just because I'm a pastor doesn't mean that we are exempt from this sort of thing. The death of our son Christopher in 2008 was the greatest trial of our lives, and we have clung to the Lord and to each other as never before. Through it all, as dark as it has been at times, I have come to value and appreciate my wife more than ever before, and I trust that she feels the same about me.

Listen, every marriage will go through storms. People should realize this and be ready for it. But so many seem to be completely taken by surprise. When that first blast of cold wind comes over the horizon, riding on a mass of dark clouds, too many husbands and wives want to throw in the towel. "This is hard!" they'll say, as if they are totally blown away by the idea of a marriage enduring some hardship. "I don't know if I can handle this."

But here is the thing. You can handle it. You and your wife can handle *anything* if you have built your marriage on the right foundation.

At the end of the Sermon on the Mount, Jesus gave an unforgettable word picture:

> "Anyone who listens to my teaching and follows it is wise, like a person who builds a house on solid rock. Though the rain comes in torrents and the floodwaters rise and the winds beat against that house, it won't collapse because it is built on bedrock. But anyone who hears my teaching and doesn't obey it is foolish, like a person who builds a house on sand. When the rains and floods come and the winds beat against that house, it will collapse with a mighty crash." (Matthew 7:24-27, NLT)

Is your marriage on the Rock? Or is it on the rocks? Is it built on Jesus Christ or on the shifting sand of human emotion? It is not a matter of *if* the storms will come; it is only a matter of *when* and *how many*. But if you build your marriage and family on the Lord and His Word, your marriage will still be standing when the storm is only a distant memory.

As a pastor, I have spent a great deal of time with people who are about to enter eternity. And when life reaches its final days and hours, really only three things matter. I can tell you right up front that money isn't one of those things. People on their deathbeds aren't thinking about the money they have in the bank, their stock portfolio, their sports cars, or their expensive collections of this or that. No, there are three things that seem to bubble up to the top when someone looks back over his or her life: faith, family, and friends.

Concerning faith, believers will have one of two reactions. They either will be clinging to the Lord as their faith grows stronger, knowing they soon will be seeing Him face-to-face, or they will be wondering why they didn't spend more time in their lives pursuing God.

Family is a close second. And so often in those last moments, I hear regrets. People sigh and say how they wish they had done this, said that, or spent more time here or there. And to a lesser degree, people also think of their friends in those final moments.

But you never will hear people saying, "I wish I'd spent more time in the office" or "I wish I'd made that promotion" or "I wish I'd spent more time on the golf course."

You don't want to approach your last hours on earth filled with regret because you ruined your home or neglected your love relationship with your husband or wife. Trust me, that is not how you want to end your life.

Thankfully, knowing full well how prone you and I would be to shipwreck our lives and lose any chance at happiness, Jesus turned His attention to marriage—and divorce—in His Sermon on the Mount.

A FRESH LOOK AT THE ORIGINAL PLAN

I love how Jesus suddenly seemed to shift gears and transition into teaching on marriage and divorce. In Matthew 5:21-30, He talked about matters of the heart, the spiritual danger of holding on to hatred toward your brother, and the perils of allowing lust to take root. And then, in verse 31, He turned quickly to a subject His audience probably wasn't expecting at all—the relationship between a husband and wife and the tragedy of divorce:

> "Furthermore it has been said, 'Whoever divorces his wife, let him give her a certificate of divorce.' But I say to you that whoever divorces his wife for any reason except sexual immorality causes her to commit adultery; and whoever marries a woman who is divorced commits adultery." (verses 31-32)

What a bombshell that must have been. But let's keep a marker here in Matthew 5 and fast-forward to Matthew 19—another occasion when Jesus addressed the same subject. In that setting, He added a few words that I think are very important for us to consider:

The Pharisees also came to Him, testing Him, and saying to Him, "Is it lawful for a man to divorce his wife for
just any reason?"

And He answered and said to them, "Have you not
read that He who made them at the beginning 'made
them male and female,' and said, 'For this reason a man
shall leave his father and mother and be joined to his
wife, and the two shall become one flesh'? So then,
they are no longer two but one flesh. Therefore what
God has joined together, let not man separate."

They said to Him, "Why then did Moses command
to give a certificate of divorce, and to put her away?"

He said to them, "Moses, because of the hardness
of your hearts, permitted you to divorce your wives,
but from the beginning it was not so. And I say to you,
whoever divorces his wife, except for sexual immorality, and marries another, commits adultery; and
whoever marries her who is divorced commits adultery." (verses 3-9)

It is interesting to me how the Lord answers their question
by taking them all the way back to the book of Genesis, to
Adam and Eve, and to God's original plan.

Of course, we all know that Adam had the ultimate setup
in the Garden of Eden. Talk about the best bachelor pad ever!
Perfect weather, light work, incredible fruit trees on every side,
and the whole animal kingdom as companions. Best of all, the
Lord God Himself would come walking through the garden in
the cool of day to enjoy close fellowship and personal conversation with Adam.

It couldn't be better! And yet—believe it or not—

something was missing in Adam's life. More specifically, someone was missing. Adam was homesick for someone he had never seen or met, someone who didn't even exist yet.

God understood Adam's heart and said, "It is not good that man should be alone; I will make him a helper comparable to him" (Genesis 2:18). The phrase "helper comparable to him" also could be translated "someone who comes to rescue another."

What followed was a little divine surgery. And God knew that Adam would be thrilled with the results.

And the LORD God caused a deep sleep to fall on Adam, and he slept; and He took one of his ribs, and closed up the flesh in its place. Then the rib which the LORD God had taken from man He made into a woman, and He brought her to the man.

And Adam said:

"This is now bone of my bones
And flesh of my flesh;
She shall be called Woman,
Because she was taken out of Man."

Therefore a man shall leave his father and mother and be joined to his wife, and they shall become one flesh. (Genesis 2:21-24)

Commentator Matthew Henry said that Eve was made by God "not out of [Adam's] head to rule over him, nor out of his feet to be trampled upon by him, but out of his side to be equal with him, under his arm to be protected, and near his heart to be beloved."

When you get down to it, Adam and Eve had everything you could want for an ideal marriage. She never would have to hear about the way his mother cooked, and he didn't have to hear about all the other men she could have married.

The purpose of a man and a woman coming together is to leave and cleave (as the wording goes in the old King James Version). This is the most basic premise in marriage, dating back to when the first man and woman came together in that garden long ago.

But it is strange that to this day, I meet married couples who never have gotten this basic premise of marriage down.

The word *cleave* means "to glue, cling, or join together." The biblical pattern is to leave and cleave, sever and bond, loosen and secure, depart from and attach to.

Marriage begins with the leaving—a leaving of all other relationships. The closest relationship outside of marriage is specified here when God says that a man and woman must leave their parents. If that is true, then it is certainly true that all lesser ties must be broken, changed, or left behind.

What does it mean to "leave" your old family structure? Let me explain a little. You are still a son or a daughter to your parents, and you are still a sibling to your brothers and sisters. But now a new family has started, and you are a husband or wife. Therefore (and it doesn't get any more basic than this), a husband's primary commitment must be to his wife, and a wife's primary commitment must be to her husband.

Yes, you are to honor your parents, but now the relationship has changed, and a leaving must take place. If it doesn't, this could be detrimental to the marriage.

The word *cleave*, on the other hand, means "to glue or bond together," and it is the picture of what God intends for a husband and wife. In Malachi 2:14 we read these words: "The LORD has been witness between you and the wife of your youth, with whom you have dealt treacherously; yet she is your companion and your wife by covenant."

God says to the husband, "Your wife is your companion and friend. Be good to her. Be faithful to her!" That word *companion* means "one to whom you are united in thoughts, goals, plans, and efforts." Husbands, are you united with your wife in that way? Your wife should be your best friend in the whole world. And wives, your husband should be your very best and closest friend.

Stick together. Leave and cleave. Be attached. That is what Scripture says, and that is the biblical worldview for a husband and wife.

When Jesus quoted this "leave and cleave" verse in the Sermon on the Mount, He used a term that speaks of being glued or even welded together—so the two parts cannot be separated without doing serious damage to both.

And so it is.

Have you ever used superglue? That stuff freaks me out a little bit. It doesn't even look like glue; it looks more like water. You wonder whether it will even work, but then if you're not careful, you can glue your fingers together.

The verb in the original language, however, means more than simply getting stuck together. It also speaks of deliberately holding on to or clinging to something. So it is not like, "Well, I guess I'm stuck."

It is more like, "I'm holding on for dear life!" In fact, you are holding on to each other. That is how it should be in your marriage right now.

Are you leaving and cleaving? One way to maintain this

is through constant communication. Without question, communication is the lifeblood of any relationship. A survey among divorced couples asked them why their marriage failed, and 86 percent of the couples indicated the main problem was deficient communication.

Consider this. Experts say that a woman speaks 50,000 words every day. (I believe this. I've witnessed this.) Men supposedly speak 25,000 words—half as many. So here is the problem: Women are more communicative by nature. They are simply more adept and gifted in this area. And men? Well, not so much. We feel things, but we just don't express those emotions very well.

If you're a man, when was the last time you told your wife that you love her? If you're a woman, when was the last time you said that to your husband? Even a hug now and then would be nice.

I heard about a couple who was having some marital difficulties, so they went to see their pastor. They had a few sessions with him, and he asked a lot of questions. After a time he said, "I think I've got this figured out. I know what the problem is in your marriage."

The pastor got up from behind his desk, walked up to the man's wife, and gave her a big hug. Then he turned to the husband and said, "Sir, this is what your wife needs every single day."

The husband thought about that for a moment, looked up at the pastor, and said, "So what time do you want me to bring her by tomorrow?"

Yes, this guy missed the point a little, didn't he? But you don't have to.

Leave and cleave. Sever and bond.

BUT WHAT ABOUT DIVORCE?

What is the number-one reason cited for people getting divorces? Irreconcilable differences.

That drives me just a little bit crazy. Irreconcilable differences? Are you kidding me? Everybody has irreconcilable differences. My wife and I have had them for thirty-eight years now. She is very neat, and I'm often messy. She is sometimes late, and I'm usually early. She likes the toilet seat down, and I like it up. (I'm working on that. Even my little granddaughter is scolding me: "Papa, put the toilet seat down!")

It is a funny thing, but sometimes the very things that attracted you to your mate in the beginning become the things that divide. Why did you like her in the first place? She was different than you. She is outgoing and talkative, while you are more quiet and reserved—or the other way around. Back when you were courting, you loved those differences in your personalities. But now they are driving you crazy.

Bottom line, I don't believe in irreconcilable differences. Sometimes you have to just square your shoulders and say, "Okay, this thing that sometimes bothers me probably will never change, but I'm going to love my mate anyway." The Bible doesn't recognize these so-called "irreconcilable differences" as justification to dissolve a marriage.

Are there legitimate biblical reasons for divorce? We'll look into that in a moment, but first consider the attitude toward marriage and divorce back in Israel in that day. In fact, the attitude was very lax. A guy could pretty much divorce his wife for anything. For sure, divorce laws all favored the man.

According to a liberal rabbi of that day named Hillel, a man could divorce his wife for "incompatibility of temperament." (Sounds a little like irreconcilable differences, stated another way.) A man also could divorce his wife for such trivial things as burning his meal, embarrassing him in front of his friends, or even if a more attractive woman came along.

Absurd! Yet this was the prevalent background and culture when the Pharisees posed this question to Christ about divorce. In Matthew 19:7, they said to Him, "Why then did Moses command to give a certificate of divorce, and to put her away?"

In verse 8, Jesus replied, "Moses, because of the hardness of your hearts, permitted you to divorce your wives, but from the beginning it was not so."

Note the difference between these two statements. The Pharisees used the word *commanded* in reference to divorce, but Jesus used the word *permitted*. There's a big difference between those words.

Jesus went on to add, "And I say to you, whoever divorces his wife, except for sexual immorality, and marries another, commits adultery; and whoever marries her who is divorced commits adultery" (verse 9).

Moses didn't command divorce; he permitted it, giving men and women a release clause because their hearts were so hard and callous. Generally, Moses allowed it because the woman was being taken advantage of. It was to protect her from the hardship (and nightmare) of endeavoring to carry on in a home where she was unloved and unwanted, because a man had failed to realize the high ideal of marriage.

So yes, there is a way out. But it is nothing to celebrate.

WHEN IS DIVORCE ALLOWED?

Divorce is allowed when sexual immorality takes place.
Again, in Matthew 19:9, Jesus said, "I say to you, whoever

divorces his wife, except for sexual immorality, and marries another, commits adultery." Back in our original text from the Sermon on the Mount in Matthew 5:32, He said, "Whoever divorces his wife for any reason except sexual immorality causes her to commit adultery."

What is sexual immorality? It comes from the Greek word *pornea*. Any guesses what English word we get from that term? That's right . . . pornography. The word speaks of extramarital sexual relations, including the so-called affair. It also would cover incest, prostitution, and homosexuality.

Why is immorality a potential deal-breaker in a marriage? It is because the oneness of the marriage bond is violated. Paul even said that when you have sex with a prostitute, you become one flesh with her (see 1 Corinthians 6:16).

Oh, I know people call it a one-night stand and say that "it really didn't mean anything."

But that is a lie. It does mean something. It means a great deal to God, and it should mean a lot to you, as well. If you are married, sex outside of marriage is a direct violation of your oneness with your spouse.

Having said that, it doesn't mean you have to get a divorce over an occurrence of adultery. In fact, I would say that every effort should be made to restore the marriage, carefully examining the steps that led to this sin and applying some preventative measures.

By all means, try to save the marriage. Immorality is not only grounds for divorce, but it is also grounds for forgiveness.

God allows for divorce in the case of abandonment or desertion. In 1 Corinthians 7:13, Paul made this statement: "A woman who has a husband who does not believe, if he is willing to live with her, let her not divorce him."

Let's play this out a little. This is speaking about a woman who is married to a non-Christian guy or vice versa.

How does this happen? Sometimes it happens because of out-and-out disobedience. A single Christian gets impatient waiting for God's best choice for his or her life and decides to marry an unbeliever. After a little while, however, the Christian comes to regret that decision and doesn't want to stay in the marriage anymore. What's more, he or she may have met some nice Christian man or woman at church and wants to marry that person instead.

People have said to me, "Greg, I married a nonbeliever, and he doesn't love God, won't go to church with me, and won't pray with me. Then I met this kind, loving Christian man in church, and the Lord spoke to me and said, 'Dump that heathen nonbeliever and marry the man of God.' So what do you think?"

What I think is unimportant. What matters is what the Bible says. And that is where 1 Corinthians 7:13 comes in. Your job description now is to win that nonbelieving husband or wife to Christ. Your job is to reach your spouse for the Lord.

But let's just say the nonbeliever departs and abandons the believing mate. Paul went on to say in verse 15, "But if the unbeliever departs, let him depart; a brother or a sister is not under bondage in such cases. But God has called us to peace."

The Greek term translated "under bondage" here means "held by consent of agreement, or to be a slave of." So if the nonbeliever leaves you, you are free.

But what if he claims to be a Christian? It doesn't matter. Quite frankly, if a man or woman would abandon a spouse, claiming the Lord's leading, when that spouse doesn't want to separate, I would have to question whether that person is actually a believer at all. The Bible clearly tells us, "But if anyone does not provide for his own, and especially for those of his household, he has denied the faith and is worse than an unbeliever" (1 Timothy 5:8). So if that person abandons you, according to Scripture, you are not held to the agreement any longer.

Having cited these allowances for divorce, however, let me say this: Legitimate divorces that have a scriptural basis are very, very rare. Most divorces I have seen could have been avoided if the people would have applied themselves.

Here is my strong advice: Take careful stock of your marriage, and periodically examine your relationship to see if there is anything—anything at all—that might be bringing division between you and your spouse. And then, whatever that thing might be, get rid of it, because your goal in Christ is to leave and cleave . . . until death.

WHO WE REALLY LONG FOR

A little earlier, I mentioned how little girls grow up wanting to be princesses, and wanting their prince to come rescue them. Boys, too, grow up with romantic notions of meeting some girl who will satisfy the deepest needs of their lives.

But let's get real for a moment. What you really long for is God.

Yes, for a woman, a good man can greatly enrich her life. If you're a man, a godly woman can bring great joy—and her price is above rubies. But that man or woman, that husband or wife, can't meet the deepest, most profound needs of your life.

Only Jesus can do that. He is the one you really long for. And every one of us was created to be fulfilled by and in Him.

He is the one who will help you to be the single person He called you to be, and He is the one who will show you how to bond with your spouse, even in the darkest of times.

Cry out to Him for help, and He will give you more help than you ever could have imagined.

MONEY, POSSESSIONS, AND GIVING

You have stuff, I have stuff, everyone has stuff—and most of us have more of it than we know what to do with.

Guys pack all kinds of notes and receipts in their wallets, cram their wallets into their back pockets, and dislocate their hips in the process. Women have purses, an even bigger place to carry even more of who-knows-what kind of stuff.

Our cars have stuff in the glove boxes and trunks and probably under the seats. Our houses and garages have stuff in corners, stuff in boxes and bins, stuff in attics and basements, stuff in crowded closets, and stuff shoved under the beds. Some of us rent extra room at a storage facility to keep even more of our stuff.

Comedian George Carlin suggested that is what a house is really for: It's a place to keep your stuff. In fact, if you didn't have so much stuff, you wouldn't even *need* a house. A house is just a pile of stuff with a cover on top of it.

So one day, you look at your overflowing garage and closets and drawers, and realize you have way too much stuff and need to get rid of some of it. So you sell off your stuff, which usually works, because there is always someone out there who wants used stuff at a bargain. They are driving around on Saturday, looking for more stuff to buy, so they purchase your stuff.

Then what do you do? With your earnings in hand, you go out and buy some new stuff to replace your old stuff.

Believe it or not, the Bible addresses our love affair with stuff. In fact, Jesus told a story about a well-off man who had lots and lots of stuff. As the story goes, he was so successful in business that he ended up with more stuff than he could possibly store.

After thinking about this dilemma, he hit on a solution. It wasn't a very good solution at all, but he never bothered to ask God about it and went for it anyway. Here is what happened:

> "He said to himself, 'What shall I do, for I have no room to store this harvest of mine?' Then he said, 'I know what I'll do. I'll pull down my barns and build bigger ones where I can store all my grain and my goods and I can say to my soul, Soul, you have plenty of good things stored up there for years to come. Relax! Eat, drink and have a good time!' But God said to him, 'You fool, this very night you will be asked for *your soul*! Then, who is going to possess all that you have prepared?' That is what happens to the man who hoards things for himself and is not rich in the eyes of God."
> (Luke 12:17-21, PH)

Just before He told this story, Jesus looked around at the crowd who had gathered to hear Him speak and said, "Life is not measured by how much you own" (verse 15, NLT).

A common bumper sticker might read, "He who dies with the most toys wins," but that is just one more lie from the father of lies. Possessions are not the measure of a successful life and never will be.

Jesus talked quite a bit about possessions. It might surprise you to learn that 15 percent of everything Jesus said related to the topic of money and possessions—more than all of His teachings on heaven and hell combined. What's more, half of the parables He told dealt with possessions and money. Beyond the words of Jesus Himself, one out of every seven verses in the entire New Testament deals with this very topic.

As the pastor of a church, however, I know that preachers talking about money can seem like a risky thing. You can almost see the guys in the congregation reach down to feel for their wallets, just to make sure they are still there.

Why do we feel that way? Why are we so protective of our possessions? It may be because we think of the money we possess as *our* money and all the stuff in our lives as *our* stuff.

But it really isn't. The Bible, filled as it is with sometimes uncomfortable truths, reminds us that we—everything we are and have—belong to God.

Paul makes that point very, very clear in 1 Corinthians 6:19-20, where he wrote, "Don't you realize that your body is the temple of the Holy Spirit, who lives in you and was given to you by God? You do not belong to yourself, for God bought you with a high price. So you must honor God with your body" (NLT).

You belong to God, and I belong to God, bought and paid for! If I have good health (and thank God, I do), it is a gift to me from God. The breath I draw into my lungs right now, even as I write these words, is a gift to me from God. The beat of my heart is a gift to me from God.

One time the Pharisees came to Jesus, seeking to trap Him with His own words. Acting oh-so-innocently interested and concerned, they asked Him, "Is it lawful to pay taxes to Caesar, or not?"

Jesus saw right through their deception. If He had said, "Yes, pay taxes to Caesar," they would have said, "Don't you think we Jews are being overtaxed by Rome?" But if He said, "Don't pay taxes to Caesar," then they would have replied, "Oh, so you are a rebel and an insurrectionist. You ought to be arrested."

So Jesus said neither. Instead, He surprised them by saying, "Show Me the tax money." And someone produced a coin bearing the face of Caesar.

Jesus said, "Whose image and inscription is this?"

"Caesar's," they replied.

He said, "Render therefore to Caesar the things that are Caesar's, and to God the things that are God's" (see Matthew 22:17-21).

You and I bear the imprint of our Creator God, just as a quarter bears the image of George Washington. You were made after His image and His heart. For that reason, we should glorify God with our lives—with everything we have and are. Even if our possessions and bank accounts are the result of our natural talents and the hard work of years, every bit of that bounty has been given to us by the Lord.

In Haggai 2:8, God said, "The silver is Mine, and the gold is Mine." You say, "But, Greg, wait a second here. I've acquired my possessions through strategic investments and countless hours of hard labor." Yes, that may be true. But again, it is the Lord who gave you the opportunity and the ability to do all of those things.

Proverbs 10:22 says, "The blessing of the LORD makes one rich, and He adds no sorrow with it." And we read in Deuteronomy 8:18, "But remember the LORD your God, for it is he who gives you the ability to produce wealth, and so confirms his covenant" (NIV).

You say, "Greg, I think you might be talking to the wrong person, because I've never been wealthy. I'm pretty low on the economic ladder."

So you're not wealthy? Many in the world—perhaps most —might disagree with you. It depends on whom we're comparing ourselves to, doesn't it? Are you comparing yourself to a professional athlete or celebrity living in Beverly Hills? Then yes, compared to a person like that, you might not be wealthy.

But then again, maybe someone in Beverly Hills would say, "Being rich isn't so easy these days. And I'm not wealthy compared to a megamillionaire." And then the megamillionaire says, "Okay, I'm fairly well off. But look at Bill Gates!"

On it goes. There always will be someone higher on the economic ladder than we are. But guess what? There will be many, many more people who are a great deal lower on that ladder than you. It is my belief that the very lowest rung on our American economic ladder would be considered rich in comparison to a good portion of humanity.

Someone once said, "If you have money in the bank, in your wallet, and spare change in a dish somewhere, you are among the top 8 percent of the world's wealthy."

That changes the perspective on things, doesn't it? You may be more wealthy than you imagined. The issue is, you have stuff, and all those things you now possess were given to you by God. How, then, are you living in view of these truths? What does the Bible say?

In his first letter to Timothy, the apostle Paul wrote,

> Command those who are rich in this present world not
> to be arrogant nor to put their hope in wealth, which is
> so uncertain, but to put their hope in God, who richly
> provides us with everything for our enjoyment.
> Command them to do good, to be rich in good deeds,
> and to be generous and willing to share. (6:17-18, NIV)

Paul set forth three principles in his counsel to young
Pastor Timothy.

THREE POINTS FOR A PERSON WITH RESOURCES

***1. Don't be arrogant, and don't place ultimate hope in
wealth.*** I heard the story of a wealthy man who was very near
death. He had worked very hard for his money and desperately wanted to take some of it with him to heaven. So he
prayed and specifically asked God if he might be an exception
to the rule and take a few valuables to heaven. God thought
about it, and then said, "All right. One suitcase only."

So the man loaded up a suitcase with solid gold bars. After
he died, he stood at the gate of heaven and was greeted by
(who else?) Peter. The man explained the arrangement he had
made with God and asked to check his suitcase so he could
look around a little.

Sometime later, someone asked Peter, "What was in that
guy's suitcase, anyway?" Peter shook his head and said, "You
know, it's the funniest thing. I don't get it. He went to all of
that effort to bring in a suitcase full of pavement."

Apparently, that's what gold is good for in heaven — to

pave the streets. The fact is, that which is regarded as valuable on earth has no value in heaven. And often that which is undervalued on earth has maximum value in heaven.

2. *Enjoy what God has given you.* Does that surprise you? It shouldn't. That is exactly what it says in the text. *"God . . . richly provides us with everything for our enjoyment."* We should enjoy what God has given us without feeling guilty.

Sometimes people will suggest there is virtue in poverty. But the Bible doesn't teach that. The Bible tells us that God can and will bless a person, and that can include monetary blessing. No, I don't subscribe to the teaching of those who claim that God wants every believer to be healthy and wealthy all the time. On the other hand, I don't believe God wants every believer to be impoverished either. God can certainly bless a person materially, as He did with Abraham, Job, David, Solomon, Joseph of Arimathea, Mary of Bethany, and Barnabas, in varying degrees.

Sometimes people will quote the story of the rich young ruler in Mark 10:17-22 and remind us that Jesus told him to give up everything he had and follow Him.

But that is no prerequisite for being a Christian. Jesus only said that to one man, one time. And the reason he said that to him in particular was because he was a young man trapped and ruled by his possessions. He couldn't go any further in seeking God until he let them go.

God says that if He has blessed you with an abundance, go ahead and enjoy it, and do so with a thankful heart.

"But, Greg," someone says, "doesn't the Bible say that money is the root of all evil?"

Actually no, the Bible does not say that. Here is what the Bible says, in 1 Timothy 6:10: "The love of money is a root of all kinds of evil, for which some have strayed from the faith in their greediness, and pierced themselves through with many sorrows."

There is a difference. You can have money—even a great deal of money—and not love it. It is also possible to have just a little money and love it a great deal. It isn't an issue of how much you have; it's your attitude toward what you have.

Money itself is neutral, neither moral nor immoral. The problem with wealth is not in having it. The problem occurs when it has you. The issue is with how we get money, guard money, and give money. It can be used for worthy or very unworthy purposes.

3. Use your money to do good. The text in the New Living Translation says, "Tell them to use their money to do good. They should be rich in good works and generous to those in need, always being ready to share with others" (1 Timothy 6:18).

You can tell quite a bit about a person's spirituality by his or her giving—or the lack thereof. Jesus said, "Where your treasure is, there your heart will be also" (Matthew 6:21).

The fact is that if we are true followers of Jesus, we should give sacrificially to the work of the kingdom of God. It has been said that we should give until it hurts. Jesus, however, teaches that it should hurt when we cease to give. Giving is a real test of our faithfulness to God. Jesus said, "If you are untrustworthy about worldly wealth, who will trust you with the true riches of heaven? And if you are not faithful with other people's things, why should you be trusted with things of your own?" (Luke 16:11-12, NLT).

In the Sermon on the Mount, Jesus pulls it all together for us.

WHAT THE FATHER SEES IN SECRET

"Take heed that you do not do your charitable deeds before men, to be seen by them. Otherwise you have no reward from your Father in heaven. Therefore, when you do a charitable deed, do not sound a trumpet before you as the hypocrites do in the synagogues and in the streets, that they may have glory from men. Assuredly, I say to you, they have their reward. But when you do a charitable deed, do not let your left hand know what your right hand is doing, that your charitable deed may be in secret; and your Father who sees in secret will Himself reward you openly." (Matthew 6:1-4)

Don't forget that the theme running through the Sermon on the Mount is *the heart*. Jesus already had made the point that hating someone in your heart is like murdering them, and lusting after someone in your heart is like committing adultery with them. And now He is saying to those who loved to make a big show of their offerings and gifts that they ought to do those things in secret—not out in the open to gain attention.

If someone sees you giving something, that is okay. But never do it in a way that deliberately draws attention to yourself. Why? Your heavenly Father sees what you do in secret—for His eyes only—and will reward you openly. God watches everything we do; He always has His eye on us. The book of Proverbs says: "God is closely watching you, and he weighs carefully everything you do" (5:21, TLB).

In another passage, we read how Jesus went over to the collection box in the temple and sat and watched as the crowds dropped in their money. Many rich people put in large amounts—and the coins clattering into the box must have made quite a racket.

Then a poor widow came along who dropped in two pennies. It must have made a tiny little sound like *ka-plink . . . ka-plink.*

At that moment, Jesus called His disciples over to Him and said, "I tell you the truth, this poor widow has given more than all the others who are making contributions. For they gave a tiny part of their surplus, but she, poor as she is, has given everything she had to live on" (Mark 12:43-44, NLT).

I find it interesting that Jesus sat by the collection box . . . and just watched. He actually went over and sat down with the express purpose of observing how people gave. He noticed how the wealthy would come and throw in an offering that was a significant amount of money to a normal person—but not to them, because they had so much more. And then this woman came with her two pennies. Not a lot of money, but it was everything she had to live on—with none left for even a piece of bread for supper that night.

Jesus saved His praise for her. He didn't condemn the others; He just praised her. The wealthy men had given much, but had much, much more to spare. But she gave everything and had nothing left. It hadn't been a performance. She probably had no idea that anyone was even watching. But Jesus was watching. And He watches what we give as well.

Back in Matthew 6, Jesus said the hypocrites gave, wanting "glory from men" (verse 2). In other words, they wanted applause and recognition. They wanted people to see them and say, "Oh my, what a fine fellow you are."

These are the people who are always boasting about their accomplishments and how much they have done for the kingdom of God. They make sure you know all of the great sacrifices they have made.

That's fine. But if they are posturing themselves to receive the approval and applause of others, that is all they will get. Jesus said, "They have their reward" (verse 2). By the way, that word *reward* means "paid in full and receipted." Those who are searching for the spotlight and want so badly to be acknowledged have already been paid.

By contrast, Jesus said here is the way to give: "Do not let your left hand know what your right hand is doing" (verse 3). When you make up your mind to do a charitable deed, don't do it in a way that draws any attention to yourself. Do it for the glory of God alone. Let your act of compassion be done in secret, "and your Father who sees in secret will Himself reward you openly" (verse 4).

God will not be your debtor. And whatever you have given up for the kingdom of God is duly noted by the Lord Himself. If we remember, God will forget. But if we forget, God will remember.

In other words, if we feel it is necessary to keep reminding ourselves (and others), "I did this for God. I did that for God," the Lord will reply, "I think you already were paid for that. You got your reward by telling everyone how much you did." But if you do something for God in a discreet way, deliberately avoiding attention, God will take careful note of that and reward you. You may even forget about what you did, but He won't.

And no one ever outgives the Lord.

Over in the book of 2 Corinthians, the apostle Paul expands our worldview on possessions even further by teaching about giving—and the attitude of our hearts.

WHAT GOD LOVES

Remember this — a farmer who plants only a few seeds will get a small crop. But the one who plants generously will get a generous crop. You must each decide in your heart how much to give. And don't give reluctantly or in response to pressure. "For God loves a person who gives cheerfully." And God will generously provide all you need. Then you will always have everything you need and plenty left over to share with others. As the Scriptures say,

> "They share freely and give generously to the poor.
> Their good deeds will be remembered forever."

For God is the one who provides seed for the farmer and then bread to eat. In the same way, he will provide and increase your resources and then produce a great harvest of generosity in you. (2 Corinthians 9:6-10, NLT)

So what do we learn from this?

God loves cheerful giving. The Bible has quite a lot to say about what God hates, and frankly, I want to learn all I can about those things. It is a terrible thought that I might someday find myself occupied in something and then hear God say, "I hate that." I already know that He hates lying, evil, slander, discord, and divorce, so I want to walk carefully in life and avoid those things that displease Him.

But I am also interested in what God *loves*. What gives Him pleasure? What are the activities that prompt Him to say, "I just love that."

According to 2 Corinthians 9:7, "God loves a cheerful

giver." The word translated *cheerful* also could be translated "hilarious." He loves a hilarious giver, because that is a person who has discovered the joy of giving. Remember, Jesus said, "It is more blessed to give than to receive" (Acts 20:35). Have you discovered that to be true yet?

When you are a child, you may have a hard time believing that. You may feel pretty sure that it's more blessed to receive than to give. Right? When you have a birthday coming up or it's almost Christmas, you draw up detailed maps to your favorite toy store and the aisle where your parents can find that wonderful thing you want.

As you get older, however, you begin to enter into the joy of giving. You start to enjoy the look of delight on the face of your spouse or child when they open the present you picked out for them. And to be perfectly honest, it really is a more joyful experience than receiving something yourself. The glow lasts longer, and the satisfaction goes so much deeper.

But kids don't understand that. Kids don't like to give — or share. You can have two very small children who haven't even learned to talk yet and maybe know just a few words between them. But if one child grabs a toy the other had been interested in, an all-out battle can ensue. And they begin saying the one word they learned before "Da-da" or "Mama." *Mine!*

But adults can get that mixed up, too, can't we? We look at the things God has blessed us with and begin to think, "These are mine. I earned them. I deserve them. They belong to me." But as we noted earlier, everything you have ever had, have, or will have belongs to God. Why? You don't even belong to yourself. You — and all you are and have — belong to Him.

So what should my perspective be? Here's how the Lord Himself phrased it: "Do not lay up for yourselves treasures on earth, where moth and rust destroy and where thieves break in and steal; but lay up for yourselves treasures in heaven, where neither moth nor rust destroys and where thieves do not break in and steal" (Matthew 6:19-20).

Have you ever been ripped off? Have you ever had anyone break into your house or your car or steal your wallet? I had my wallet stolen recently—right out of my back pocket. What a major production that turned out to be. Quickly calling my credit card company, I found out that someone had started making charges on my card *within three minutes* after stealing it. So I had to shut everything down, get a new driver's license, and the whole nine yards. The experience, if you have ever been through it, makes you feel angry and sick inside. We all have to go to a lot of trouble and expense to protect our possessions.

Jesus, however, reminded us that what we send on ahead to heaven can never be stolen, never lose value in a bad market, and never deteriorate in any way. Those riches, transformed into heavenly currency, will be waiting for you when you cross over to the other side. No, you can't take them with you, like that foolish man with his suitcase of gold wanted to do, but you can send them on ahead.

How do I send it on ahead? It works like this: Every sacrifice that I make for the kingdom, every gift that I invest, every prayer that I pray, and every time I share the gospel—in fact, everything I do here on earth for the glory of God—results in treasures in heaven.

It is a blessing to give. Many believers haven't yet discovered this blessing. In 2 Corinthians 8:4, Paul spoke about a group of believers from Macedonia who just loved to give. The apostle wrote: "They begged us again and again for the privilege of sharing in the gift for the believers in Jerusalem" (NLT).

They were begging to give. They were saying, in effect, "What can we give to now? That was great, but now we want another project. Who is in need? How can we help people?" That is what you call hilarious giving. The Macedonian believers loved giving to God, and God loved their heart in giving.

As we give to God, God will give even more to us. Let's consider Paul's words to the Corinthians in another translation:

> But remember this — if you give little, you will get little. A farmer who plants just a few seeds will get only a small crop, but if he plants much, he will reap much. Everyone must make up his own mind as to how much he should give. Don't force anyone to give more than he really wants to, for cheerful givers are the ones God prizes. God is able to make it up to you by giving you everything you need and more so that there will not only be enough for your own needs but plenty left over to give joyfully to others. (2 Corinthians 9:6-8, TLB)

Some people choose to give the very least possible, and that is their choice. It is a good thing to be careful and prudent and wise in our giving—but Scripture makes it clear that it delights God's heart when we are generous. We all know people who don't want to give anything. When you go out to dinner with them and the check comes, they suddenly get paralysis of the hand when it comes time to reach for their wallet. They are always just a step or two slow, leaving you with the bill.

But there are other people who jump in right away and say, "Here! Let me get that." And they have their money out and on the table before you can even protest.

It's a strange phenomenon, but I have often found that people who have the most tend to give the least. And people who have very little at all are the most ready to give. But they never will be the loser for their generosity; God Himself will see to that. Many promises in the Bible clearly state that if we will faithfully give to the work of the kingdom of God, we always will have more than enough resources for our own needs. For instance, the book of Proverbs tells us, "Honor the LORD with your possessions, and with the firstfruits of all your increase; so your barns will be filled with plenty, and your vats will overflow with new wine" (3:9-10).

You may say, "I can't really afford to give."

The truth is, you can't afford *not* to give.

I heard the story of a preacher who asked a farmer in his congregation, "Farmer, if you had $200, would you give $100 to the Lord?"

The farmer answered, "Yes, preacher, I would."

"And if you had two cows, would you give one of those cows to the Lord?"

"Yes," the farmer replied. "I would do that."

Then the preacher said, "If you had two pigs, would you give one of them to the Lord?"

The farmer replied, "Now, you know very well that isn't fair, because I *do* have two pigs."

In other words, giving to God may be great when it's theoretical. *If I had this much money, I'd do thus and so with it.* But what about what you have now? God won't hold you responsible for what you don't have, but He will hold you responsible for what you do have—and what you do with it.

One day soon, you and I will leave *everything* behind, whether we have accumulated much or very little. As Solomon wrote: "Cast but a glance at riches, and they are gone, for they will surely sprout wings and fly off to the sky like an eagle" (Proverbs 23:5, NIV).

It's true, isn't it? We open the newspaper and see that our 401(k) went in the tank, or a surefire investment went south, or we realize we have simply spent way more than we had intended to.

Wealth will either leave us while we live or leave us when we die. Either way, it will leave us. When John Rockefeller, one of the wealthiest men who ever lived, passed away, someone asked his accountant, "How much did Mr. Rockefeller leave?"

The accountant replied, "He left all of it."

Here is what it comes down to: One day you will depart this earth and leave everything behind. The government will get a chunk of it, and maybe the rest will go to someone you didn't even want to get it. But you won't be worried about that, because you will be standing before God, giving an account of your life and what He gave you to steward and invest.

Here is a happy solution: Invest every dollar you can in God's work. Invest your energy in spreading His gospel and advancing His kingdom.

Five seconds after you open your eyes in heaven, you will be very glad—even hilarious—that you did.

OUR FATHER IN HEAVEN

When Father's Day rolls around, sometimes we feel some mixed emotions. Mother's Day is usually much easier to talk about and celebrate, because almost every child loves his or her mom.

When some college or pro football player makes a big play, and the camera goes in for a tight shot, sometimes we can see him mouthing, "Hi, Mom."

When a child falls and gets hurt, the first word that comes out of his or her mouth is "Mommy!" That's even if Dad happens to be standing right there. And we dads sometimes wonder to ourselves, *So what am I, chopped liver?*

Here is the answer. If Mom is there, then yes, you are chopped liver. Get used to it.

Mothers always seem to trump dads. Do you know what day of the year more phone calls are made than any other? Christmas? Thanksgiving? No, it's Mother's Day. (And the one day of the year when the most *collect* calls are made is Father's Day.)

Some reading these words will have had hands-on fathers, men of God who were or are the spiritual leaders in their homes. We all thank the Lord for such men.

Others had fathers who were somewhat distant or disinterested and not really engaged in their lives. Sadly, others have dads who abandoned them altogether, and they have had very little, if any, contact with them.

Every believer in Christ, however, has one thing in common: No matter what kind of dad you have or had on earth, you have a Father in heaven. Regardless of how your father on earth has treated you, for better or for worse, you have a Father in heaven who has always been there for you and always will be there for you.

Psalm 68:5 says that God is a Father of the fatherless. And David wrote in Psalm 27:10, "When my father and my mother forsake me, then the LORD will take care of me."

Yes, we have a heavenly Father who loves us. And the way we communicate with Him is through prayer.

"MY FATHER AND YOUR FATHER"

The Lord's Prayer is contained in the Sermon on the Mount, the greatest sermon ever preached. And in that prayer, Jesus taught us to pray as follows: "Our Father in heaven, hallowed be Your name" (Matthew 6:9).

"Father in heaven"? That sounds common enough to you and me, but it was a revolutionary thought for a Jewish person in Jesus' day. The Hebrews so feared God and attached such sacredness to His name that they wouldn't even utter it aloud. And you certainly didn't hear these Hebrews referring to God as "Father." Yes, He is called Father seven times in the Old Testament, but even then the references are indirect or somewhat remote.

In fact, when Jesus referred to God as His Father, He was accused of blasphemy. And one of the reasons they crucified Him was because He spoke of this special relationship He had with His Father.

Now, because of our Lord's death and resurrection, we, too, have a Father in heaven. You may remember that after His resurrection, Jesus said to Mary Magdalene, "Go to My brethren and say to them, 'I am ascending to My Father and your Father, and to My God and your God'" (John 20:17).

Each of us might respond a little differently to the concept of a Father in heaven, depending on what sort of father we had on earth. If you had a passive, mostly disengaged father, you might think God is that way: mostly disconnected and oblivious to what's going on in your life. Then again, if your dad was involved, loving, nurturing, and affirming, you might carry over some of those impressions to your view of God the Father.

These comparisons aren't really very helpful. What we need to do is develop our view of God based on how He is presented in Scripture, rather than comparing Him to a human father.

WHAT IS THE FATHER LIKE?

Not only does God tell us in His Word to address Him as Father, but we are to do so in an intimate way. Romans 8:15-16 says, "For you did not receive the spirit of bondage again to fear, but you received the Spirit of adoption by whom we cry out, 'Abba, Father.' The Spirit Himself bears witness with our spirit that we are children of God."

The word *Abba* speaks of a tender intimacy, like calling

your father Daddy or Papa. The idea is that we are invited into an intimate, privileged, affectionate relationship with Him.

My granddaughters call me "Papa." Little Lucy, who, at this writing, is just beginning to walk and talk, has just started calling me that. And when she wants to get out of her high-chair or be picked up, she will lift her hands up and say, "Uppy, Papa!" It's very cute, and how in the world could anyone resist that? I certainly can't resist it, so I pick her "uppy" every time.

If you really want to know what kind of Father we have in heaven, you have only to look at Jesus. Because Jesus said in John 14:9, "He who has seen Me has seen the Father." He also said in John 8:19, "If you knew me, you would also know my Father" (NLT).

So what is God the Father like? Just look at Jesus with the little children in His arms, blessing them. Look at Jesus with tears streaming down His face at the grave of His friend, Lazarus. Look at Jesus washing His disciples' feet in the Upper Room. That is what your Father in heaven is like.

If you want an accurate snapshot of God, a proper portrait of the Father, look carefully at the story of the prodigal son in Luke 15. In this story, Jesus presents the Father as an engaged, loving, affectionate Dad who loves His sons.

As you may remember in that story, the father had two sons. One day, the youngest said to his dad, "Father, give me the portion of goods that falls to me" (verse 12). In other words, "I want my portion of the inheritance *now*. I don't want to wait until you die."

So the father divided up the estate and gave the boy what he wanted. Then that youngest son went off to a distant country, lived like a fool, and soon blew through all his inheritance money. He ended up in a literal pigpen, feeding the animals and wishing he could eat some of the stuff they were giving to the pigs.

Finally, he came to his senses and returned to his father. Instead of portraying that father as angry and vengeful, Jesus speaks of a heartsick father who longs for his son's return. And when he sees the boy in the distance, looking so sad and bedraggled, he runs down the road to meet him and throws his arms around the young man, kissing him over and over:

> When he was still a long way off, his father saw him. His heart pounding, he ran out, embraced him, and kissed him. The son started his speech: "Father, I've sinned against God, I've sinned before you; I don't deserve to be called your son ever again."
>
> But the father wasn't listening. He was calling to the servants, "Quick. Bring a clean set of clothes and dress him. Put the family ring on his finger and sandals on his feet. Then get a grain-fed heifer and roast it. We're going to feast! We're going to have a wonderful time! My son is here — given up for dead and now alive! Given up for lost and now found!" And they began to have a wonderful time. (verses 20-24, MSG)

That is your Father. So Jesus said, "In this manner, therefore, pray: 'Our Father in heaven.' " Jesus didn't say we should call Him "Our Creator in heaven." He is our Creator, but that is not how we are to address Him. Nor should we even say, "Our God in heaven," though He is our God. No, we are encouraged to use the word *Father*, implying a relationship, intimacy, closeness, and affection.

The fatherhood of God is featured prominently in the

Sermon on the Mount. Jesus mentions the Father seventeen times—and ten of those references include the word *heaven* or *heavenly*.

So Jesus is saying that He is your Father in heaven.

Before we look at the Lord's Prayer itself, however, let's consider the words that immediately precede it.

IN THE SECRET PLACE

"And when you pray, you shall not be like the hypocrites. For they love to pray standing in the synagogues and on the corners of the streets, that they may be seen by men. Assuredly, I say to you, they have their reward. But you, when you pray, go into your room, and when you have shut your door, pray to your Father who is in the secret place; and your Father who sees in secret will reward you openly. And when you pray, do not use vain repetitions as the heathen do. For they think that they will be heard for their many words.

"Therefore do not be like them. For your Father knows the things you have need of before you ask Him." (Matthew 6:5-8)

Notice that Jesus refers to the Pharisees as "hypocrites."

It's a word we throw around a lot. When someone stumbles or makes a mistake, we will sometimes say (or think), "What a hypocrite."

But that is not an accurate use of this term. To be a hypocrite doesn't mean you make mistakes or fail to always live up to what you believe.

That is not hypocrisy. That is called *humanity*.

Every one of us will fall short, saying things we wish we hadn't said and doing things we wish we hadn't done. We will find ourselves apologizing to people, regretting choices we've made, and wondering how we got so far off track.

Again, that is not hypocrisy. That is just a struggling Christian trying to live out what he or she really believes.

Being a hypocrite is different.

When it was used in its original context, the word *hypocrite* meant "an actor." In fact, in Greek culture it had no negative connotation whatsoever. If you were describing someone in a play who was wearing a costume or a mask, you would speak of them as a hypocrite. It was just another way to say actor.

It's much the same today. We may see a particular movie, view some actor in a stirring, inspirational role, and develop some admiration toward that person. Then we might happen to see that same individual being interviewed on late-night TV, and think to ourselves, *He's not the person I thought he was.* Or, *She isn't anything like that role she played in the movie.*

Without their makeup, costumes, and cleverly written lines, we realize these people are *not* the characters they play. They are just actors. They are pretending—and very skillfully—to be something or someone they are not.

That is what a hypocrite is. The problem with the Pharisees and religious leaders of that day is they were showmen. They were putting on an act for men and women to see. It was theater, they were actors, and they would put on their robes, say their lines, and pray their prayers.

When they gave gifts, they did it in a dramatic, theatrical way to garner maximum attention, seeking to show how devout, pious, and holy they were.

But Jesus was saying, "Don't do that. Don't act that way." Jesus even condemned the rote, ritualized prayers these guys repeated all the time.

Why? Because they weren't really praying, they were *acting*. It was all for show.

That is why I've never been fond of repeating some sort of memorized prayer. Now, there's nothing wrong with praying the Lord's Prayer, if it's coming from your heart. It *is* a magnificent prayer.

Sometimes, however, some people think it is some kind of megaprayer, with extra influence in heaven. In other words, if all else fails, this one will get through.

It's like one of those fire alarms you see in certain buildings, where it says, "In case of emergency, break glass." So the emergency comes, you pull the alarm, and you say, "Our-Father-who-art-in-heaven-hallowed-be-Thy-name." I don't mean to make fun of anyone who has ever prayed this prayer in a crisis, because it is a powerful prayer. And if your heart is engaged, I'm sure the Lord will honor it. But this prayer Jesus gave us in the Sermon on the Mount is more than just a memorized prayer to repeat; it is a template, or a model for all prayer. (More about that later.)

Beware of memorized prayers that you can rattle off without thinking. Be careful about saying formula prayers, whether you're thanking God for a meal or praying with your child before bedtime.

Our God is a *personal* God, and a loving Father. He wants to hear and respond to our real concerns and needs. The psalmist said, "Trust in him at all times, you people; *pour out your hearts to him,* for God is our refuge" (Psalm 62:8, NIV, emphasis added).

In Matthew 6:7, Jesus said, "When you pray, do not use vain repetitions as the heathen do."

Again, God doesn't want you to pray ritualized, repeated, memorized prayers, because He wants you to speak to Him from your heart. He is your *Father*. And the truth is, you can repeat memorized prayers or beautiful poetic prayers written by someone else without any thought of God whatsoever.

We've all done that. We've all "prayed," rattling off a bunch of words, without really thinking about God. Why? For one thing, we become distracted in prayer sometimes, and we forget who we are talking to. Maybe we will be thinking about lunch instead, and a particular hamburger at our favorite diner.

Sometimes people will use prayer as an opportunity to brag about their accomplishments, and the prayer is more about themselves than God: "Lord, I thank You for waking me up at 4:00 a.m., and Lord, You know I've been on my knees for hours. This thirty-day fast I'm on has been really hard, Lord, but I thank You for the opportunity to share the gospel with twelve people yesterday. . . ."

Oh, please. Just stop. That is not prayer; that is a performance for the ears of others. Don't pretend that you are praying to God when your prayer is all about you.

At other times we may use prayer as an opportunity to gossip: "Lord, You know that Jim has been cheating on his wife. . . ." And suddenly people in your little group can't wait to get out of that prayer meeting to tell other people what they have just heard.

Others use prayer as an opportunity to impress, with flowery words that sound like they came right out of the old King James Bible: "Our most gracious heavenly Father, we come before Thee this day. . . ." And they go on and on and pray too long. Jesus spoke of those who "rattle off long prayers" and "think they will be heard because they use so many words" (Matthew 6:7, PH).

Bottom line? Don't pray long prayers in public. Make them as long as you like when you're alone with the Lord, but keep them short when you're with others. You will find that most of the public prayers in the Bible were short and to the point.

In Matthew 6:8, the Lord reminded us, "Your Father knows the things you have need of before you ask Him."

If that is the case . . . then why pray at all? Isn't the objective of prayer to get God to do what I want Him to do?

Actually, no. Prayer is not moving God your way; prayer is moving you God's way. Prayer is not getting your will in heaven; prayer is getting God's will on earth. God invites us to pray so that we will remember our dependence on Him and see our regular need for His help.

Obviously, God could give me everything I ever needed all at once, in one big delivery with a bow around it—all the security . . . all the wisdom . . . all the provision . . . all the help. But if He did that, then I might not feel the need to come to Him each day, humble my heart before Him, and tell Him all my needs and desires in detail. And I would be the biggest loser.

As it is, God gives me things as I need them and works with me day by day, hour by hour. And in the moment of great trial, He is there with all the grace I need to make it through.

It's the same for you. When you hit that financial crisis, get bad news from the doctor, or find yourself crushed in spirit from relationship issues, you go to your Father and tell Him all about it, asking for His help.

He loves that, and it's the best thing in the world for you. Our Father is generous with His help, and He loves to provide for you.

In the final analysis, however, prayer isn't meant to bend the arm of God, but rather to bend our will to His. True prayer isn't overcoming God's reluctance; it is taking hold of His willingness.

THE LORD'S PRAYER

> In this manner, therefore, pray:
> Our Father in heaven,
> Hallowed be Your name.
> Your kingdom come.
> Your will be done
> On earth as it is in heaven.
> Give us this day our daily bread.
> And forgive us our debts,
> As we forgive our debtors.
> And do not lead us into temptation,
> But deliver us from the evil one.
> For Yours is the kingdom and the power and the glory
> forever. Amen. (Matthew 6:9-13)

What we call the Lord's Prayer can be divided into two sections. The first three requests have to do with the glory of God, and the final three deal with the needs of people.

As I said already, the Lord's Prayer isn't so much a word-for-word prayer to repeat, as much as it is a template or guide for prayer. And notice how it starts.

"OUR FATHER IN HEAVEN"

Yes, God is a Father who loves us. But He is our Father in *heaven*. When we pray, we approach the awesome King of the universe, whose throne is in heaven.

In other words, our prayers ought to start with Him and a realization of who He is—and not with ourselves. This is God Almighty! This is the Creator of all.

This also will help us get our own problems into perspective. Sometimes when we come to God with our problems, they seem huge and overwhelming to us. So we lug these gigantic questions and troubles and needs into His presence, and we can hardly see around them or over them.

But here's the problem: If we're focused on how big our problems are, our God will seem small, barely able to help us. But if we begin by focusing on the greatness, might, majesty, and awesomeness of our eternal God, our problems won't seem so big at all. If you realize how big your God is, your problems will seem very, very small in comparison.

Prayer, then, helps you gain perspective as you contemplate and rehearse to yourself the glory of God. As you thank and praise the Lord out loud, it's also a reminder to yourself of how He has cared for you, helped you, and protected you in times past. *Father, You are so glorious. You are so powerful. You are the one who created the world. You are the one who raises the dead. Lord, You have been so faithful to me.*

And then (it's amazing how this works), as we say those words honoring God and rehearsing His greatness and His kindness toward us, our perspective begins to change. It's as though we are lifted up in the Goodyear Blimp and see our life from a whole different angle.

So don't just go into God's presence and say, "Our Father

in heaven, . . . give us this day our daily bread." That is how many of us pray. We skip right to our needs and wants. We say, "Good morning, Lord. Now here's my list of stuff I want to speak to You about. . . ."

But that is not what the template of the Lord's Prayer teaches us. No, we start by saying, "Our Father in heaven, hallowed be Your name."

What do those words mean? *Hallowed* isn't a term most of us would use in everyday speech. What it means is "to set apart." It means that God is set apart in my life, above everything and everyone else. He is Lord of all. It means that in my life and character, I want to set Jesus Christ above all else and live a holy life.

These thoughts lead me to look more closely at my ambitions, interests, pursuits, and goals, and ask myself some important questions: *Is what I'm doing for the glory of God? What about my career choice? What about this upcoming business decision? What about this dating relationship or the people I hang out with? Can I write "hallowed be Your name" over these things?*

Martin Luther said, "How is God's name hallowed among us? It is when both our doctrine and living are truly Christian."

Here is our problem, however: Sometimes we'll just plunge on ahead and formulate our plans and make our decisions without consulting God at all. And then, almost as an afterthought, we'll say, "Lord, please bless these plans I've just made and this direction I've just committed myself to."

But that is not the spirit of the Lord's Prayer.

We pray, "Father in heaven, Your name be above all else. I lay everything in my life at Your feet. I want Your will above all else. Guide my steps today, Father. Open the doors You want to open and close the doors You want to close."

When I pray, "Your kingdom come, Your will be done on earth as it is in heaven," that is a multi-faceted request with different shades of meaning.

First, it is a request for the return of Jesus Christ to the earth. I am praying, "Lord, come back to planet Earth." The word used here for *kingdom* doesn't speak primarily of a geographical territory, but rather of sovereignty and domin- ion. So when I pray, "Your kingdom come," I'm praying for God's rule on earth. The word *come* speaks of a sudden, instan- taneous coming. "Oh, Lord, come back to rule and reign on this broken planet of ours. Come quickly, Lord! I'm looking forward to Your return. I long for that day!"

Have you ever prayed a prayer like that? A strong belief that Jesus could return to earth at any moment will have a purifying effect on your life spiritually. In 1 John 3:3, the apostle said, "Everyone who has this hope in Him [the hope of the Lord's soon return] purifies himself, just as He is pure."

Second, it is a personal request. When I pray, "Your kingdom come. Your will be done on earth as it is in heaven," I am asking for the kingdom of God to come into my own life. What is the kingdom of God? It is the rule and reign of Christ when He returns, yes. But it is also the rule and reign of Christ in my own life.

Later on in the Sermon on the Mount, Jesus said, "Seek first the kingdom of God and His righteousness, and all these things shall be added to you" (Matthew 6:33). In other words, put God's kingdom above your own. So I am saying, "Lord, I truly want Your rule, Your kingdom, and Your sovereignty in my life."

Before I can pray, "Your kingdom come," however, I must pray, "My kingdom go."

Third, it is an evangelistic prayer. By praying, "Your kingdom come," I am also asking for the salvation of those who don't know the Lord. As His kingdom rules and reigns in my life, I can play a part in bringing that kingdom to others. In fact, one way God's kingdom is brought to this earth is each time a new soul receives Jesus Christ as Lord.

We know it is God's will for people to believe. The Scriptures tell us, "The Lord is . . . not willing that any should perish but that all should come to repentance" (2 Peter 3:9). In response to this, we should pray every day for nonbelievers, that they might find life and salvation in Christ.

This heart for the lost is also modeled for us in Isaiah 53, a prophetic passage that points to Jesus as the coming Savior. In verse 12 we read that Jesus "poured out his life unto death, and was numbered with the transgressors. For he bore the sin of many, and made intercession for the transgressors" (NIV).

As He hung on the cross, His first words from Calvary were, "Father, forgive them, for they do not know what they do" (Luke 23:34).

Jesus prayed for nonbelievers. Do you?

We see a striking illustration of this in the death of young Stephen, the church's first martyr. The book of Acts records how Stephen was hauled before the Sanhedrin, how he boldly proclaimed the gospel to them, and how he was subsequently stoned to death. As he was being martyred, Scripture says, as the rocks were flying and death drew near, he prayed, "Lord, do not charge them with this sin" (7:60).

In fact, those were his last words. He prayed for the people who were in the process of taking his life. And presiding over this horrific event was a man known as Saul of Tarsus. Saul was a Jewish scholar and leader who had dedicated his life to hunting down, torturing, and murdering followers of Jesus.

In Stephen's last moments, could it be that he directed his prayer to God for Saul, the man at the end of the mob who was holding people's coats? Maybe as Stephen was dying, he prayed, "And, Lord, save that guy there—that guy in charge, Lord. Get hold of his heart!"

Praying for your own murderer? Isn't that crazy? And why waste your breath on someone like Saul, who had no chance of becoming a believer?

Right?

Wrong!

You know the rest of that story. Out on the Damascus Road, Saul of Tarsus met Jesus of Nazareth, and in the course of time became the great apostle Paul.

Why do I bring this up? I'm guessing you know someone who is so stubborn, so arrogant, so entrenched in his or her sin that you could never imagine that individual's coming to Christ. She may be mean and utterly self-centered. He may be profane—a militant atheist with Darwin stickers on his ecologically correct car. This may be an individual who goes out of his way to harass you.

Start praying for her. Bring him before the Lord every day. Pray that God will get hold of that life. No one is beyond the reach of prayer, and the way is open for anyone and everyone to come to Jesus.

Jesus taught us to pray, "Your will be done on earth as it is in heaven." And that is how it was once. Before sin entered the world, heaven and earth existed in perfect harmony. When God looked down at His creation, He said that it was good. God's will was the dominant will, and the result was . . . paradise!

After the rebellion of Lucifer, however, who later became Satan, other wills were introduced that brought division between heaven and earth. Lusting after the top position, Satan lost his place in heaven and fell, drawing a third of the angels with him. And now lost sinners, the devil, a host of demonic beings, and even Christians sometimes rebel against God and want their own way.

But it won't always be like this. One day, God's will on earth once again will be just as it is in heaven. Until that day comes, however, we are to pray and work toward that goal. As I said already, prayer is not a means to get our will in heaven, but to accomplish God's will on earth. True prayer is a partnership between heaven and earth.

So how is God's will accomplished on earth? Primarily through us. We accomplish it by the way we pray, the way we live, and the way we share the gospel.

The fact is, it is not always easy to do or to accept the will of God. When the Lord answers our prayers for financial provision or healing or strength, we love the will of God.

But what about when you lose your job, the sickness doesn't go away, or the crisis gets worse instead of better? What about when you find out you have only six months to live? What then? Some crisis slams into your life, and you find yourself asking, "Could *this* be the will of God? Is God paying attention?"

Those are the moments when we need to pray, as Jesus prayed, "Nevertheless not My will, but Yours, be done" (Luke 22:42). Don't you love this about Jesus? He didn't just preach this stuff, He *lived* it. And there in the darkness, beneath those gnarled olive trees of Gethsemane, He prayed that prayer. He said, "Father, if it is Your will, take this cup away from Me;

nevertheless not My will, but Yours, be done."

What cup was Jesus speaking of? It was the cup of the wrath of God He was about to drink—right down to the dregs. The pressure on Jesus was so intense at this particular time that the writer Luke, a physician by trade, tells us His sweat was like great drops of blood.

Jesus was in deep sorrow and anguish, and His disciples never had seen Him that way before. But they would not forget hearing Him pray, in effect, "Lord, if there is any other way for this to be accomplished, that's what I want. Nevertheless not My will, but Yours, be done."

Jesus gave us a model of what to do in a time of uncertainty. The truth is, we don't always know the will of God in every situation, do we? And there are times when we do know it—and don't like it. There are times when we are experiencing the will of God, and it makes no sense to us at all, as in the case of Job.

Sometime we read Job's story and think to ourselves, *Come on, Job. Get a grip. What's up with all that complaining? Why can't you just trust God?* What we forget is that Job was living out these tragedies in real time. Job didn't have the opportunity (at that point) to read the end of the book of Job. All he knew was that one day his world was humming along nicely, and the next day he lost his possessions, his family, and his health. He didn't have any idea how it would all work out. To him, it must have seemed like the end of the world.

The point is, we can't always see or understand the whys or wherefores of what God allows into our lives. We're still in the middle of the story. Then again, we may be closer than we realize to the end of the story.

Either way, the story isn't done yet.

We may say, "I liked the first chapters of my life. I like the way the book read back then. Chapters 1, 2, 3, and 4 were fantastic. And now, *this* chapter makes no sense at all."

No, it may not. But then again, you aren't at the end of the book yet. God still has more chapters to write—and some of those may not be finished until after you leave this life for heaven. But God has promised that He will work everything together for good to those who love Him (see Romans 8:28). So you need to continue praying, "Not my will, but Yours, be done."

Never be afraid to commit an unknown future to a known God. There will be a Gethsemane event, if you will, for every believer—a place that is beyond our comprehension, a place we can't begin to handle on our own, a place where we must simply surrender in every way to the will of God, a place where we pray, "Not my will, but Yours, be done." Don't be afraid to say that to God.

In Ecclesiastes 3:11, Solomon wrote, "God has made everything beautiful for its own time. He has planted eternity in the human heart, but even so, people cannot see the whole scope of God's work from beginning to end" (NLT).

No, we can't. No human being can do that. But God can. And He has a plan and a purpose. Each of His plans has a beginning, a middle, and an end. And in the end, we will all agree that what He has done is very good. Until that day, we say, "Not my will, but Yours, be done."

Has the Lord shown you His will? Then do it to the best of your ability. Are you running from the will of God? Don't. Your Father loves you and has a plan for your life beyond anything you could dream up on your own.

You may have grown up with a dad who let you down a lot

and didn't keep his word.

But you have a heavenly Father who never will let you down and will always keep His word—both now and forever.

THE LORD'S PRAYER

Have you ever been in what appeared to be an impossible situation with no way out? Have you ever desperately needed or wanted something, but it seemed as though there was no way that you ever would have it, reach it, or attain it? Or have you ever thought there was no future for you, that for you, it was just too late?

If so, you need to know about the power of God that can be released through prayer. One thing that comes out very clearly in the pages of Scripture is the fact that prayer can dramatically change situations, people, and sometimes even the very course of nature. It has been said that if you are swept off your feet, it's time to get on your knees.

More than anything else, however, the thing that prayer changes the most is you. You change when you pray and as you pray. As we noted in the last chapter, the objective of prayer is not to change God or persuade Him to move in a certain direction; the objective of prayer is to align ourselves with His will and purposes.

God will allow hardship, challenges, need, and sometimes even tragedy to enter our lives so He can reveal Himself to us in fresh ways and put His power and glory on display.

Why do we need to pray? We need to pray because we are weak. If we understood that fact better, if we realized just how weak we truly are, maybe we would pray more than we do. We imagine ourselves to be strong and resourceful and tend to think of getting on our knees before God as a last resort. We will say, "I've tried everything I know to do, and I've called all of my contacts. I guess all I can do now is pray."

But prayer shouldn't be the last resort; it should be the *first* resort. The first thing we should do in our need is to pray and seek the Lord's help, direction, and provision.

In all my days, I never have prayed as much as I do now, in this season of my life. I don't write that to impress you, because I still don't pray nearly enough. It is just that I never have sensed such need in my life, and I never have been aware of such weakness.

But it is a funny thing. When we catch a glimpse of our profound weakness, we also find ourselves in a better vantage point to glimpse the strength of God. In fact, the weaker that we see we are, the greater we see that God really is.

Paul put it like this in 2 Corinthians 12:10: "That's why I take pleasure in my weaknesses, and in the insults, hardships, persecutions, and troubles that I suffer for Christ. For when I am weak, then I am strong" (NLT).

Paul was referring to the fact that he had been suffering with some unnamed thorn in the flesh and had asked God on three different occasions to remove it. But each time he asked, God gave him the same answer: "My grace is enough for you."

Finally, Paul concluded (loosely paraphrased here), "You know what? I'm okay with that. And I'll tell you why. Because when I am weak, I am strong. And I am seeing God's greatness in all of this as never before."

So what should you do if you are suffering? You should pray.

What should you do if life is going really well? You should pray (see James 5:13-14).

And who was a greater example of prayer than Jesus Himself? He often would spend long nights alone with the Father in prayer. So it was really only natural that His disciples would come to Him one day and say, "Lord, teach us to pray." *We want to pray like You, Jesus. We want to understand what prayer really is.*

It was as if He was just waiting for them to ask, because He immediately gave them the template and pattern for what we call the Lord's Prayer. He said,

> "When you pray, say:
>
> Our Father in heaven,
> Hallowed be Your name.
> Your kingdom come.
> Your will be done
> On earth as it is in heaven.
> Give us day by day our daily bread.
> And forgive us our sins,
> For we also forgive everyone who is indebted to us.
> And do not lead us into temptation,
> But deliver us from the evil one." (Luke 11:2-4)

We call this the Lord's Prayer, but it never was really *His* prayer. It was a prayer He gave to the disciples and to us. This is obviously not a prayer Jesus would have prayed Himself.

How do we know that? Jesus never would have prayed, "Forgive us our sins," because He had no sins to be forgiven! So this is a prayer for you and me, because we do need our sins forgiven.

If you want to read the *real* Lord's Prayer—the prayer that only Jesus could pray—that can be found in John 17. Nevertheless, even though the prayer Jesus taught us could more accurately be called "the disciple's prayer," we will continue to refer to it in the way most familiar to all of us: the Lord's Prayer.

In the last chapter we saw how this prayer can be divided into two sections, the first dealing with the glory of God and the second dealing with the needs of men.

That second section is what we will concentrate on in this chapter.

THE THREE PETITIONS

Our Daily Needs
"Give us this day our daily bread." (Matthew 6:11)

Bread was a staple for the first-century Jew and a part of every meal. (No one was running away from carbs in those days.) Bread was regarded as essential, and everyone utilized it every day. Satan himself brought bread into the conversation when he challenged Jesus to turn stones into Wonder Bread in the wilderness.

I've always had a weakness for bread. I can resist a dessert, but if I'm around freshly baked bread slathered with melted butter, well, it is all over. I can't resist it. And if I see a fresh biscuit? It is the same result.

When the Bible speaks of bread or our daily bread, it is not just referring to that particular food item. It is speaking of food in general. When we pray, "Give us this day our daily bread," we are essentially saying, "Lord, provide me with all the food that I need."

But it is really more than food, too. "Daily bread" speaks of our human needs and includes clothing, shelter, and all that I need in life. Back in the 1960s, we used to call money "bread." We would say, "Hey, man, you got any bread?" So it is really a phrase that speaks of God's provision in general. Within this template for prayer that Jesus gives us, then, we need to ask God to provide for our needs.

Why should we pray for that every day? God wants us to come before Him in prayer and make our requests. This is clearly taught in Scripture. James 4:2 says: "You do not have because you do not ask God" (NIV).

That verse makes you stop and think a little, doesn't it? There may be many things in our lives that we don't have but could have had, simply because we haven't talked to God about them.

Go to the Lord with your needs. Talk to Him about what is on your heart. Bring what you regard as impossibilities in your life, realizing that with God, nothing is impossible. He is your Father, and He loves to talk to you and hear your voice.

Charles Spurgeon said, "Whether we like it or not, asking is the rule of the kingdom."

So yes, we can certainly ask for His provision, and nothing is too big or too small or insignificant to bring to God. This is the God who knows the number of hairs on your head (for me, that wouldn't be a big chore) and takes note of every little bird that falls to the ground.

Is He into details? Yes, He is.

Most of us do this as parents, right? If my son Jonathan comes to me with a big problem, I will make time to help him as best I can. If one of my granddaughters comes to me with what seems like a big problem to her, I will help her out. You had better believe I will!

The other day Stella came to me, showing me that her doll had lost its head. For her, that was a big-time problem. I spent half an hour trying to get that head back on again, but couldn't do it. So I told her, "Stella, let's go buy a new doll, okay?"

As earthly parents, we take time for our kids and grand-kids. How much more will our heavenly Father take time for us? Jesus said,

> "Which of you fathers, if your son asks for a fish, will give him a snake instead? Or if he asks for an egg, will give him a scorpion? If you then, though you are evil, know how to give good gifts to your children, how much more will your Father in heaven give the Holy Spirit to those who ask him!" (Luke 11:11-13, NIV)

If you as a parent know how to provide and meet your kids' needs, how much more will Your Father provide for your needs? Notice that word *needs*. I didn't say *greeds*.

The Bible doesn't promise that God will meet our every desire. There are times when He will overrule our requests and say, "No, son; no, daughter; you don't really need that right now. In fact, it wouldn't be good for you."

Now, having established the fact that God willingly provides for us, it doesn't mean we should sit around, be inactive, and neglect to work. Don't be a lazy bum and say, "Well, the Lord will provide."

No, the Bible is clear on this. God expects us to work hard. In 2 Thessalonians 3:10 Paul wrote, "If anyone will not work, neither shall he eat."

"But Greg," you say, "I don't have a job."

Fair enough. That is true for many people these days. But if that's the case, you need to work just as hard at looking for a job as you would if you were on the job. Work where you can, don't look down on lesser jobs, and be as responsible as you can be.

By praying, "Give us this day our daily bread," I am acknowledging that everything I have comes from God, both today and in all the days He gives me on this planet. Furthermore, He wants me to speak to Him about this provision on a daily basis and just stay connected with Him as my Father and Provider.

I also would add that I need to be a good steward of what He does provide for me. And I need to faithfully give back to Him and invest in the work of the kingdom of God. The Scriptures clearly point out—in Malachi 3:8-11 and other passages—that if I am faithful in my tithes and offerings, the Lord will richly provide for my needs.

Forgiving and Being Forgiven
"Forgive us our debts, as we forgive our debtors." (Matthew 6:12)

We need to pray for the forgiveness of sins, and in the process of receiving that forgiveness, forgive others.

That doesn't mean you run up debt on your credit cards and then say, "Lord, forgive my debts." God may, but the credit card company probably won't.

No, this word *debt* could better be translated "sins." *Forgive our sins. Forgive us our trespasses—our shortcomings or our resentments or what we owe to You for the wrong we have done.*

Some people say, "I don't need forgiveness. I don't think I have sinned today." Trust me on this: You *have*. And so have I.

Sometimes I like to wear a pair of white pants. But it is strange, because I always see stains on them before the day is over. Why do I always spill stuff on my nice white pants? To be honest, I think I spill stuff all the time. I just notice those stains when my pants are white. When I wear jeans, my coffee stains or burrito stains are somewhat camouflaged by the dark material, and I don't see them.

In the same way, we fail to see many of our sins on any given day. We might even come to the end of the day and congratulate ourselves a little, thinking, *I've had it together today. I don't think I've sinned today.* (And there is a stain right there. It's called pride.)

Here is a newsflash: You haven't been sinless today. If you think you have, then you are deceived. The Bible says, "If we say that we have no sin, we deceive ourselves, and the truth is not in us" (1 John 1:8). Thoughts that went through your mind left a stain. Little flashes of attitude passed through, leaving more stains. And you did things you don't even remember doing. Even if you didn't break a specific commandment of God, you certainly fell short of the standard of God. Maybe it was the sin of omission, where you failed to do good that you could have (and should have) done.

I'm not saying these things to make you feel bad. I'm just pointing out that we need to ask God every day to forgive us for our sins.

But as we receive that forgiveness, we also should extend it to others. As our debts are forgiven, we are to forgive our debtors, or those who have sinned against us.

According to Jesus, our generous and constant forgiveness of others should be the natural result of understanding the forgiveness God has extended to us. Here's an even simpler way to put it: Forgiven people ought to be forgiving people.

Why do I need to be a forgiving person? People are going to hurt me, and I am going to hurt them. There is really no getting around it. And sometimes little things turn into big things. Have you noticed that?

Maybe you have heard of the Hatfields and the McCoys. This was one of the longest running blood feuds in American history. They were two pioneer families; one lived in West Virginia, and the other in Kentucky. They fought on opposite sides during the Civil War, and after the war conflicts developed. A Hatfield was killed, and in retribution, a McCoy was slain. And so it went for years. At the end, twenty-four people were dead—twelve from each family.

Most of us think that sounds insane now, but the truth is, people still get into crazy feuds with other people. And sometimes people even forget why they had been angry at each other in the first place or what in the world started the fight. Even so, one thing leads to another, lines are drawn, and people end up hating each other for no good reason.

John thinks Joe can't do anything right. Jane thinks Jill is wrong in everything she does. They look at each other through the dark lenses of cynicism and mistrust and criticism, and both parties grow increasingly bitter.

Not content to be embittered with each other, however, two feuding people can't seem to keep the poison to themselves. They spread the bitterness around, and it grows more and more toxic.

The Bible strongly warns against this. In Hebrews 12:15 we read: "See to it that no one falls short of the grace of God and that no bitter root grows up to cause trouble and defile many" (NIV).

When I hold grudges, when I hate, when I fail to forgive, I grieve the Holy Spirit of God. What does that mean? It means to make Him sad and sorrowful. Ephesians 4:31-32 says, "Get rid of all bitterness, rage and anger, brawling and slander, along with every form of malice. Be kind and compassionate to one another, forgiving each other, just as in Christ God forgave you" (NIV). And if you refuse to do that, Paul points out in verse 30 that you bring sorrow to God's Holy Spirit by the way you live.

We live in a society that doesn't value forgiveness. In fact, forgiveness is often seen as a sign of weakness rather than strength. Our culture esteems vengeance and payback. We believe in the old adage, "I don't get mad; I get even."

You may want to keep your distance from a person with a bumper sticker that reads: "Kill them all, and let God sort them out." I wouldn't recommend tailgating that guy or cutting him off in traffic — especially if he has a sticker on the other side of his bumper that says, "Protected by Smith & Wesson." (It might be a good time to change lanes.)

The Bible says that we are to be forgiving, extending this forgiveness over and over again. And here is a little tip that I will throw in for free: If you forgive, you might *live* longer.

Extensive research has been done on the subject of forgiveness over the years, and recent studies suggest that those who don't forgive are more likely to experience high blood pressure, bouts of depression, and problems with anger, stress, and anxiety.

You might say, "But, Greg, you don't know what happened. This person doesn't *deserve* forgiveness."

My response is, *do you?*

Yet God forgave you anyway, didn't He? You, in turn, must forgive others.

C. S. Lewis summed it up pretty well when he wrote, "Everyone says forgiveness is a lovely idea, until they have something to forgive."[1] Isn't that true? "Oh yes. I'm all for forgiveness—except for that rat over there who stabbed me in the back last week!"

No, Scripture doesn't allow for any exceptions. Forgive as God has forgiven you.

"Lord, Don't Let Me Fall!"

"And do not lead us into temptation, but
deliver us from the evil one." (Matthew 6:13)

I need to pray to not fall into temptation. In this prayer we are asking God for specific guidance that will keep us in His will, and guard us from unnecessarily placing ourselves in the way of temptation. When I pray this, I am essentially saying, "Lord, don't let me be tempted above my capacity to resist."

And He won't, of course. As Paul wrote in 1 Corinthians 10:13, "No temptation has overtaken you except such as is common to man; but God is faithful, who will not allow you to be tempted beyond what you are able, but with the temptation will also make the way of escape, that you may be able to bear it."

In other words, God will never give you more than you can handle.

Even so, here's the interesting thing about temptation. It's so . . . *tempting*. Satan is like an expert fisherman alongside a trout stream. He knows just the right bait or lure that will attract you most. That is why we need to pray every day of our lives, "Father, keep me from falling. Guard me from the temptations I will encounter today."

The fact is, we can be quick to condemn sin in someone else's life at the same time we are rationalizing sin or compromised behavior in our own life.

Sometimes we find ourselves in one of those so-called gray areas, and we wonder, *Is it all right for a Christian to do this?* Here is a little litmus test you can apply, if you wonder if something is an enticement to evil or not. (I dare you to try this.) If you're wondering about a particular activity, bring it into the clear light of the presence of God, and specifically pray about it.

Can you ever hear yourself saying, "Lord, please bless us as we go and party tonight and get drunk. And, Lord, could You please close the eyes of the police, so we don't get a DUI on the way home?" Or how about this: "Lord, please bless me tonight as I have sex with this girl (or guy) I'm not married to."

Would you ever pray prayers like that? No? Then why would you ever go in that direction?

Here is another example or two. Would you ever pray this? "Father, I ask You to bless me and prosper me as I sue my Christian brother. I know I don't have cause to do it, Lord, and I know I really haven't tried to resolve the whole issue. But I've decided to take him to court anyway, and I ask that You would be with me."

You wouldn't pray that? Then how about this? "Lord, I come to You and ask You to bless me as I divorce my devoted wife and marry another woman."

We couldn't pray prayers like these, because we know that what we are doing is wrong and displeases the Lord. We know we can't lay that activity before the Lord and say, "Hallowed be Your name" over it. Knowing these things, then, we must turn away from these destructive and dead-end roads.

Here's another question you might ask yourself if you are contemplating a questionable activity: *How would this look if some other Christian gave into it?* If you saw another believer doing what you are doing right now, how would you feel about it? Would it look wrong to you? Would it have what the Bible describes as "the appearance of evil"? Then don't do it.

You and I will not walk through this life and somehow avoid temptation to sin. Those lusts and temptations will come every day, in one form or another. That is why our prayer needs to be, "Lord, don't let me foolishly put myself unnecessarily in the way of going astray." It is a direct appeal to God to place a watch over our eyes, ears, mouth, feet, hands, and thoughts.

In this way, then, the Lord's Prayer is a model, or pattern, for the sort of prayers we should offer every day. I approach a God who isn't just some distant deity, but a heavenly Father to me. I realize that although He is my Father, He is a mighty and awesome God, worthy of my respect and submission. I ask for His will in every area of my life. I ask for His provision for my daily needs. I admit my sins, turn from them, and ask for His forgiveness. I determine in my mind to forgive all those who have offended me. And I plead with Him to help me avoid temptation, because I know it would both hurt me and grieve His great heart.

In the gospel of Luke, Jesus tells a story after giving His disciples the Lord's Prayer. It goes like this:

"Which of you shall have a friend, and go to him at midnight and say to him, 'Friend, lend me three loaves; for a friend of mine has come to me on his journey, and I have nothing to set before him'; and he will answer from within and say, 'Do not trouble me; the door is now shut, and my children are with me in bed; I cannot rise and give to you'? I say to you, though he will not rise and give to him because he is his friend, yet because of his persistence he will rise and give him as many as he needs.

"So I say to you, ask, and it will be given to you; seek, and you will find; knock, and it will be opened to you." (Luke 11:5-9)

Often in prayer we will ask God for something once or maybe twice. Then, if He doesn't seem to answer in the affirmative, we tend to give up and conclude, "Well, it must not be His will." Jesus, however, encourages us to keep on praying and not give up.

This story He told would have been well understood by the people of that day. In biblical times, family members didn't have their own rooms, as we do today. They would sleep in one great room—mom and dad, son and daughter, grandma and grandpa, and maybe even Uncle Harry and Aunt Matilda too. So imagine everyone has turned in for the night, and you are all lying there in a single room, trying to sleep.

Suddenly, someone bangs on your door—loudly.

The man of the house doesn't want to get up, because by

stirring around, he will end up rousing everyone else, maybe tripping over his son or stepping on Uncle Harry's head.

So he says, "Do you have any idea what time it is? Go away!"

This neighbor, however (and can you believe this guy's nerve?), keeps on knocking. He says, "Hey, please open up. I've just had someone come from out of town. They need some bread. Can you spare me a loaf of bread?"

"Okay. Fine."

So the man answers the door and gives his neighbor what he asks.

Jesus isn't saying here that the Father is like that man who doesn't want to answer. The Father does want to answer, but He wants you to be persistent and keep on asking.

When Jesus said to ask, seek, and knock, it showed an ascending intensity. The word *ask* implies requesting assistance. We realize our need, and we ask God for help. It has the feel of being low-key, doesn't it? We might compare it to being in a restaurant, and when the waitress goes by you say, "Excuse me, could I get some more coffee?" You are polite, soft-spoken, and not overly aggressive.

But what if she doesn't pay any attention to you, and walks on by?

That brings us to the next word. You begin to *seek* after the coffee. That denotes asking, plus a little action. You don't just express your need, but you get up and look around for a little help. It involves some effort. So you stand up, walk around the corner maybe, and say to the waitress, "Hi there. Could I get some more coffee over here?" And you hold up your empty cup for her to see.

The next word, *knock*, implies asking plus acting plus

persevering. It is the idea of pounding on a closed door. You've asked politely, you've asked a little more aggressively, and now you are knocking, making a little noise. You are not taking no for an answer. Going back to our restaurant analogy, you probably find the coffee pot and just go over and pour your own coffee. (But I wouldn't recommend it.)

The idea here is that we say to God, "Father, I'm not backing down on this, because I believe this is Your will. This prodigal child of mine needs to turn back to You, and I'm not going to stop praying for this answer, this provision."

This comes close to another huge aspect of praying, known as intercessory prayer. More than simply asking, this is when you stand in the gap for someone, interceding for someone's life or someone's salvation, and refuse to give up.

Do you pray like that? Do you put that kind of passion into prayers for nonbelievers? Or, are your prayers more like, "Lord, please save the world. Amen. That should about cover it."

If you don't put any heart into your prayers, don't expect God to put much heart into answering those prayers. But if you will ask, seek, and knock, praying with passion, patience, and persistence, then you will see more prayers answered in the affirmative.

J. Sidlow Baxter once said, "Men may spurn our appeals, reject our message, oppose our arguments, despise our person, but they are helpless against our prayers."

What a privilege prayer is!

Nevertheless, I will tell you one thing that can stop prayer cold, and that is unconfessed sin. In Isaiah 59:2, God tells us, "Your iniquities have separated you from your God; and your sins have hidden His face from you, so that He will not hear."

We need to pray as David prayed in Psalm 139:23-24, "Search me, O God, and know my heart; try me, and know my anxieties; and see if there is any wicked way in me, and lead me in the way everlasting."

Ask God to search your heart and reveal any sins or attitudes that displease Him. And then, as You receive His forgiveness, make sure that you are ready to extend that forgiveness to those who have hurt or offended you.

This is part of the life-transforming model that Jesus gave us for prayer. We have probably known it all our lives as the Lord's Prayer. But it is really more like the Lord's gift to each one of us, a daily pattern for prayer that will keep us close to the Father through all our days—until we finally stand in His presence.

13

WORRY AND ANXIETY

Most of us worry in some way, shape, or form, or find ourselves playing that never-ending what-if game.

Something happens in your life or your circumstances, and the more you turn it over in your mind, the more it seems to escalate.

Granted, there is no lack of things to worry about in our culture today. Just open the morning newspaper or your favorite news website, and look at all the scary things happening in the world.

And what about our terrible economy? Despite all our government's reassurances, things don't really seem to be improving at all. You could get the dreaded pink slip. Your 401(k) could go in the tank. And what if you missed a mortgage payment? Would you lose your house?

Then there are all those personal worries—your health, your family, your job, and much, much more.

A recent poll asked a group of Americans, "What do you worry about the most?" The number-one response? "My appearance." Don't you love that? *I may lose my house and my life savings, or I might get wiped off the earth in a nuclear blast, but how do I look in this outfit?*

What do *you* worry about most? What causes you the greatest stress? It reminds me of an old fable I heard about a man who came face-to-face with the dangers of worry. As the story is told, Death was walking toward a city one morning when an alarmed man accosted him and asked, "Where are you going? What are you intending to do?"

Death said, "Today I'm going into that city, where I will take one hundred people."

"That's horrible!" the man said.

"Well, that is what I do," Death replied. "That's the way it is."

As a result, the man quickly ran ahead of Death (who moved at his own steady pace) and warned everyone about Death's plan.

That evening, as Death was coming out of the city, the same man met Death again. He said, "You told me you only were going to take one hundred people. Why did a thousand die?"

"I kept my word," Death responded, "I only took one hundred people. Worry took the rest."

That is how it often works in life. Statistics tell us that half of all the people occupying America's hospital beds today are constant worriers. Forty-three percent of all adults suffer health effects due to worry and stress. And research has found that 75 percent to 90 percent of all visits to primary care physicians are stress-related complaints or disorders.

You could write on countless American gravestones this epitaph: "Hurried. Worried. Buried." We spend our lives full of anxiety, frustration, and worry. The truth is, however, most of what you and I worry about actually never happens.

In the Sermon on the Mount, Jesus gives the biblical worldview on anxiety and worry—and tackles the subject head-on:

"Therefore I say to you, do not worry about your life, what you will eat or what you will drink; nor about your body, what you will put on. Is not life more than food and the body more than clothing? Look at the birds of the air, for they neither sow nor reap nor gather into barns; yet your heavenly Father feeds them. Are you not of more value than they? Which of you by worrying can add one cubit to his stature?

"So why do you worry about clothing? Consider the lilies of the field, how they grow: they neither toil nor spin; and yet I say to you that even Solomon in all his glory was not arrayed like one of these. Now if God so clothes the grass of the field, which today is, and tomorrow is thrown into the oven, will He not much more clothe you, O you of little faith?

"Therefore do not worry, saying, 'What shall we eat?' or 'What shall we drink?' or 'What shall we wear?' For after all these things the Gentiles seek. For your heavenly Father knows that you need all these things. But seek first the kingdom of God and His righteousness, and all these things shall be added to you. Therefore do not worry about tomorrow, for tomorrow will worry about its own things. Sufficient for the day is its own trouble." (Matthew 6:25-34)

So what do we learn from these words of Jesus about anxiety and worry?

The Believer Shouldn't Worry
"Therefore I say to you, do not worry about your life."
(Matthew 6:25)

Jesus wasn't saying that a Christian shouldn't think about or be concerned with the basic needs of life like food or clothing. He didn't say, "Don't think about food. Don't concern yourself with clothing."

No. What He said was, "Don't *worry* about those things."

Yes, you need to think about a roof over your head, clothes on your back, food in your stomach, and how you will provide for your family. Of course you do. In fact, the Bible has many admonitions about saving money, investing wisely, and working hard for a living. So Jesus wasn't saying not to consider these things. What He was saying is not to be *obsessed* with these daily human needs. Don't let anxiety about them tie you into knots.

The simple fact is, worrying doesn't make anything better. In fact, it makes a situation worse. It is a completely worthless activity. It is like being in a rocking chair—always moving, but never getting anywhere. As Corrie ten Boom once observed, "Worry doesn't empty today of its sorrow. It empties tomorrow of its strength." It diminishes you, hurts you, and tries to choke the life out of you. That is why Jesus warns us against it.

In the gospel of John, Martha is a classic example of someone who became overly anxious. Martha, her sister Mary, and her brother Lazarus were special friends of Jesus. They lived in Bethany, near Jerusalem, and Jesus and His disciples often visited their home.

Can you imagine how hard it would be not to brag about

the fact that Jesus came and hung around your house? "Just last night when we were with Jesus Christ (the Creator of the universe), He said these words to us. . . ."

But it was true. Jesus was a friend to this family and would often show up at their house unannounced, with twelve of His hungry buddies. It is understandable, then, that when Jesus came through the front door, Martha would hurry into her kitchen to prepare a feast fit for a king. (In this case, *the* King.)

On one particular occasion, Martha was slaving away in the kitchen, feeling rushed, distracted, and bothered. What irritated her most was that her sister Mary was in the living room, sitting at Jesus' feet, leaving Martha to handle all the preparation.

Finally she came storming out of the kitchen. (Can you see her in your mind's eye, with a spoon in her hand and wearing a food-splattered apron?) "Lord," she blurted out, "tell her to help me."

Jesus looked at her and said, "Martha, Martha, you are worried and troubled about many things. But one thing is needed, and Mary has chosen that good part, which will not be taken away from her" (Luke 10:41-42).

In other words, there is a time for work and there is a time for worship. Mary recognized the Son of God was in her house, perhaps sensed that His time on earth was brief, and wanted to just sit at His feet. Martha, however, thought this might be a good time to create a meat loaf.

In this instance, Martha had it wrong. The meat loaf wasn't as important as soaking in the words of Jesus. She needed to just relax and take advantage of Jesus' being a few feet away from her in her own home.

Let's face it. We are a lot more like Martha than Mary

sometimes, aren't we? We run around in frenzied circles, like chickens with their heads cut off.

By the way, headless chickens really do run in circles. I personally observed this when I was five years old, living with my grandparents in the Yucca Valley. When my grandfather got hungry for fried chicken, my grandmother didn't go to the market like any normal person and buy a few frozen chicken breasts for dinner.

No, it had to be fresh — very fresh, as in just killed.

So she sent my grandfather, Daddy Charles, out to chop the head off a chicken. Apparently, he thought this would be a good thing for a five-year-old boy to witness, so he took me with him.

We strolled into the chicken pen, and I still didn't know what was happening. Quick as anything, he grabbed a chicken, put it on the chopping block, and brought down the hatchet. Boom! The body rolled off, blood spurted, and the headless chicken ran around, flapping its wings. (I still break out in a cold sweat when I walk by a Kentucky Fried Chicken outlet.)

Anyway, it has become a metaphor for the way we act when we get worried and stressed. Sometimes we are just running around in circles, and we don't even know what we are doing.

If someone points out that we're worrying too much, we might even try to justify it. We will say, "Well, I worry because I care."

That won't fly, because worry is not a virtue. In fact, let me take it a step further. Worry actually can be a sin. In Matthew 6:25, Jesus said, "Do not worry about your life."

In the Greek, this could be translated, "Stop worrying about your life," because they were already worrying. In other words, the Lord was essentially saying, "You have been worrying a lot, and I am telling you right now to stop it! It's not good for you."

The word *worry* comes from a Greek term that means "to choke or strangle." And that is what worry will do to you. It won't help your situation. It will only aggravate it and make it worse.

Martyn Lloyd-Jones said, "The result of worrying about the future is that you are crippling yourself in the present."[1]

The great theologian Charlie Brown of the *Peanuts* comic strip once said, "I have developed a new philosophy. I only dread one day at a time."

The Bible says, "Each day has enough trouble of its own" (Matthew 6:34, NIV). There are enough troubles waiting there tomorrow and the day after and the day after. Don't even think about those right now. Just take the troubles of today and put them into the hands of God.

Yes, we live in a world filled with trouble. As we live our lives, we can encounter situations that cause great anxiety, and I face those as well. No one is exempt from these things. So it is not an issue of *will* we have trouble; the question is, what will we do with that trouble *when* it comes? Jesus was effectively saying, "I will tell you what you shouldn't do. You shouldn't worry."

Why can worry be a sin? It is a lack of trusting in God. It is a refusal to rest in the providence of God. What is the providence of God? It is the belief that God controls the universe. Specifically as a Christian, it means that I believe there are no accidents or coincidences in my life. Nothing touches me that has not first passed through His hands.

The Old Testament prophet Daniel is a classic example of a man who trusted in God's providence. If you know his story, you will remember the Israelites had been conquered by the Babylonians, with many of them marched off into captivity in Babylon for seventy years. During that time, Darius came into power after Nebuchadnezzar, and Daniel—one of the Hebrew prophets—had ascended to a place of influencing this mighty king. So much so that the king really liked Daniel and relied on his wise and insightful counsel.

As you might imagine, that didn't go over so well with Darius's other counselors, who were filled with toxic envy toward this upstart Hebrew. They wanted Daniel removed, by any means possible. At first, they sent out the private investigators and tabloid news reporters to dig up some dirt on Daniel. Imagine how stunned they were when they could find *nothing*. Zero! No skeletons in his closet. No charges of sexual harassment. No embezzling. No scandals. No sins at all that they could identify. Daniel was just who he seemed to be: a man of moral integrity with no weak spots.

So what did they do? They persuaded the king to issue a foolish edict, signing into law a statement declaring that no one could pray to any god except him (the king) or they would be thrown into a den of lions. This was all aimed at Daniel, of course. His enemies knew very well that he prayed openly to God every single day, probably at an open window, facing Jerusalem.

Sure enough, Daniel prayed as he always had. And the king had to enact this law. As powerful as that monarch may have been, he couldn't change a law already in motion—not even to save a good man who had become a friend. And so Daniel was sent to a den of lions, where he most certainly wouldn't survive the night. It was sad, but he would be killed—probably instantly.

Yet what do we read? Daniel slept peacefully while the distraught king was up all night. Isn't that interesting? The child of God in the den of lions slept peacefully, and the man without faith, resting on a soft bed in the palace with all its luxuries, was worried and stressed out.

The Bible says in Psalm 127:2, "He gives His beloved sleep."

And so it is for the person who puts his or her trust in God and His providence. What does it mean, then, when I worry and stew and fret? It means that I don't believe God is really in control or that He isn't paying attention. Somehow, God has taken His eyes off the ball, so now I'm in trouble.

But God never takes His eye off the ball. Not for a millisecond.

Why should I refuse to worry? Jesus gave us some illustrations. First of all, He said, "Look at the birds" (Matthew 6:26). He was outdoors near the Sea of Galilee when He preached the Sermon on the Mount. As He spoke, He probably gestured to some birds flying by. He was saying, "Take a look at those birds flying over your head. Do they look worried? Have you ever seen a bird with a little bottle of Valium under its wing? Or maybe chewing on his little toenails? Or on a little couch getting psychoanalyzed by an owl?"

Birds don't do that. And yet birds don't have the promises we have. Birds aren't created in the image of God. Birds aren't promised eternal life. And yet every morning, just like clockwork, they are up at the break of dawn, singing their hearts out.

Jesus was saying, "If God takes care of birds, won't He take care of you?" That doesn't mean the birds don't go out and get their food. Some eat vegetation, others eat bugs or seeds or fish. The rest hang out at McDonald's and wait for you to drop your fries. Birds take care of business and don't worry about it. And that is the point Jesus was making.

It reminds me of the old poem that says,

Said the robin to the sparrow,
"I would really like to know
Why these anxious human beings
Rush around and worry so."

Said the sparrow to the robin,
"Friend, I think that it must be
That they have no Heavenly Father
Such as cares for you and me."

Then the Lord shifted gears and talked about flowers. Flowers don't worry. Why should you? Matthew 6:28 says, "Why do you worry about clothing? Consider the lilies of the field, how they grow: they neither toil nor spin; and yet I say to you that even Solomon in all his glory was not arrayed like one of these."

Even Solomon, in his royal robes, surrounded by his lavish furniture encrusted in gold, wasn't as beautiful as a simple, humble wildflower. Maybe Jesus plucked up a little wildflower as He spoke. "Look how beautiful it is," He was saying, "and it isn't worried about a thing."

You and I, however, get concerned about what we are going to wear. *Does this look good? Is this in style? Is this too wrinkled? Do I look fat in this?*

The Bible isn't saying don't be attractive or try to look your best. It is saying don't be obsessed with your looks. (Frankly, some people ought to think a little bit more about their looks.

There is a place for that too.)

There's nothing wrong with a woman wanting to look attractive or a guy wanting to look good. Those aren't sinful things. But if that pursuit to be beautiful becomes more important to you than your spiritual life, and you spend all of your time on your outward appearance while neglecting your soul, then your life is out of balance.

In the book of 1 Peter, the apostle wrote,

> Your beauty should not come from outward adornment, such as elaborate hairstyles and the wearing of gold jewelry or fine clothes. Rather, it should be that of your inner self, the unfading beauty of a gentle and quiet spirit, which is of great worth in God's sight. For this is the way the holy women of the past who put their hope in God used to adorn themselves. (3:3-5, NIV)

Why is that so important? One day this body will be gone, but the soul will live forever. It was Erma Bombeck who once said, "Sooner or later, dust wins."

The real you and me, however, will live on. So if the greater thing (life everlasting) is in His control, I can leave the lesser thing (my physical appearance) to Him as well. Don't stress yourself and worry yourself sick about all these externals.

Worry Won't Add to Your Life — It Will Subtract
"Which of you by worrying can add one cubit to his stature?"
(Matthew 6:27)

The Greek word used here for *stature* means length or duration of life. So effectively Jesus was saying, "How many of you through worry and anxiety can extend the length of your life?"

Answer: No one.

In fact, worry can *shorten* your life—or at least make it more difficult. We live in a culture, however, that is obsessed with trying to lengthen life. Those who worry about these things exercise regularly, eat the right foods, supplement their diets with vitamins and minerals, and get regular physical checkups in the hope of extending their lives for a few more years.

Now, I am not making light of any of this. It is a wise and prudent idea to take care of your body, because you want to live as long as you can and stay as healthy as you can. So there is a place for taking care of yourself physically, and you don't want to neglect that. In 1 Timothy 4:8 the Bible says, "Physical training is good, but training for godliness is much better, promising benefits in this life and in the life to come" (NLT).

You can go too far either way. You can put too much emphasis on the physical while neglecting the spiritual, but you can also put so much emphasis on the spiritual that you neglect your body and your health.

Here is the bottom line: God entrusted you with an eternal soul, encased in a human body, and He expects you to take care of both of them. But understand that worrying and fretting and obsessing over your health won't lengthen your life a single day—but may shorten it instead.

The simple fact is that you will live as long as God wants you to live—not less, not more. You and I don't get to determine the day of our birth or the day of our death (no matter how many bran muffins and how much tofu we consume). What we do have a lot to say about is that little dash between our birth and death. That is why Psalm 90:12 says, "So teach us to number our days, that we may gain a heart of wisdom." Another translation renders this: "Teach us to number our days and recognize how few they are; help us to spend them as we should" (TLB).

Live your life carefully and prayerfully, and recognize that anxiety and worry will do nothing to lengthen your days or contribute to their quality.

Worry Indicates a Lack of Faith

"Now if God so clothes the grass of the field, which today is, and tomorrow is thrown into the oven, will He not much more clothe you, O you of little faith?" (Matthew 6:30)

These are words directed to those who have already placed their faith in Christ. Jesus didn't say, "You of no faith." He said, "You of *little* faith." In other words, there are people today who believe that God will save their souls, but they have a hard time believing He will provide for their needs . . . or resolve their problems . . . or even answer their prayers. They believe in Jesus for salvation, but they struggle when it comes to believing Him for the circumstances of everyday life.

Martyn Lloyd-Jones said, "To be 'of little faith' means, first of all, that we are mastered by our circumstances instead of mastering them."[2] As a result, people of little faith get bowled over by the challenges and tests that come their way. We need to grow in our faith and not live out our years being spiritual lightweights.

How do you get more faith? One way is by reading and hearing the Word of God. The Bible itself says, "Faith comes by hearing, and hearing by the word of God" (Romans 10:17).

But it is not just hearing it, like background noise. No,

what Scripture is talking about here is *attention with intention.* We all know there are different ways to listen. You can listen and let your mind wander, which really isn't listening at all. But if you hear God's Word and internalize God's Word, then your faith will grow.

Your faith also grows by simply using it—by taking God's Word and applying it directly to daily life, with all its rough edges. Sometimes we treat faith like a fragile little egg that might crumble if we blow on it, when it is really more like a muscle that grows stronger through use.

This very term, *little faith,* was once used to describe Simon Peter. We all remember the story of Jesus' walking on the water. Peter, seeing Him standing out there in the wind and the waves, said, "Lord, if it is You, command me to come to You on the water" (Matthew 14:28).

And Jesus said, "Come."

Sometimes you hear people criticize Peter for walking a few steps on the water and then sinking. But how many of the other disciples climbed out of the boat that night? How many other people in the history of the world actually walked on the top of water?

After Jesus gave Peter permission to come, this disciple actually did the impossible and took steps on the Sea of Galilee. Then, when anxiety and fear began to kick in, he started to sink. Immediately he cried out, "Lord, save me!" (verse 30).

Jesus, of course, pulled him back on his feet again and said, "O you of little faith, why did you doubt?" (verse 31). In other words, "Hey, Peter, you were doing so well. You were really doing great. I was so proud of you. You could have made it."

Even so, Peter did take a step of faith that night, when no one else would dare. We are very much like Peter, aren't we?

Sometimes we step out with our "little faith" and see the Lord enable us and use us, and at other times, we experience lapses in our trust and shrink back in fear and worry.

The only logical solution is to get back up and try again. Remember this: With Jesus holding his hand, Peter walked back to the boat *on the water.*

Put God and His Will First in Your Life
"But seek first the kingdom of God and His righteousness, and all these things shall be added to you." (Matthew 6:33)

So what does that mean? Let's first define what we are talking about here. In a nutshell, God's kingdom is the rule and reign of Christ in your life.

Jesus taught us to pray, "Your kingdom come. Your will be done on earth as it is in heaven" (verse 10). In that prayer, we are praying for a day when the Lord will bring heaven to earth—His literal, physical rule on our planet. The Bible tells us that He will indeed reign as King of the earth and that we will reign with Him. That is our future and our destiny.

But when I pray, "Your kingdom come. Your will be done on earth as it is in heaven," I must remember this: I am also praying for the rule and reign of God's kingdom in my daily life.

What is the kingdom of God? It is when Jesus is in charge. When you are under His lordship and He is in control of your life, you are experiencing the kingdom of God within you. It is not some list of rules and regulations. Far from it! The apostle Paul said, "The kingdom of God is not eating and drinking, but righteousness and peace and joy in the Holy Spirit" (Romans 14:17).

That is what we want in our lives. In fact, there is no better life than that. We need to seek first God's rule and reign in our lives.

When I Put God and His Kingdom First, My Life Will Find Its Proper Balance

"But seek first the kingdom of God and His righteousness, and all these things shall be added to you." (Matthew 6:33)

What things? In the context of Matthew 6, it is what you wear, what you eat, and what you drink. But obviously it is more than that. It is also where you work, where you live, whether you will remain single, or whom you will marry one day. God will take care of the basic issues of life when we put Him first.

When David and Bathsheba's son, Solomon, ascended the throne of Israel, he was still a young man and quite naturally felt overwhelmed by the task ahead of him. One night after Solomon had been praying and worshipping the Lord, God appeared to him in a dream, and said, "Ask! What shall I give you?" (1 Kings 3:5).

Can you imagine? What if God came to you tonight and said, "What do you want? Whatever you want, I will give it to you right now." What would you pray for?

The text doesn't tell us how long Solomon took to answer the Lord's question. But his eventual reply was a wise one and pleased the Lord. He said, in essence, "Lord, I'm overwhelmed by the size of the task before me. I need wisdom to rule your people."

Listen to the Lord's reply:

"Because you have asked for wisdom in governing my people and haven't asked for a long life, or riches for yourself, or the defeat of your enemies — yes, I'll give you what you asked for! I will give you a wiser mind than anyone else has ever had or ever will have! And I will also give you what you didn't ask for — riches and honor! And no one in all the world will be as rich and famous as you for the rest of your life! And I will give you a long life if you follow me and obey my laws as your father David did." (1 Kings 3:11-14, TLB)

Solomon had his priorities in order. In the language of the Sermon on the Mount, he sought first the kingdom of God, and all of those things — many, many things — were added to him.

The Best Antidote to Worry Is Prayer

Do not be anxious about anything, but in every situation, by prayer and petition, with thanksgiving, present your requests to God. (Philippians 4:6, NIV)

In other words, don't worry, but pray.

Life is filled with trouble, and we can't control that, no matter who we are or how we might try. The Bible assures us that trouble will come our way through the years of our lives, and our natural inclination is to allow ourselves to overcome by stress and worry.

But it doesn't have to be that way, and we don't have to follow our natural inclination. We can pray instead.

Worry is like a natural reflex for many of us. It is like when the doctor taps your knee with his little rubber hammer and your leg jumps. It is like when a child touches something hot and instantly recoils. These are natural reflexes, and we can see them in many of our actions.

But there is also something called a conditioned reflex that we learn through time and repetition. For instance, when you first learned to drive a car, it seemed like there were dozens of things to remember, and you were conscious of doing every one of them.

Okay, now I'm looking in the rearview mirror.
Now I'm putting the car into drive.
Now I'm using the turn signal.
Now I'm turning off the turn signal.
Now I'm putting on the brake.

If you happened to learn on a car with a manual transmission, there were even more things to remember. It seemed almost overwhelming.

But now what happens when you drive? Do you think about each one of those individual actions? No, you just drive. It almost feels automatic. You just hop in the car and off you go.

In the spiritual life, worry is a natural reflex, but prayer is a conditioned reflex. Let's say you get some bad news on the phone. Your natural, physical reflex is to respond with fear and become locked up with worry and anxiety. But you don't have to let that happen. Instead, you can use each such opportunity to pray instead. And the more you do that, the deeper the conditioning will become.

When trouble comes, right in that moment, turn to prayer. When you get the bad news and hang up the phone, immediately speak to God: *Lord, I commit this situation into Your hands. This is too much for me to handle. I'm asking You to step into this situation, Lord, with grace and help and power and healing and wisdom.*

When worry comes your way, don't embrace it; instead,

pray about it. When your knees start knocking, kneel on them.

Let the Lord be the first one you turn to. Many people turn to friends and family in a crisis. As soon as trouble comes, they immediately begin making calls or sending texts or posting something on social media. They want everyone who knows them to know. And yes, there is a place for that. But people can let you down. People have their own problems to deal with. People can give you wrong advice or turn you in an unwise direction. Go first to God. Seek the Lord immediately, and talk to others later.

Others turn to alcohol when trouble comes, which only creates new problems rather than solving old problems.

Still others retreat into denial and close the door behind them. They try to tune it all out and pretend it isn't happening. But that is a dead-end street, and it will only make matters worse.

Take your hardships and trials and concerns to God. Run to Him . . . His arms are wide open. As Peter wrote, "You can throw the whole weight of your anxieties upon him, for you are his personal concern" (1 Peter 5:7, PH).

I don't know how I could have gotten through so many things I have had to face in my life without the Lord. I don't even like to contemplate what might have happened to me. Without the Lord, I think I would have been like a bug on the windshield. But He has been there for me, every time, through every circumstance, and He has walked with me through the most difficult days and nights of my life.

He will do the same for you. Yes, He will!

If you are a believer, no matter what comes your way in life, God will be there for you. Put aside your worry, and rest in Him.

THE NONBELIEVER'S FAVORITE VERSE

What do you think a nonbeliever's favorite verse might be? How about John 3:16: "For God so loved the world that He gave His only begotten Son, that whoever believes in Him should not perish but have everlasting life"?

No, it is not that one. (But it ought to be.)

Maybe it would be 1 John 1:9, with its promise of forgiveness and cleansing: "If we confess our sins, He is faithful and just to forgive us our sins and to cleanse us from all unrighteousness."

No, that's not it either.

What about Romans 8:28? That is a verse everyone could love: "And we know that all things work together for good to those who love God, to those who are the called according to His purpose."

No? Then how about Jeremiah 29:11? "For I know the thoughts that I think toward you, says the LORD, thoughts of peace and not of evil, to give you a future and a hope."

Those are all wonderful verses, but none of them is the

nonbeliever's favorite verse. As a matter of fact, the verse we are looking for comes right in the middle of the Sermon on the Mount, the passage we have been studying in this book.

Here it is: "Judge not, that you be not judged" (Matthew 7:1).

It seems like every nonbeliever knows that verse, usually quoted in the old King James English: "Judge not, that ye be not judged."

Why do nonbelievers quote this particular verse? It usually comes up in a conversation that goes something like this. The Christian approaches a nonbeliever (or a compromising Christian) and talks to the individual about his or her need to make a change in behavior and turn to Christ.

The nonbeliever invariably replies, "Who are *you* to judge *me?* Doesn't the Bible itself say, 'Judge not, that you be not judged'?" And how do you answer that? Is that person right? In your desire to share the gospel with that individual, were you somehow judging them?

What do these words of our Lord really mean?

IS THERE A PLACE FOR JUDGING?

Is Jesus suggesting that we are never to speak frankly and truthfully to someone, even if what they are doing is wrong? Is that being judgmental? What does the Lord want to communicate in His words, "Judge not, that you be not judged"?

Clearly, there are people who are very condemning of others and who seem to delight in pointing out wrong in someone's life.

It reminds me of the young man who brought a girl home to meet his mother. He was in love with this young lady and hoped to marry her. But alas, his mom didn't like her. So he went and met another girl and brought her home one day to his mother, but she didn't like this one either. So then he went and found a girl who looked like his mother, dressed like his mother, and talked liked his mother. And his dad didn't like her. That is how some people are. They just like to find fault.

So here is the question: Is there a place for judging? Are we to judge one another? And if so, on what basis?

Let's read the words of Jesus again in their Sermon on the Mount context:

> "Judge not, that you be not judged. For with what judgment you judge, you will be judged; and with the measure you use, it will be measured back to you. And why do you look at the speck in your brother's eye, but do not consider the plank in your own eye? Or how can you say to your brother, 'Let me remove the speck from your eye'; and look, a plank is in your own eye? Hypocrite! First remove the plank from your own eye, and then you will see clearly to remove the speck from your brother's eye.
>
> "Do not give what is holy to the dogs; nor cast your pearls before swine, lest they trample them under their feet, and turn and tear you in pieces." (Matthew 7:1-6)

As Jesus wraps up this greatest sermon ever, the message points us to the fact that our brief life on earth is a journey. All in all, whether we live to be sixty, seventy, or one hundred, our days pass very quickly. Each of us is on his or her way to a great moment of judgment, an ultimate assessment before the living God, and then to a final destiny.

When all is said and done, it doesn't really matter very much what other people think of us. The important thing is, what does our Creator think of us? As Maximus said to his troops in the movie, *Gladiator*, "What we do in life echoes in eternity."

It's true. Everything we do — in fact, every word we say — during our brief time on earth has ramifications that will go on forever. What we do in time will matter in eternity. That is what we need to keep in mind as we live out our daily lives, making our decisions and choices.

So how do we apply this in a practical way as we seek to please the Lord with our lives and share the Good News of salvation with others?

We Should Be Discerning, but Not Condemning

"Judge not, that you be not judged. For with what judgment you judge, you will be judged; and with the measure you use, it will be measured back to you." (Matthew 7:1-2)

Again, does this mean that Christians are never to be critical or make an evaluation? Some people think that being a Christian means you must be tolerant of everything and love and accept everyone. And by the way, you are never supposed to register an opinion either. We should all put our arms around each other, sway back and forth, and sing "Kumbaya."

Does that describe a real Christian?

No, it really doesn't. In fact, that description actually contradicts what we read in many other passages of the Bible.

People often refer to Jesus, our Lord and example, as a great humanitarian, because He loved and shared and cared. That is true, to a degree. But Jesus also was a revolutionary. He confronted people without fear and had hard, stinging words for the religious hypocrites of the day. He called the Pharisees vipers, hypocrites, and dead men walking, and He asked, "How can you escape the condemnation of hell?" (Matthew 23:33).

So Jesus didn't walk through His years on earth throwing rose petals or whistling a happy tune. When confrontation was necessary, Jesus would speak the truth to a person — even when that truth seemed hard. And we must do the same.

We must indeed communicate truth, but the Bible tells us to do so lovingly. Ephesians 4:15 says we are to speak the truth in love.

How do we treat people we love? We tell them the truth. We refuse to deceive them.

Would you let your friend go out to dinner with a big stain on the back of her white blouse? No, you would tell her what you see that she can't see. If your friend has spinach stuck in his teeth, do you discreetly tell him about it, or let him find out later that night when he looks in the mirror?

What if your friend has stumbled into some destructive sin? Will you close your eyes to it? Will you look away and pretend you don't see? No, because that would be damaging to your friend — and wouldn't be love at all. Of course you have to say something.

Look at Proverbs 27:5-6: "Open rebuke is better than love carefully concealed. Faithful are the wounds of a friend, but the kisses of an enemy are deceitful."

Those are powerful verses. How dare you say that you love someone if you won't tell them when something is wrong in their life? If you really love them, you will speak truth to them to help them — even at the risk of offending them.

We have all known people who will be all sweetness and light to our face, but will stab us in the back when we are not looking. A true friend stabs you in the front (if you need stabbing), instead of the back. He or she will say what needs to be said to your face: "You know what? I love you. And because I love you, I'm going to tell you something right now for your own good—because I care about your soul."

That is what a true Christian does. So yes, as believers we are to make judgments.

So what do you do when someone quotes Matthew 7:1 to you? "Doesn't the Bible say, 'Judge not, that you be not judged'?"

What is your response? Maybe it is something like this: "Yes, it does say that. But I don't think you understand the meaning of that statement."

The reality is that Christians are to make judgments—and we all make them every day.

Jesus gave an example of making such a judgment in this very passage. In verse 6, He said, "Do not give what is holy to the dogs."

Now what on earth does that mean? Who are the dogs? Are these people with flea collars? What does this mean? Actually, this is an evaluation, and the Lord is calling on us to make it. Jesus used this picture to describe someone who has no interest at all in what you have to say. In other words, this is an individual who has closed his or her ears to the gospel, refusing to even listen to you. So you have to make a quick evaluation: Will this person be open to the gospel message, or is he as insensible to the message as a dog?

Jesus went on to say, "Nor cast your pearls before swine." Why would you give pearls to a pig? Do you think a pig would value such a gift? Of course not. He doesn't want your pearls; he wants your garbage. Give him garbage, and he will be happy.

I remember years ago when I was brand-new in the faith and was out sharing the gospel with people on the streets. On that particular day, I was with a kid who was a little bit younger than me. He was a very small guy, but bold as a lion. I remember him walking up to a big, burly, gnarly, tattooed biker and confronting him with the gospel.

The biker said, "If you don't shut up, I'm going to punch you out."

I pulled on my friend's arm and said, "Okay, let's go now." But my friend said no. In fact, the little guy was more fired up than ever. He kept talking and talking to the bigger man.

The biker growled once again, "If you say *one more word,* I'm gonna hit you in the mouth."

"Let's go, let's go," I said.

My young friend looked up at the big guy and said, "Fine. The Bible says don't cast your pearls before pigs."

And I was thinking, *We are going to die today.*

You see, these are not the most effective verses to quote to nonbelievers. You might call them more in-house verses—our Lord's counsel to His followers—and not intended to win over someone's heart.

However, don't let anyone tell you that Christians aren't supposed to judge, because we are. In fact, God calls on us to make judgments every day. Over in 1 Corinthians 6:2, the apostle Paul said, "Do you not know that the saints will judge the world? And if the world will be judged by you, are you unworthy to judge the smallest matters?" And in 1 Peter 4:17, we read that judgment begins at the house of God.

We *need* to make judgments. A judgment, after all, is simply an evaluation. It is like crossing a busy street, where you look both ways before you step out onto the road. What have you just done? You have looked at the situation and made a judgment about the safety of making that crossing.

You also must make judgments and evaluations about people in the course of a given day. *Is this person on the level? Is she telling me the truth? Is he ready to hear this? Can I count on her to follow through?*

The Bible tells us that we need to be very careful in these last days; one of the signs of the end times will be false teachers leading people astray. Just because someone gets up, waves a Bible around, and says, "Thus saith the Lord," doesn't mean you should believe them. You need to take everything they say and lay it alongside the teachings of Scripture.

So you see, we are to make judgments and evaluations. Jesus once warned His followers to "be wise as serpents and harmless as doves" (Matthew 10:16). The apostle John said, "Beloved, do not believe every spirit, but test the spirits, whether they are of God; because many false prophets have gone out into the world" (1 John 4:1).

It isn't correct to say that Christians should never judge. No, followers of Jesus Christ should and must judge and make evaluations.

What, then, did Jesus mean when He said, "Judge not"?

The Greek word used for *judge* here means to separate, choose, select, or determine. In the context, we see that Jesus is dealing primarily with motives.

When push comes to shove, you really can't judge my motives, nor can I judge yours. You might say, "That guy is so full of pride," but you don't really know that, do you? You can't see that man's motives. Only God sees into the heart, and He never appointed you to be judge, jury, and executioner over one of His sons or daughters.

It would be a better translation of Matthew 7:1 to say, "Condemn not, that you be not condemned." Yes, I am to make judgments and evaluations, but I'm not to condemn a brother.

You say, "Well, I think he's going to hell."

Maybe he will and maybe he won't, but you're not God, and that is *His* call. It is not for you to say.

I heard about an old codger who didn't like Christians. He'd heard that the local preacher was planning to repair his roof, so he went over to the pastor's house, pulled up a lawn chair, and just sat and watched him as he worked.

The pastor paused for a moment in his nailing and called down to the man in the chair, "Friend, did you come here to get some carpentry tips?"

The old man replied, "No. I'm just waiting to see what you say when that hammer hits your thumb."

He was waiting to see the preacher mess up, and that is all he cared about. There are people out there who are doing the same with you, and they are not all nonbelievers. Sadly, there are Christians who have fallen into the habit of making snap decisions and jumping to conclusions about fellow believers. Don't be one of them!

The great preacher J. Vernon McGee once said the only exercise some Christians get is jumping to conclusions and running down others.

It's true, isn't it? Sometimes we are so quick to condemn and so ready to believe the worst about a person instead of the best. This is what Jesus was saying here: "Don't do that. Don't be quick to condemn a brother or sister. Pray for them instead of talking about them."

I came across an old poem by a woman named Mary Wilder Tileston, and it goes like this:

> Judge not the workings of his brain,
> And of his heart you cannot see.
> What looks to thy dim eyes a stain,
> In God's pure light may only be
> A scar brought from some well-won field
> Where thou wouldst only faint and yield.

Our objective never should be to condemn and put down our fellow believers. On the contrary, it is our job to help and restore them.

Our Desire Should Be to Restore, Not Condemn, a Person in Sin

Brothers and sisters, if someone is caught in a sin, you who live by the Spirit should restore that person gently. But watch yourselves, or you also may be tempted. Carry each other's burdens, and in this way you will fulfill the law of Christ.
(Galatians 6:1-2, NIV)

This is an interesting statement here, because the phrase "caught in a sin" implies it wasn't premeditated. In other words, this isn't the picture of a person who set out intentionally and deliberately to commit a sin, as some people certainly do. This is different. This is a man or woman who stumbled into a sin. They slipped, and they fell. It wasn't intentional.

They must still take responsibility for their sin, whether

they fell into it or walked into it with eyes wide open. Either way, I should take no delight in their failure but do all I can to restore them.

The first step to restoration, however, sometimes involves confrontation. I have to speak gently but clearly to this individual and say, "My friend, I think you've become trapped in this sin."

"Well," she might reply, "I don't think it is a sin."

"Yes, it is," you say, "and here is what the Bible says about it."

You have to help this person come to her senses, because you can't restore an individual who doesn't want restoration. In humility and with God's help, you have to help her see her sin, and then encourage her to set it right. In fact, the Greek word used here for *restore* means to set a broken bone or put a dislocated limb back in place. As any physician would tell you, you have to do that carefully so that you don't end up doing more harm.

Earlier in the chapter, I pointed out that we are to speak the truth in love (see Ephesians 4:15). Sometimes, you and I get half of that right. We speak the truth all right, but it is not in love. Our information might be correct, but we confront an individual in a careless or heavy-handed way.

Then again, at other times, we might have love in our hearts, but we shrink back from speaking the truth. Both elements need to be present when we are seeking to restore a fallen brother or sister.

I Can't See a Speck in My Friend's Eye
If I Have a Telephone Pole in Mine

"And why do you look at the speck in your brother's eye, but do not consider the plank in your own eye? Or how can you say to your brother, 'Let me remove the speck from your eye'; and look, a plank is in your own eye?" (Matthew 7:3-4)

Jesus used a little humor here. The word He used for *plank* speaks of a very large piece of wood—in contrast to the speck, which is like a tiny grain of sawdust. So in a loose paraphrase, we might say, "How can you get the sawdust out of your brother's eye if you have a telephone pole in your own?"

Here is another interesting twist in this word picture: The terms *speck* and *plank* indicate they are from the same substance, the same piece of wood. In other words, the reason some people are so adept at finding fault in the lives of other people is because they are so familiar with it in their own lives. They can spot certain things in others, because they are guilty of the same sin—and perhaps in an even greater way.

So here is the reality: Sometimes the people who nitpick sins in others are guilty of far worse themselves.

We can see this in the life of King David. He had committed adultery with the wife of one of his most loyal soldiers and then ended up arranging that soldier's death on the battlefield. After that, he did his best to cover up the sin and pretend like it had never happened.

Then the prophet Nathan walked into the throne room with a little story to tell the king:

"There were two men in a certain city, one very rich, owning many flocks of sheep and herds of goats; and the other very poor, owning nothing but a little lamb he had managed to buy. It was his children's pet, and he fed it from his own plate and let it drink from his own cup; he cuddled it in his arms like a baby daughter. Recently a guest arrived at the home of the rich man. But instead of killing a lamb from his own flocks for food for the traveler, he took the poor man's lamb and roasted it and served it." (2 Samuel 12:1-4, TLB)

When David heard this story, his blood boiled. "The man who has done this shall surely die!" he raged (verse 5).

Really? For swiping a sheep? Isn't that a little harsh?

At that moment, when David was so hot with indignation, Nathan boldly pointed his finger in his boss's face and said, "You are the man!" (verse 7).

Busted!

But here is the interesting thing about that story: David had wanted to kill a man for a relatively minor offense, and yet he was guilty of adultery and murder. He had taken another man's wife and arranged for her soldier husband to be placed in a killing zone, where he died. Yet there he was, raging over a purloined little lamb.

The fact is, we are quick to dish out judgment to others, yet are we willing to be judged in the same way? In Matthew 7:2, Jesus warned about that, saying, "With what judgment you judge, you will be judged; and with the measure you use, it will be measured back to you." So be careful about being overly harsh in your thoughts or remarks about a fellow believer. Ask yourself, *Am I prepared to be judged by God in the same way that I am judging this person?* That is the central question here.

So first get the plank out of your own eye before you try to help your brother with the speck of sawdust in his. (You will see so much better!) Jesus did not say, "Don't try to help your brother" or "Ignore the speck in his eye." He just said to get the board out of your own eye first.

The simple fact is that if you know anything of being forgiven by God, you will be a forgiving person.

Sometimes People Just Don't Want Our Help

"Do not give what is holy to the dogs; nor cast your pearls before swine, lest they trample them under their feet, and turn and tear you in pieces." (Matthew 7:6)

We have looked at this verse briefly already. The bottom line here is that sometimes people don't want help, and you can't make them take what they don't want. The very person you are trying so hard to help or save may turn on you. More than one lifeguard has been drowned by the person they were trying to save.

I remember snorkeling years ago in Hawaii. We went out with one of the local boys there who knew the water really well. We were cruising along in our masks and fins, and there was a net in front of us—with a shark in it. Was it dead? We didn't really know. It was just lying there, not moving, so we moved in pretty close to get a better view. After all, how often do you get a chance to see a shark in the wild?

As we were looking at the shark, the Hawaiian pulled out his knife and began cutting the net to let the shark out. We were thinking, *This is great. This is cool. We're going to see a shark up close.*

Then suddenly, the shark came back to life. He began

shaking and twitching. If people could walk on water, we would have done it right there. In fact, we would have been running across the ocean in the opposite direction, as fast as we could go. As it was, we swam away in a panic.

Since that time, however, I have thought about that local guy trying to help the shark. Did he expect the shark to be grateful? Did he expect it to act meek and humble? In fact, the very animal he was trying to save turned on him and began swimming toward him. I think the shark would have eaten him (or me), if it had been given the chance.

That is how some people are. You try to help them, and they turn on you. That's what is behind this whole word picture of giving what is holy to dogs or casting pearls before swine.

Sometimes people just flat-out don't want to hear what we have to say.

Let's imagine this scenario. You are out in public somewhere, talking to a man about your faith.

In the middle of your testimony, the man looks at you and says, "Okay, just stop. I really don't want to hear about Jesus Christ, and I don't want you to quote the Bible to me anymore. So just go away and bother someone else, okay?"

Your natural inclination in this situation might be to press on, to tell that man about God whether he wants to hear you or not. But there comes a point when you simply have to wish him a good day and walk away. He doesn't want your pearls. He doesn't care about your pearls. And if you keep offering him your pearls, he will knock them out of your hand and step on them.

It wasn't the Lord's intent to insult people by calling them dogs or swine. What He was saying is that dogs and pigs don't really appreciate holy words or lovely pearls. If someone doesn't want to hear the holy truths of God, don't waste your time or your breath. Just move on, because there will be someone else down the road who really does want to hear the holy words and check out those beautiful pearls.

At other times, however, people will be pushing you away with one hand and beckoning you with the other, because they really do want to hear. It's as though they are going through a little dance of opposition, but don't really mean it. Why? Because they truly want to believe what you are saying to be true, but they can't quite believe it.

A good example of this in Scripture is the woman at the well in Samaria, in John 4. As Jesus began a conversation with her, she was somewhat flippant, sarcastic, and not totally respectful of Jesus. But He pressed on, and she began to believe. Jesus wasn't casting His pearls before swine. This was a woman with a hungry heart who really wanted to hope and to believe.

It was a similar story between Jesus and Nicodemus. The Lord took time with this distinguished teacher, drawing word pictures for him and reasoning with him. And even if he didn't believe right away, Nicodemus was very interested and trying to track with Jesus.

On the other hand, when Jesus was bound as a prisoner and brought before King Herod, Jesus wouldn't say a word to the king. Not one word! Why? Herod wasn't interested in the truth, and Jesus knew that. The king wanted to see a sideshow; he wanted Jesus to perform a miracle, like some kind of parlor trick. But Jesus would have none of it.

We need to pray for discernment as we are speaking to someone. Are they putting up a show of resistance when they really do want to hear, or are they genuinely closed to the message? The Holy Spirit will show us, if we are depending on Him for wisdom and help.

"Enter by the Narrow Gate"

"Enter by the narrow gate; for wide is the gate and broad is the way that leads to destruction, and there are many who go in by it. Because narrow is the gate and difficult is the way which leads to life, and there are few who find it." (Matthew 7:13-14)

The narrow gate here speaks of the person who walks day by day with God. Jesus was saying this is a difficult road. Sometimes it won't be easy to be a Christian. You will find yourself left out and excluded from certain activities and associations. You will be scorned for your beliefs. The road at times will seem narrow compared to the road that nonbelievers travel.

Our culture doesn't like that word *narrow.* It doesn't sound right to twenty-first-century ears. *Narrow.* When you hear the word used these days, it usually means intolerant, bigoted, or insensitive. We hear someone described as narrow-minded, which generally means they are stupid, prejudiced, or both.

In the Lord's words, however, we read that the narrow way leads to life. So what do we do with that?

Should we be ashamed to have people describe us as narrow-minded? It depends. If we are acting smug or arrogant, or if we come across as self-righteous know-it-alls, then yes, we should be ashamed of that.

On the other hand, if we share the good news with humility and grace, pointing out that Jesus is the only way to God, then no, that sort of narrow-mindedness is very good.

To enter at the narrow gate means we have recognized that we must walk a specific road to reach a particular destination. It's really as simple as that.

When you think about it, in life we really like and appreciate narrow-minded people. Would you want a broad-minded pilot if you were flying to Hawaii? After all, Hawaii is just a speck in the middle of a big, blue ocean.

How would you feel if the airline pilot got on the intercom system just after takeoff and said, "Hello, ladies and gentlemen. Welcome to Flight 343 with direct service to Honolulu, Hawaii. By the way, folks, I'm not so sure about this whole navigation thing. Some pilots are really into their maps and hardware and electronics. Not me. I'm not into that. I'm more laid-back. In fact, I'm actually a little drunk right now. But here is my philosophy, ladies and gentlemen. I believe that all roads lead to Hawaii. So buckle up. Enjoy your mai tais, and off we go."

You would say, "This guy is crazy! Get me off this plane! I want a narrow-minded pilot who knows what he's doing and where he's going!"

How would you feel if you were being wheeled into the operating room for surgery, and you heard the surgeon saying words like these, right before you went under? "I don't know, dudes. Do you really want to do this surgery today? I'm so sick of this procedure. Let's just do a new one! I read about a cool one in a magazine yesterday. Let's try that. Or maybe let's mess around a little and do some plastic surgery. That would be interesting."

No, I don't want a surgeon like that, and neither do you. I want a narrow-minded surgeon who follows the rules and does it right.

As important as it might be to land in Hawaii or have a successful surgery, however, there is something much more important than either of those things. It is the question of where you will spend your *eternity*.

Are you willing to take a chance on that? Are you willing to say, "Maybe all roads lead to God. Who knows? What counts is that a person is sincere."

Are you serious? Do you really want a broad-minded answer about how to get to heaven? Jesus said, "Difficult is the way which leads to life, and there are few who find it."

And what is that narrow way? It is the way through Jesus Himself. He said, "I am the door. If anyone enters by Me, he will be saved, and will go in and out and find pasture" (John 10:9). He also said, "I am the way, the truth, and the life. No one comes to the Father except through Me" (John 14:6).

On that final day when we stand before God, it is not going to be about good people and bad people. It is going to be about who walked the narrow road and entered at the narrow gate.

By contrast, Jesus spoke of a broad way that leads to destruction. That is the popular road. That is the road everyone wants to travel. People in our culture set a high value on being broad thinkers and broad-minded. In the eyes of the world, broad is good and narrow is bad.

The road Jesus asks us to travel isn't popular or trendy. But it is the road that leads to life.

There is something else implied by the word *narrow* in the original language. It's the idea that it is so narrow, only one person gets through at a time.

Think of a turnstile in a store or at a ballgame. Turnstiles are designed to admit one person at a time. Two people can't walk through a turnstile at one time. (You can try later and experiment if you like, but it is not going to work very well.)

So it is with the narrow road that leads to life. It admits one person at a time. When you stand before God on that final day, you will be alone. You won't be there with your friends. You won't be there with your family. You will be there all by yourself. And if you have believed in the Lord Jesus Christ, then you can know with certainty that you will be welcomed into heaven. But if you tried to walk the broad road, the popular road, the ultracool road, the whatever-it-is road, you will find that it has led you to destruction. But in that moment, there will be no turning back.

Choose the narrow road while the way is still wide open.

THE FOUNDATION OF LIFE

heard a story about a young businessman who was just starting his own firm. Wanting to make a big impression on potential clients, he leased a beautiful office suite in a prime location and then went out and bought some classy office furniture and a few choice antiques to furnish the space.

Sitting at his brand-new desk (with no clients yet and nothing much to do), he caught a glimpse of a man who had walked into the outer office. The young man thought to himself, *I want to impress this guy*. Picking up the phone, the would-be executive launched into a phony conversation with an imaginary person on the other end. Wanting to appear like a big shot, he started throwing around some big numbers, and then said, "All right, then. We're going to do this. All right. It's a deal."

After hanging up the phone (with authority), he pretended to notice the man in the outer office for the first time, and he said briskly, "Yes, can I help you?"

"Yeah," the man said. "Um, I'm here to activate your phone line."

So we all know what that man sitting at the brand-new

desk was, don't we? He was a *poser*. You know what a poser is. It's someone who pretends to be something they are really not.

Have you ever noticed those people who like to pose as bikers? They wear black leather jackets, sport a Harley tattoo on their arm, and have a chain on their pants connected to their wallet. And then, when you're not looking, they go climb onto a Vespa scooter in the parking lot.

A scooter, of course, won't cut it. To be an *authentic* biker, you have to have a motorcycle—more specifically, a Harley. (Just kidding.)

Where I live in Southern California, people like to pose as surfers. They have boards on top of the car and all the right stickers on the back window. They have all the lingo down too: "Hey, I'm really stoked, dude. Great swell coming in."

But the problem is, they don't surf. And they never have. They're posers.

Or maybe you have seen those guards who work at the mall and like to think they're police officers. They have the dark blue uniforms with the patch on the shoulder and a cute little fake badge. And they drive around the mall parking lot in these glorified golf carts with little flashing lights on top.

Honestly, is that supposed to intimidate me if I'm a bad guy? It's the opposite of intimidating. It makes me want to laugh. (And I never want to laugh at real officers of the law.)

And guess what? There are posers in the church as well. They sit in the seats next to us, sing the same songs, pray the same prayers, mark up their Bibles, and know all the Christian lingo too: "Praise the Lord! . . . Hallelujah! . . . God bless you" . . . and so on. They come off like they're Christians, but they're not.

Let me say something here that might seem controversial

to some people. Did you know that it's possible to pray, believe in miracles, even perform miracles, live a good life, be baptized, keep the Ten Commandments, go to church, and not necessarily be a Christian? Now, if you are a Christian, you should do all of the things I just mentioned. But doing them in and of themselves doesn't mean you are a believer. In fact, you might be a poser.

Jesus spoke to this topic directly as He wrapped up the Sermon on the Mount—the greatest sermon ever preached.

THE IMITATORS

"Not everyone who says to Me, 'Lord, Lord,' shall enter the kingdom of heaven, but he who does the will of My Father in heaven. Many will say to Me in that day, 'Lord, Lord, have we not prophesied in Your name, cast out demons in Your name, and done many wonders in Your name?' And then I will declare to them, 'I never knew you; depart from Me, you who practice lawlessness!'

"Therefore whoever hears these sayings of Mine, and does them, I will liken him to a wise man who built his house on the rock: and the rain descended, the floods came, and the winds blew and beat on that house; and it did not fall, for it was founded on the rock.

"But everyone who hears these sayings of Mine, and does not do them, will be like a foolish man who built his house on the sand: and the rain descended, the floods came, and the winds blew and beat on that house; and it fell. And great was its fall." (Matthew 7:21-27)

Whenever something good comes along, you can always be certain that imitations and knock-offs will follow on its heels.

Years ago in the mid-1960s, pop music went through a radical transformation when four guys from England burst onto the scene. They were from Liverpool, a city many of us had never heard of, and they called themselves the Beatles. They even talked funny. We were accustomed to Elvis and the way he said, "Thank you, thank you very much." But then we found ourselves dealing with a Liverpool accent and funny haircuts.

But man, were they talented! Where did these guys come from? Their sound was distinctive and like nothing we had heard before. I remember thinking it was fantastic, and I still think that to this day.

But then after the Beatles came all of these other British bands, riding on the coattails of their success: Herman's Hermits, the Animals, The Dave Clark Five, Gerry and the Pacemakers. It went on and on. They called it "the British Invasion" at the time, but in reality it was all about the Beatles and a host of imitators.

Believe it or not, some of these bands are still playing today—all these years later. Remember the Herman's Hermits song "Mrs. Brown, You've Got a Lovely Daughter"? It was a big hit, but now it has been updated a bit. They call it "Mrs. Brown, You've Got a Lovely Walker."

Do you remember the first cell phones? In March 1983, Motorola released the first portable phone into the market, and it became known (appropriately) as the brick phone. It was about as big as a handheld vacuum cleaner, had a battery life of about four minutes (or so it seemed), and sold for $3,995 retail.

Years later, Steve Jobs from Apple came along with a whole new concept called the iPhone, which would allow you to text, e-mail, and browse the Internet as well as make phone calls. Now, of course, there are countless imitations, all with their claims to be as good as or better than the iPhone.

That is always the way it is. Whenever something good comes along, there always will be imitators.

In the spiritual realm, that is what the devil is. He's an imitator, and he always has been.

A PROLIFERATION OF FAKES

To illustrate Satan's counterfeiting strategy, Jesus told a story that we call the parable of the wheat and the tares. It's the story of a farmer who went out and planted a crop of wheat. Soon after that, however, in the middle of the night, his enemy came along and planted tares—or weeds—alongside the wheat. The attack didn't become obvious until the little plants broke through the soil together, and you could see the weeds growing up with the wheat. In fact, the weeds actually uprooted the wheat.

That is how it's going to be, Jesus told us, leading up to the time of His return in the last days. The genuine and the imitation will be side by side. The real article will be right next to the fake.

I read an interesting article on the CNN website recently that spoke of fake Christians. The title of the article was, "More Teens Are Becoming Fake Christians." Kenda Creasy Dean of Princeton University warned of a mutant form of Christianity. She said more American teenagers are embracing what she calls "moralistic therapeutic deism." Translation? It's a watered-down faith that portrays God as a divine therapist, whose chief goal is to boost people's self-esteem. They concluded that many teenagers thought God simply wanted them to feel good and do good.[1] Fake Christians.

For the next few pages, I want you to consider the words of Jesus and ask yourself the question, "Am I a fake Christian?"

Now let me back up a step or two and explain something. When I speak of a fake Christian, I am not talking about a *struggling* Christian, because every Christian struggles. And if you know Christians who say they don't struggle, they are lying. The apostle James said that "we all stumble in many ways" (James 3:2, NIV). Every Christian falls short, every Christian sins, and every Christian misses the mark of God's righteous standards. That is not a fake Christian.

A fake Christian is a poser. A fake Christian is an imitator and an actor, someone who is putting on a performance. These men and women are one thing sitting in the pew on Sunday, but something else altogether in day-to-day living. These are the people of whom the Lord speaks as He wraps up His sermon. In essence, He leaves the people with a sober warning: Make sure your life matches up to your words.

That brings us to our first point.

1. Just because people say, "Lord, Lord," doesn't mean they are Christians.

"Not everyone who says to Me, 'Lord, Lord,' shall enter the kingdom of heaven, but he who does the will of My Father in heaven. Many will say to Me in that day, 'Lord, Lord, have we not prophesied in Your name, cast out demons in Your name, and done many wonders in Your name?'" (Matthew 7:21-22)

Jesus wasn't speaking here of your garden-variety non-believers. These are deeply religious people with more than a passing confession of faith.

First of all, they address Jesus as "Lord." This is a respectful title that comes from the Greek term *kurios*, which implies divinity. It's a proper title for Christ, and it is like saying, "Lord Jesus Christ." So they are respectful and acknowledge that Jesus is divine.

Not only that, there is passion in their words. They say, "Lord, Lord," not just "Lord." These aren't people just going through the motions; they have emotion and fervor in their voices. Also, note that this is a public profession. They are saying right out loud that they prophesied and did miracles in the name of Jesus.

Those are all good and worthwhile activities. But they don't make you a believer.

2. Just because people see miracles in their lives doesn't necessarily mean they are believers. The Scriptures say these people spoke prophetic words in the name of Jesus, cast out demons in the name of Jesus, and did wonders in the name of Jesus. How could false believers do that? Don't the miracles themselves prove they are Christians?

Not necessarily.

Sometimes God can choose to work through flawed vessels. He spoke prophecies and blessings through Balaam, a pagan prophet who ended up selling Israel down the river. We know that King Saul prophesied, but he was a wicked man who ultimately consulted with a witch and died in rebellion against God. Judas Iscariot was sent out with the disciples initially, and he presumably cast out demons along with the others. Yet we know that he ultimately betrayed the Lord for thirty pieces of silver. God's power can work through an individual despite that individual. Sometimes God works despite who we are or what we are.

On the other hand, the display of miraculous powers could have been from Satan. Did you know the devil can do "miracles"? No, they are not the same kind of miracles as the ones God would do. But they resemble them. The devil can do signs and wonders too. Remember when Moses went into the court of Pharaoh and used certain God-ordained signs to confirm that he had been sent from God? He turned water from the Nile into blood before Pharaoh, and when he threw down his staff, it turned into a snake—and then back into a staff again. And yet Pharaoh's magicians were able to duplicate those miracles (although they were unable to duplicate all of them).

It is a lesson to us that we can't let miracles alone convince us that an individual has been sent by God. In fact, the Bible tells us that when the Antichrist comes on the scene in the end times, he will deceive people through lying wonders and devilish miracles.

If, then, some preacher comes along and says, "You have to hear what I have to say, because I'm doing miracles by the hand of God," be careful! His "miracles" may be from hell. In the end, you have to measure what that person says, laying it alongside the unchanging Word of God.

Then again, the claims of miracles in this passage might have been false claims. They said they cast out demons and did wonders, but maybe they didn't. Maybe they were illusionists who were very good at their craft and sleight of hand.

Our family went to a so-called magic show recently. But the performer was a Christian and never pretended to be doing real magic—just clever illusions. He seemed to make things appear and disappear at will, and even when you watched carefully, it was difficult to figure out how he did it. Afterward I asked him about a couple of the jaw-dropping things he did. But, of course, he only smiled and wouldn't tell me his secrets. He was a superb illusionist who kept his audience amazed.

Were these "Christians" in Matthew 7:22 illusionists? Did they really do miracles? Maybe they did, and maybe they didn't, but Jesus said they didn't belong to Him, even though they professed to belong to Him.

3. Just because people pray in a crisis, it doesn't make them Christians. So here is the real question we have to ask ourselves: *What do you have to do to become a genuine Christian?* Imagine that you and I went out on the street right now and randomly interviewed people, asking them what a person needs to do to become a Christian and go to heaven after he or she dies.

We would probably get answers like "Go to church," "Read the Bible," "Obey the Golden Rule," "Follow the Ten Commandments," "Pray," or maybe even "Believe that Jesus Christ is the Son of God."

But the fact is, you can do all of those things and still miss heaven. If you are truly a believer, you *ought* to do those things. But those activities and beliefs, in and of themselves, won't make you a Christian.

For instance, you can pray and not necessarily be a Christian. Nine out of every ten Americans pray. Many people call out to God when the chips are down. As it has been said, there are no atheists in foxholes. (I don't know if that is completely true. I think there actually are some atheists in foxholes.) For the most part, however, people cry out to God when they suddenly find themselves in a crisis. You hear it all the time. When something dramatic happens, people yell, "Oh, my God!"

But are they truly calling out to God or just mouthing words?

One thing for sure, God knows.

We find a good example of this sort of calling out to the Lord in the book of Jonah, when the rebellious prophet was running from the Lord. He had boarded a ship headed in the opposite direction from where God had commanded him to go. Then he went below to his quarters and fell asleep. Running from the Lord must have been tiring work, because the prophet slept right through the mother of all storms, with the ship in great danger of foundering in the shrieking wind and high seas.

As this was happening, the Bible says the terrified pagan sailors began to cry out to their various gods. Then they woke up Jonah and told him to pray too. That is the way most people are. When big trouble arrives on the doorstep, they get serious about praying.

But praying in a crisis doesn't mean you are a believer or that you are following Jesus Christ. Many people teach their children a prayer to say before they go to sleep at night. You have probably prayed it too: "Now I lay me down to sleep, I pray the Lord my soul to keep. And if I should die before I wake, I pray the Lord my soul to take."

We can teach children to repeat little prayers from the time they first speak. But have we taught them how to talk to the true and living God who knows and loves them? Have we taught them how to pray or just how to say a prayer?

When the disciples observed Jesus praying, they didn't come to Him and say, "Lord, teach us a little prayer." Rather, they said, "Lord, teach us to pray" (Luke 11:1).

Here is the stark fact in all of this: You can go through your petitions and offer your ritualistic, memorized prayers and then get up from your knees without having had any communication with God whatsoever.

The psalmist said, "If I regard iniquity in my heart, the Lord will not hear me" (Psalm 66:18, KJV). In Hebrew, that word translated *regard* means "to hold on to." Let me break that down for you. If you are doing something right now that you know is a sin before God, and you persist in doing that thing, don't expect God to answer your prayers.

God says, "The LORD's arm is not too weak to save you, nor is his ear too deaf to hear you call. It's your sins that have cut you off from God. Because of your sins, he has turned away and will not listen anymore" (Isaiah 59:1-2, NLT). It's as though you are having a conversation with God on your cell phone, and then you hit "end." You stop the call. You terminate the conversation. That is what you do when you have unconfessed sin in your life.

4. Just because people make visible changes in their lives, it doesn't mean they are Christians. The book of Acts tells the story of Simon the sorcerer, who had been leading the people of Samaria astray. They even had a nickname for him: "The Great One." He was the man! And then Philip showed up and began preaching the gospel. People in the town started turning to Jesus, and they weren't following Simon anymore. (Maybe they had begun to see that "The Great One" wasn't so great after all.)

Simon must have been incensed that he was no longer the center of attention and wondered how he might recapture some of that limelight. So (as far as we can tell) he faked a conversion, was baptized, and began acting like one of the new believers.

Sometime later, Peter and John rolled into town to encourage the newly born church of Samaria. In the process, they prayed for some of the believers to receive the power of the Holy Spirit. Simon was impressed and apparently thought to himself, *Man, that was cool! I've got to add that to my bag of tricks.* He approached Peter, rattling his money bag, and said, "Give me this power also" (Acts 8:19).

The Phillips translation puts Peter's words in blunt terms:

> To hell with you and your money! How dare you think you could buy the gift of God for money! You can have no share or part in this matter, for your heart is not honest before God. All you can do now is to repent of this wickedness of yours and pray earnestly to the Lord that if possible the evil intention of your heart may be forgiven. For I can see inside you, and I see a man bitter with jealousy and bound with his own sin! (verses 20-23)

Simon's heart wasn't right before God, and Peter told him, "You can have no share or part in this matter." He had looked like a believer, even to the point of being baptized, but he had evidently never surrendered his heart to Jesus.

I'm also reminded of King Herod, who had been greatly influenced by the preaching of John the Baptist. He liked John and believed his words. No one had ever spoken to the king so fearlessly and forthrightly before. The Bible even says the reprobate old king made some changes in his life. I don't know what those changes were, and the Bible doesn't say. Maybe he didn't torture as many people that week, or he didn't execute people on Tuesdays. Whatever it was, he was starting to make some changes in response to John's dynamic teaching.

There are people like that today. They will say, "Let's go to church. It's good to get a little religion, and I like the way that guy preaches." I even had one man come up to me after a church service and say, "That was a hell of a message, Reverend."

People will act like they have been converted when they aren't converted at all. Why? Maybe it is to get something. Isn't it interesting how some politicians begin talking about their so-called faith as it gets closer to election time? And then as soon as they are elected, we don't hear anything more about God or their faith until the next election comes along.

Have you ever been buying a used car, listening to the sales guy cussing up a blue streak? Then, when he finds out you are a Christian, all of a sudden it is, "Praise the Lord, brother" and "God bless you." I can't stand it when people do that, when they fake it. And Jesus doesn't like it either.

You can even keep the Ten Commandments and not be a Christian. Earlier in this book, we spoke about the rich young ruler who came to Jesus and said, "Good Teacher, what shall I do to inherit eternal life?" (Luke 18:18).

Jesus went over a number of commandments with him, and he said, "All these things I have kept from my youth" (verse 21). Then Jesus told him what to do next, and he essentially said, "Oh . . . sorry. No, I can't do that."

He went away sad, and he also went away *lost*. He had come very, very close to Jesus—kneeling right before Him—but he wouldn't take the all-important next step.

Putting all this together, you could summarize by saying that true conversion doesn't always precede Christian activity.

While it is true that faith without works is dead (see James 2:17-20), it could also be said that works without faith are dead. Despite how impressive people might be in an outward sense, they could still be a million miles from God in their hearts.

If you are a real Christian, it will show in the way you live.

In Matthew 7:23, Jesus said, "And then I will declare to them, 'I never knew you; depart from Me, you who practice lawlessness!'"

The Greek term translated *lawlessness* here speaks of a continuous, regular action. Jesus was saying, "You continually and habitually practice lawlessness and sin." In other words, beneath this veneer of spirituality beats a heart that is dark in rebellion to God. And Jesus will utter those awful, frightening words: "I never knew you."

The phrase "knew you" speaks of intimacy; it was often used to describe marital intimacy. The Lord is saying, "I never had a relationship with you."

"But we knew You, Lord!"

"No. I don't even know who you are."

That brings us to the very foundation upon which we are to build our lives.

A REAL CHRISTIAN BUILDS LIFE ON THE RIGHT FOUNDATION

Jesus illustrated this with a story of two men building houses. Apparently, both of these men had the same desire. They wanted to construct a house they could live in with their family. They thought about the same thing, they were interested in the same thing, and the two men may have even been close to each other, perhaps sharing the very same floor plan.

Have you ever been in a housing tract where all of the homes look pretty much alike? That is the picture here. These homes are right next to each other, and they look almost identical. Outwardly, they both look great.

In the Lord's story, however, there was one major difference: One of the houses was built on the right foundation, and the other was not.

And that makes all the difference in the world.

When you're building anything, there is no more important investment than the time you spend laying the foundation. Why? Because if you don't get that right, nothing else will matter. The fun part may be deciding paint colors, moldings, or countertops, but if you don't get them right, you can easily have a do-over. But you don't get a do-over on laying a good foundation or installing wiring and plumbing. If you don't have the basics right, all the money you spend on furnishings won't matter much.

In 1172, the Italian architect Pisano began work on his most famous project—a magnificent tower that would stand next to the cathedral. But apparently, the builders were in a rush to get the work done, because they made a crucial discovery after the tower had been finished. As it happened, the soil below the tower was softer than anyone had guessed. As a result, the tower still stands today . . . eighteen feet off center. People come from around the world to look at it in the Italian city of Pisa. It's called the Leaning Tower of Pisa. People who measure such things say the tower is tilting a little more every year. Unless the structure is somehow shorn up, it eventually will collapse.

Instead of being a creation of wonder and beauty as it was

intended, it has become a curiosity and an object of derision and mockery. Here were some guys who spent years designing and building this tower, but they didn't get the foundation right.

Sadly, this can happen with our lives too. If you build your life on the right foundation, it will stand the test of time. But if you don't, there will be a devastating collapse in your future.

The collapse doesn't necessarily happen right away. It can happen over a period of time. Today you may be leaning a little bit. A year from now, your lean will be more pronounced. If ten years from now you bump into someone you know well today, they may be shocked at how far your life has tilted off center. The fact is, if you don't allow the Lord to change you, one day you will just drop over, because you haven't built your life on the right foundation.

What is the right foundation? The answer is in 1 Corinthians 3:11: "No other foundation can anyone lay than that which is laid, which is Jesus Christ." If you build your spiritual life on anyone or anything else, you simply won't make it.

THIN SOIL, SHALLOW ROOTS

When Jesus told the story of the parable of the soils, He mentioned some seed that fell on rocky ground. It may have had a thin layer of dirt on the surface, but just underneath was embedded rock. The little plants shot up quickly out of the thin soil but were unable to develop any root system. As a result, as soon as the blazing sun rose into the sky, the plants withered and died.

Jesus went on to explain that this rocky soil represents those who hear the message, receive it with enthusiasm and joy, but never develop any roots. In other words, they don't go very deep. They might cruise along on emotion for a while and seemingly get along all right, but as soon as they run into some serious problems or persecution, they wilt. They have no roots, no real foundation beneath them.

On what have you built your life? Some people build their foundation on somebody else's relationship with God. A husband's relationship with God may hinge on how close his wife stays to the Lord. He goes to church because she does, but if she didn't, he wouldn't. Or maybe a teenager goes to church because his parents do, but as soon as he moves out, that is the end of it.

Maybe you have a close friend who has influenced you through the years to read the Bible or pray or attend church. That is a good friend to have, and a positive influence for sure, but what if he or she moves away? Or, what if your godly spouse dies? Or, what if you are a young person on your own and miles away from home and your parents? What will happen to your walk with God? Did you build your spiritual foundation on another believer, or did you build it on the Lord?

Some people build their foundation on their local church. All they can talk about is their friends at church or the worship at church or the Bible studies at church or their pastor, and they can go on and on about it. But chances are, at some point something will happen at their church that they won't like. A new pastor will come along, and there will be changes and new things that don't light their fire anymore. What then?

It's dangerous, of course, to build your foundation on some pastor or teacher or spiritual leader, because they are human, just like you. They can let you down or fall into immorality or make some decision that you don't like at all.

Here is the reality of life on this side of heaven: Emotions will go up and down, people will change, churches will change, and human leaders will stumble or be inconsistent. But if you build your life on the foundation of Jesus Christ, nothing will ever move you. *No other foundation can anyone lay than that which is laid, which is Jesus Christ.* He will sustain you when storms come.

Apparently, the man in the Lord's story who built on the sand didn't have time to invest in a foundation. It seems he told the builders, "Let's put the pedal to the metal and get this thing up!"

It is like people who are always looking for shortcuts in life. They don't want to watch what they eat or exercise more. Instead, they want a little pill they can swallow that will melt the fat away while they watch TV. They want to know the blessing of God, but they don't want God Himself. They want happiness, but they don't want holiness.

But shortcutting on a foundation? That is a very bad idea.

Eventually, of course, there is something that will reveal what you have built your life upon: storms.

WHAT STORMS REVEAL

In Matthew 7:25 and 27, Jesus said, "And the rain descended." It may not have been ideal, and it may not have been convenient, but those two houses by the two builders got hit by the same storm.

Storms will come, whether we like it or not. The wind will blow, the earth will shake, and the flood tides will roll in. Some storms come hard and fast, like a sudden temptation or tragedy that slams into your life from out of the blue. At other times, the storm damage may be subtle, gradually weathering, undercutting, and weakening a life, making it vulnerable.

How will you fare in that day?

Will you be left standing?

The fact is, you decide *today* how you will do tomorrow. You decide the evening of your life by what you do in the morning.

If you are young, then build your life on Christ now, and don't say, "I'll do it later." Before you know it, life will have passed by and you will have wasted opportunities. I thank God that I came to faith at the age of seventeen—over forty years ago now. I have never for a moment regretted that commitment to follow Jesus. And you won't, either. Build your life on Christ, because storms will come.

Do you doubt it? Did you think that maybe God would give you a life with no serious trials or suffering? The truth is that none of us are exempt from these things. Jesus said, "In the world you will have tribulation" (John 16:33). If you think your whole life will be a stroll through the daisies, you will have some surprises up ahead. And that is why we need to be sure of our foundation.

Tragedy, suffering, and adversity usually have one of two effects. Either you will have your faith strengthened as you run to God for comfort, or you will become angry at God and turn away from Him.

As I mentioned earlier, our family faced tragedy in the loss of our son a few summers ago. Talk about a sudden storm. Christopher's passing was such a crushing, devastating blow for all of us.

Has my faith grown weaker because of that tragedy? No, it

has grown stronger. In my weakness, I have built my life on the foundation of Jesus Christ, and He has enabled me to make it through that storm. Without Him, I would have certainly been washed away by grief. I cling to Him for life, every day of my life, and I'm never ashamed to say that I need the Lord's constant help.

"Well," someone will say, "that's just a crutch."

Actually, it's more like an entire hospital — and I need it. I need Him. If you imagine that you don't need Him, then you are a fool, because storms will come in your life, too.

Sometimes people will say they went through a great hardship or tragedy and lost their faith. But maybe they never had faith to begin with. The faith that can't be shaken is the faith that *has* been shaken. If it is real faith, it will stand up to the storm.

Here is a more modern translation of the words we have already read:

> "These words I speak to you are not incidental additions to your life, homeowner improvements to your standard of living. They are foundational words, words to build a life on. If you work these words into your life, you are like a smart carpenter who built his house on solid rock. Rain poured down, the river flooded, a tornado hit — but nothing moved that house. It was fixed to the rock.
>
> "But if you just use my words in Bible studies and don't work them into your life, you are like a stupid carpenter who built his house on the sandy beach. When a storm rolled in and the waves came up, it collapsed like a house of cards." (Matthew 7:24-27, MSG)

What is your life built on? It's the most important question anyone could ever ask.

"EXAMINE YOURSELVES"

The apostle Paul said, "Examine yourselves to see whether you are in the faith; test yourselves" (2 Corinthians 13:5, NIV). It is an important thing for every one of us to do.

I recently went to the doctor for a full physical, and he did a lot of tests on me. I never look forward to this, but it's kind of like the dentist—something that just has to be endured. They poked and prodded, hooked me up to all those little electrodes and put me on the treadmill, and did some other tests I don't even want to talk about. He checked me over for lumps or growths or anything out of the ordinary that wasn't there last year. Then I had to fill out detailed forms about this and that. Why all the bother? Because my doctor wanted to get a good, accurate read of my physical health, a snapshot of where I am in life.

He gave me a clean bill of health, which was encouraging. But I will have to go through the whole thing again next year in order to determine my physical state. It's important to me, because it's important to my wife, my family, my friends, and my church.

The Bible urges us to check up on ourselves in a spiritual sense. Are you really a Christian? Or are you just pretending to be a Christian when you really aren't at all?

There could be no more important question in coming to a truly biblical worldview. For you, this is by far the most important question of all.

"Well," you say, "I *must* be a Christian. I read my Bible

from time to time, and I go to church." Those things are wonderful and certainly should be part of your life. But those activities, in and of themselves, don't make you a Christian. You are a Christian if you have placed your faith in Jesus Christ, and Him alone, and you are trusting in Him and walking with Him day by day. That relationship, then, will make a difference in your life—you will hunger and thirst to read God's Word, you will want to be with other believers, and you will look forward to the times when you can worship the Lord alongside brothers and sisters in Christ.

Those activities, however, flow from your living relationship with Christ, not the other way around. He is the one and only foundation in all the world, and if you have built your life on Him, no storm, hurricane, earthquake, flood, or tragedy can wash you away.

That's the last word on developing a biblical worldview.

It's a worldview that will one day lead you into heaven, into the very presence of the God who loves you, and into eternal joy.

NOTES

Chapter 1: Absolute Truth

1. "New Book Describes the State of the Church in 2002," Barna Group, 2002, http://www.barna.org/barna-update/article/5-barna-update/75 -new-book-describes-the-state-of-the-church-in-2002.
2. Francis A. Schaeffer, *The Complete Works of Francis Schaeffer* (Wheaton, IL: Crossway, 1982), 254.
3. John MacArthur, *Think Biblically!* (Wheaton, IL; Crossway, 2003), 14.
4. C. S. Lewis, *The Quotable Lewis*, ed. Wayne Martindale and Jerry Root (Wheaton, IL: Tyndale, 1990), 99.
5. "Barna Studies the Research, Offers a Year-in-Review Perspective," Barna Group, 2009, http://www.barna.org/faith-spirituality/325-barna -studies-the-research-offers-a-year-in-review-perspective.
6. "The Hitchens Transcript," *Portland Monthly*, January 2010. http:// www.portlandmonthlymag.com/arts-and-entertainment/category/books -and-talks/articles/christopher-hitchens/.
7. U.S. Congress. House. *Congressional Record*, 108th Cong., 1st sess., vol. 145—Part 15 (September 5, 2003), 21335.
8. R. Albert Mohler Jr., *Words from the Fire: Hearing the Voice of God in the 10 Commandments* (Chicago: Moody, 2009), 51.
9. Martin Peers, "Apple's Hard-to-Swallow Tablet," *Wall Street Journal*, December 30, 2009.

Chapter 3: Hot-Button Issues

1. Mark Twain, *The Wit and Wisdom of Mark Twain*, ed. Alex Ayres (New York: Harper & Row, 1987), 75.
2. Max Lucado, *The Lucado Life Lessons Study Bible* (Nashville: Thomas Nelson, 2010), 370.

Chapter 4: More Absolute Truth
1. Jerry Adler, "The Thrill of Theft," *Newsweek*, vol. 139, February 25, 2002.

Chapter 5: How to Be Happy
1. Edward Ugel, *Money for Nothing* (New York: HarperCollins, 2007), 23.
2. C. S. Lewis, *Mere Christianity* (New York: HarperCollins, 2001), 50.
3. Lewis, 73.

Chapter 6: The Pursuit of Happiness
1. *Good Reads*, s.v. "Jim Carrey quotes," http://www.goodreads.com/author/quotes/329948.Jim_Carrey.
2. Cathy Lynn Grossman, "USA misses Top 10 countries in 'happiness rating,'" *USAToday.com*, June 8, 2011, http://content.usatoday.com/communities/Religion/post/2011/06/happiness-god-economy-debt/1.
3. Tony Sargent, *Gems from Martyn Lloyd-Jones: An Anthology of Quotations from "The Doctor"* (Milton Keynes, UK: Authentic Media, 2007), 46.
4. D. Martyn Lloyd-Jones, *Spiritual Depression: Its Causes and Cure* (Grand Rapids, MI: Eerdmans, 1965), 117.

Chapter 7: Make a Difference
1. Cathy Lynn Grossman, "Survey: 72% of Millennials 'more spiritual than religious,'" *USAToday.com*, October 14, 2010, http://www.usatoday.com/news/religion/2010-04-27-1Amillfaith27_ST_N.htm.
2. Chris Daino, "Early Life and Career," http://www.titanic-lore.info/Capt-Smith.htm.
3. R. Albert Mohler Jr., *Culture Shift: The Battle for the Moral Heart of America* (Colorado Springs, CO: Multnomah, 2011), xvi.

Chapter 12: The Lord's Prayer
1. C. S. Lewis, *The Complete C. S. Lewis Signature Classics* (San Francisco: HarperCollins, 2002), 66.

Chapter 13: Worry and Anxiety
1. D. Martyn Lloyd-Jones, *Studies in the Sermon on the Mount* (Grand Rapids, MI: Eerdmans, 1960), 417.
2. Lloyd-Jones, 398.

Chapter 15: The Foundation of Life
1. John Blake, "Author: More teens becoming 'fake' Christians," CNN.com, August 27, 2010, http://www.cnn.com/2010/LIVING/08/27/almost.christian/index.html?hpt=T2.

Other Books by Greg Laurie

Are We Living in the Last Days?
As I See It
Better Than Happiness
Daily Hope for Hurting Hearts
Dealing with Giants
Deepening Your Faith
Discipleship
Essentials
For Every Season, volumes 1, 2, and 3
God's Design for Christian Dating
A Handbook on Christian Dating
His Christmas Presence
Hope for Hurting Hearts
How to Know God
"I'm Going on a Diet Tomorrow"
Living Out Your Faith
Making God Known
Marriage Connections
Married. Happily.
Run to Win
Secrets to Spiritual Success
Signs of the Times
Strengthening Your Faith
Strengthening Your Marriage
Ten Things You Should Know About God and Life
The Great Compromise
The Greatest Stories Ever Told, volumes 1, 2, and 3
Upside Down Living
What Every Christian Needs to Know
Why, God?

Visit: www.kerygmapublishing.com